SNOW BUSINESS

NORDIC ADVENTURES OF A SKI REP

ANDREW REED

Matador
9 Priory Business Park,
Wistow Road, Kibworth Beauchamp,
Leicestershire. LE8 0RX
Tel: 0116 279 2299
Email: books@troubador.co.uk
Web: www.troubador.co.uk/matador
Twitter: @matadorbooks

ISBN 978 1788039 444

British Library Cataloguing in Publication Data.
A catalogue record for this book is available from the British Library.

Printed and bound in Great Britain by 4edge Limited
Typeset in 11pt Minion Pro by Troubador Publishing Ltd, Leicester, UK

Matador is an imprint of Troubador Publishing Ltd

To Jane

HAND DRAWN MAP FROM THE WELCOME PACK

ÅRE

LEGEND
1 POST OFFICE
2 SYSTEMBOLAGET
3 TOURIST INFORMATION
4 HANSONS SKI HIRE SHOP
5 FUNICULAR RAILWAY
6 SKI SCHOOL MEETING POINT
7 P+B PUBLIC TOILETS
8 SUPERMARKETS
9 SHOPPING ESPLANADE — MANESKY & PHARMACY + PHOTO SHOP
10 BANK
11 WINE SHOP
12 KEBS OFFICE
13 SKI SCHOOL

TOTT LIFTEN
SWIMMING HOTEL
ÖSTERSUND (AIRPORT)
E14
ÅRE VÄGEN
ÅRE CEMETERY
PROSTSTUGET
BJÖRNÄNGE

WORLD CUP LIFTEN
KABIN BANAN
1ST STOP
SKI SCHOOL
STJÄRN LIFTEN
TOBOGGAN RUN
E14
DUVED

PISTE
SPORT HOTELLET
HANSONS SKI HIRE SHOP
ÅRE T-PARTMENTS
DIPLOMAT SKI LODGE + APARTMENTS
ÅRE VÄGEN
ST. OLLAS VÄGEN
TRAIN STATION
INN PLAN
SKI PLAN
SPORTHOTELLVÄGEN

ICA
VIEW LINE RESTAURANT
KABIN
ÅRE TOWN SQUARE
COACH PICKUP POINT
PEAK PERFORMANCE
TOURIST INFO

MARKET
CAFÉ MISSEN
ACQUA MARKET
HOTEL ÅREGÅRDEN + COUNTRY CLUB NIGHTCLUB
ÅREGÅRDEN APTS

1

AUGUSTI

Take a Chance on Me

A hot sunny afternoon in Surbiton may seem like a strange place to start an account of a winter spent in the frozen north of Sweden, but the Sanctuary Lodge was the UK head quarters of the holiday company I was hoping to be employed by for the forthcoming winter season.

The imposing Victorian villa sheltered from the heat under tall leafy English oaks and overgrown conifers and was strangely quiet. It appeared there weren't many applicants attending the first interviews for a ski season in mid-August. I checked in with reception and was directed up the wide staircase to wait in a lobby on the first floor, where a couple of others looked up and acknowledged my arrival. I returned the nods and half smiles and took my seat by the window. I watched a squirrel flit about in the garden for a short while before I was called in to another room ahead of the others.

In the expansive but oddly empty room sat just two people behind an oversized dark wood desk with an array of papers;

application forms with passport photos pinned or stapled to the top left corner of each one. The lady that had called me in returned to her seat to the side of the desk and ushered me to the single chair with a brisk wave of her hand.

After friendly introductions were made, we went through my application form and discussed my *"need to take a career break"* as I had described it (not my current unemployed status and my strong desire, verging on desperation, to get some respite from endless job applications and rejections or indecision on the part of employers). Had I really thought what it meant to give up what they presumed to be a well paid job for a lowly paid job with very long hours? I would be living away from England and friends and sometimes dealing with stressed members of the public who had paid a lot of money for their family's once-a-year ski holiday. Err… yes, I was sure it was what I wanted to do and, if I had to live in the mountains and be paid to ski every day for it, I was ready for it.

"Of course, you won't get to ski every day, you know. There's a lot of behind the scenes paperwork and we run a very tight ship with budgets, etc," warned the man with the tweed jacket.

"That's fine," I replied. "Having worked in an office environment for a few years, I am used to keeping financial records up to date and dealing with people. I see that as the main part of the job and the skiing as a benefit." *Smart answer*, I thought, although I hoped they didn't think it too smart.

"And you are sure you want to go to Sweden?"

"Absolutely. I know people there, I've travelled around the country a bit and I like the customs and the people. And I already speak a little Swedish," I proffered, taking a bit of a gamble that none of them did. They didn't. And nor did they test the limit of my really useful sixteen Swedish words and my ability to count to ten very slowly. Apart from those basics, I could say "my hovercraft is full of eels," as I could in French, German and

Italian. Some people like to learn to say "I love you" in different languages; my friends are a little different and that phrase was one we liked to perfect. They also wouldn't be able to test my skiing ability here in Surbiton so, if I passed this interview, at the very least I would get a free week in Austria at their rep training week which would take me out of grey London. The application form had required a minimum of ten weeks' skiing. I had done only seven but, on the form, I had put eleven and had researched the locations of where and when those spurious weeks had been.

After a few more minutes' relaxed chat, they wrapped it up and thanked me for coming along, adding that I should sit outside and wait to be called in to one of the other rooms. When I returned to the lobby, some more hopeful reps had appeared fresh from their initial interviews. It wasn't long before we were divided up into groups of eight and led to various rooms where we each had to give a presentation on ourselves, do a short maths test, answer questions on the role of a resort representative, and were tested on our knowledge of the winter season brochure (where to find the information on flight times, learn to ski packages basically, *the small print*). The session finished up with a selling test, where we were each asked to sell the benefits of a particular fruit to the group. The reason being that one of the most important parts of the job was selling excursions and the more you sold, the more the holiday company made, and the more you as a rep made.

I left the building and walked back to my car feeling quite pleased with the way things had gone and thinking that surely there wouldn't be loads of people, if anyone, wanting to go to Sweden – would there? Surely all the cool people wanted to do a season in Val D'Isere or Chamonix or St Anton. No one else I had spoken to had ever heard of Åre (pronounced *oreh* or more easily *aura*) and certainly didn't know you could actually go alpine skiing there. The usual comments were "Isn't Sweden all cold and dark in the winter?" and "Don't they just go cross country skiing, eat herring and beat each other with birch twigs?" The more people held that view, the better my chances were, I reckoned.

Two weeks later, I duly received confirmation that they would like to offer me a place on their grandly named 'Winter 96/97 Overseas Representatives Training Seminar', which was planned for early December. My contract and confirmation of the resort in which I would be working was subject to the satisfactory completion of the training course. They had stressed at the interview that a place on the course was no guarantee of a job but anyone committing to the week should give serious consideration to leaving their employment. They requested a cheque for £70 and confirmation of acceptance of the offer, £35 of that was to be refunded upon the successful completion of the season *and* the return of the uniform. I would be sent further details including travel arrangements in due course.

In late October, I received a letter containing my joining instructions (should I choose to continue to accept, of course – well they had my £70 now so what choice had I?). The letter advised of the Corporate Training Day, set for Friday 29th November at Sandown Park Racecourse near Esher, following which all the staff would depart for their European training course in France, Austria or Italy. Now it was beginning to feel real and exciting but I still had some purchases to make. They suggested a shopping list, in no particular order:

Everyone

- Alarm clock (two to be on the safe side).
- Adapter plug.
- Calculator.
- Stationery e.g. stapler, ruler, coloured pens, Tippex, rubber,

scissors, Sellotape, glue (they must have got all of that straight from a *Blue Peter* annual, surely?).

- Thermal underwear (following logically on from Sellotape and glue, of course).
- Ski wear e.g. jacket, trousers, gloves, goggles, sunglasses (there was, I felt, a more than average chance I would have thrown all those things into the luggage without this helpful suggestion).
- Toiletries – especially contact lens solution (…and the title of this section was… *everyone*?).
- Money to start you off with (because they thought you were going to earn enough from selling excursions to survive – or they knew that you would, in your training week, make it your business to tap up the experienced rep for all the scams you could possibly legitimately and safely run).
- Footwear with a non-slip sole (already thought of that) – We recommend "Timberland-style" boots. (*Good product placement*, I thought. However, I had my own non-slip dark brown leather boots from Millets that I had owned for several years so I figured I'd save a bit of cash and take those, assuming they'd pass the non-slip test).
- Iron (no explanation here but I assumed they meant one for ironing clothes rather than just iron weights or vitamin tablets. There was no "e.g." so I was left slightly flummoxed. It could have been "e.g. for flattening clothes" but no clues at all, nothing).
- Dairy (I think that was a typo).

Resort Reps

- A typewriter or PC, if you have one (this was back in mid 1990s).

- Cash box (lockable) – Resort managers / Head Reps (foolishly I went out and bought one and took it out with me but never used it and have not done so to this day).
- Bum-bag / Waiter-style wallet for collecting money – ditto.

List of a few things they should have suggested:

- Season's supply of Red Bull.
- Marmite – the growing-up spread; every rep likes it, all the locals hate it.
- Mother's Christmas cake – to give you a taste of home and prolong Christmas as, although the Christmas decorations are up for longer, you will celebrate it on the wrong day (24th), it's the busiest time of the season so you are working flat out and it's back to normal rep routine the day after.
- Season's supply of headache (hangover) tablets & Berocca – to help you get through the following morning after you have partied with the guests, and then the locals, to the wee small hours, thinking it would be easy to get up early for the airport transfer.
- Earplugs – in case your room is situated above, or near, a noisy nightclub –OK for a week, maybe; not OK for six months.

They should have emphasised: We really do advise buying new "Timberland-style" boots – don't think you can get away with an old knackered pair of boots you've had for a few years.

And, for those going to work in the Scandinavian resorts, we suggest, to combat the long hours of darkness, some vitamin D tablets or a portable UV SAD desk lamp, which will work out much cheaper than regular visits to the hotel sun beds, although not as fun.

In between the letter and information arriving and the corporate day, I went to the ski show and met up with the dapper man in the tweed jacket I had met at the interview on the company's stand. In his mid-thirties, an intelligent and well-spoken man, he had a friendly face and smiley eyes. With thin wisps of brown hair brushed across his pate, he was dangerously close to sporting a comb-over. His tweed combo made him look older than his years and the stretched waistcoat revealed signs of over-indulgence in Austrian food.

I picked up a copy of the season brochure as they were making a fuss about it being Issue 2. As I flipped through it, primarily to check that my chosen resort was still featured, I found on the relevant page for Åre that it described not only how all the guests would benefit from the services of a resort representative but now – in Issue 2 – they would also have the services of a ski escort. A brightly coloured **SKI ESCORT** box by the resort guide details shouted out at me. It wasn't in bold or capitals but might as well have been. I tried to remain calm on the inside but said with outward enthusiasm, "Erm… I see you've got Ski Escorting now as part of the rep's duties for Åre?", rather hoping he might say it was a typing error but he didn't.

"Yes, you'll love it," replied dapper man. "Great fun there."

I didn't want to make the point that it wasn't there in Issue 1, in case he began to doubt my suitability for the job. Being a ski escort was a whole different ball game than just a ski rep, particularly with only seven weeks' skiing under your belt or rather, between your skis.

2

DECEMBER

Money, Money, Money

I left home early in the morning of 29th November with a fully packed travel bag and a rucksack crammed with last minute items and stuff for the long coach journey to Austria. Frankly, I felt a bit sick with apprehension, as it reminded me of the first day at a new school and wondering how easy it would be to make new friends. It was a different industry I was entering into and I wasn't totally convinced the job was really for me. On arrival at Sandown, I passed the rows of coaches all lined up in the car park ready to take the four hundred or so staff to their Alpine destinations and joined a throng of people all heading for the entrance to dump luggage in the baggage hall. Numbered areas had been marked out according to which coach you were going to travel on. Mine, I remembered, was number eight and, as I dropped my bag, I bumped into the girl who I had sat next to at the interview back in August, so we went to grab a coffee together before proceeding into the main hall. It struck me that there was a very high number of new hopeful reps, with all the excited chatter and general noise. I had presumed they were all first timers, like Kate and me, but discovered that the company insists that if you want to do a repeat season you have to go on the training week before each season. Later it was revealed that if you want to do a season in the US or Canada you have to have completed at least one season in Europe first. So far, I was impressed with the professionalism the company showed.

Kate and I nattered for a while and then found a couple of seats as others started to take their places in the Conference and Banqueting Centre. The centre began to fill up quickly now, in anticipation of all the speeches we were about to hear from the various important directors of the tour company, including (according to the timetable) an opening address by the Managing Director. I imagined we would all assemble, have a bit of an announcement, break off into our country or regional groups, and then bugger off on the coach to our various destinations, but this was serious, like a full blown conference, and it was just a ski company. Mercifully, we were spared Tina Turner's Simply the Best blasting out across the conference centre as the MD appeared, which I did endure years ago at a conference in Birmingham. I was working for a property agency that subsequently went bust. Just before things really got going, a slim girl with long dark hair, brown eyes and olive skin sat down next to me and we said "hello" to each other.

She then asked, in a rather alluring eastern European accent, "Where are you working this year?"

"It's my first season and I'm hoping to go to Sweden… you?" I replied.

"Romania," she said firmly and proudly. I nodded and then, thinking it might be her first season too and hoping to discover at least one person who might have bluffed their way to this point on the skiing, "Are you doing the escorting?"

"Yeah, of course," she said in a slightly dismissive way.

"Have you done much? I mean skiing, not escorting," starting to feel myself on the edge of a hole, I had started to excavate unintentionally.

"I was in Romanian Olympic ski team at Lillehammer Games," she answered, following with a Mona Lisa smile.

"Oh really?... wow!" nodding to her in appreciation, whilst hoping she would not ask the same of me. I was saved by the arrival on stage of the Senior Product Director for France and Switzerland and the Senior Product Director for Austria, Scandinavia, Eastern Europe and Schools, no less, amid a mixture of low key applause, cat calls, boos, and one person shouting out "wanker". I think the reception depended on whether you were a first timer or a regular season worker, as some clearly were.

The opening talks rumbled on for fifteen to twenty minutes, lauding the wonders of the company, then, after the MD had had his say, the Marketing Director came back on and spoke about "Life at the Sharp End" (i.e., us lot) and, listening between the lines, if we didn't do our job properly he wouldn't be getting his annual bonus.

After a half hour coffee break, we returned for more talks on, 1) The Role of the Reservations Team, 2) Operations, CAS (no idea?!) and Documentation Control, and 3) How the Travel Agents see us. It was starting to feel very much like a conference and didn't seem likely that we would all be heading off to the Alps later in the day. After a buffet lunch, we again resumed our places in the large room for more talk about Quality Control and Client Relations, Insurance (Guests and Reps), before another tea break. Then the head of the Scandinavian section, dapper man Bob, rounded his troops up and led us off to the canteen for a more informal chat about the specifics of our region, which saved us from the dreary sounding "Money Talks" talk by the Finance Director and the Schools Programme talk by the imaginatively titled Programme Manager.

Our small Scandinavian group barely made it back in time for the Marketing Director's Summary and at five o'clock the final speaker got up (presumably the Transport Coordinator Manager) to announce the end of the Corporate Day and advise that we were now to return to the baggage hall, collect our bags and make our way out to our pre-assigned coaches which would take us all to Dover. From there, we would all travel by ferry to Calais where, he advised, the *European* coaches would meet us on our arrival to transport us to the country training course. From Calais, we would then split up and head down to either the French or Italian Alps, or in my case to Kaprun in Austria. The "Scandies", as we were to be called, were being lumped in with those destined to work their seasons in Austria or Switzerland.

Calais docks on a cold, wet, windy November night is not the most inspiring of places to be. If you do happen to find yourself there by some quirk of fate, then make sure your onward transport is ready to take you on to your final destination. Ours wasn't. It was rather surprising, and a little disconcerting, that as a few hundred wannabe reps and chalet staff stood huddled together by the side of someone else's parked coaches and a large dockside building, our future employer, a travel company, had messed up on the travel arrangements.

To be fair, though, it didn't seem like it was their fault. Standing in the freezing darkness, trying to stay as close to the parked coach as possible to keep out of the driving rain (whilst not actually leaning on the dirty side), led me to ask the question, not for the first time in the last couple of months prior to departure, "What the hell am I doing?" The news was passed around us that our European coaches had driven to another dock, with the drivers clearly wondering where all their passengers had gone.

We stood there, our baggage's waterproof qualities being severely tested as the rain lashed down, for about an hour and a half whilst our French, Austrian and Italian coach drivers sipped at their espressos and cursed *Les Anglais* for arriving late. It seemed a simple matter to us for someone to call up and say, "They're on Quay D", and for them to drive round and pick us up. After all, the senior reps must have had a fair bit of experience of organising transport and people – that was part of the job.

Eventually, one of the senior reps came around, telling us that the coaches would be with us in the next few minutes. We were to find our bags and be ready to board our allocated coach with the same number as the one that we had taken from Epsom. They arrived in dribs and drabs, and all parked on the far side of the wide expanse of dock tarmac from where we were assembled. I only cared about locating the number eight coach to Kaprun. I stuck with my new mate, Simon (a tall, humorous and cheerful bespectacled chap hoping to get assigned to Norway) and pushed the collar of my ski jacket higher up. I squinted, trying to spot a number eight in the front window of one of the arriving coaches. The rain continued to spit down and the strong arc lights high above us shone their beams onto the glistening black tarmac, creating an effect like one of those touristy paintings of Paris you can buy where the paint has been trowelled on.

We had been advised to get as much sleep as possible on the journey and this delay was inevitably going to cut into our rest. *Still, all part of the reps' training*, we thought. We had also been warned to be on our guard for the whole week. Had the test begun already? Is the management (which included the senior reps travelling with us) already observing us and testing our reactions? At last, a coach bearing the number eight pulled up and we and thirty or so others lugged our cases, rucksacks, plastic bags, the fifty metres or so to the vehicle. It amazed me how some people had brought guitars as well as their luggage. I had never packed six months of clothing and equipment into just two bags before and ski clothing is pretty bulky, let alone all the other paraphernalia required of me. It took another full half hour to get everyone sorted out with their luggage and themselves getting on to the right coach.

I do not remember much of the journey through France, mainly because I was asleep for most of it, except when the vibration of the window would cause my head to rattle and loll about too vigorously and rouse me intermittently. However, I do recall waking up as the coach pulled into the truck stop area of a motorway service station and peering out of the window, through the dark and drizzle, towards a brightly lit forecourt, momentarily horrified to think we were still trying to find our way out of Calais docks. Reassured by others standing up and moving forward, I pulled on my ski jacket, under which I had been sleeping, and trudged off in the general direction of the lights, with one eye glued shut and my lips sealed in that half-awake pained expression. I tried my best not to become fully awake by not talking to anyone, unlike the two girls walking a little ahead of me who were nattering away and actually laughing. God knows what there was to laugh about this time of the night, or morning, or whatever it was. Some of us went to get a coffee from the shop, others, myself included, headed off for the loos and then clambered back on board as quickly as possible to try to achieve the same comfortable sleeping position again.

In the grey light of dawn, I became conscious more easily with the exciting realisation that, one, it wasn't raining anymore and, two, we had crossed the border into Austria and the flat fields either side of the road along which we were travelling were covered with lovely soft white snow. We stopped again at another service station for an Austrian breakfast of strong coffee and some kind of sausage dish in a bowl. It was too early for their pastries to be ready. Back on the coach, the daylight, general chatter, and changing scenery kept me awake as I watched the landscape reveal itself more impressively. We peeled off the motorway and began to climb higher along the narrower roads running alongside cold dark water lakes and steep-sided valleys covered with dense forests. The twists and turns of the road led us through a number of small towns and villages until, eventually, all the roof tops and walls were draped with a thick snow covering. After a spot of manoeuvring and a hiss of air brakes, the coach drew to a halt and we had arrived at our destination.

I stretched in my seat, gathered up my rucksack and ski jacket, and jumped down off the coach into the crisp mountain air and took in my surroundings. It was a true winter wonderland and I thought: *well, if I am only here for a week and then get sent home, I will have escaped rainy grey London for a while, got a bit of skiing in and not have had to pay for any of it.* Then I pulled myself together and said to myself, *No. Think more positively – there's a whole six months of this lifestyle if you really want it.*

All the reps on the training week were to stay in some of the chalets that the ski company were renting for the season. All the members of the chalet staff were also accommodated in the same chalets and had a week to hone their cooking and cleaning skills, with us reps as guinea pigs. In fact, they didn't really have any practice time at all as, although we weren't paying guests, we needed to be fed right from day one.

I checked into the Sonnenalp chalet. It was typical chalet accommodation, with a dark ornate wood balcony running around the first floor under the wide expanse of a pitched roof and plain white walls, inside and out, simply furnished with pine everywhere. I was to share a room with John, another rep who had done a few seasons, which I figured could be useful for tips and general advice on the form of what was to come in the next week. John was a professional rep, working the summer Alpine season and winter season. He looked much younger than his years being quite thin and pasty-faced with a Hugh Grant style mop of hair and ears that stuck out a bit too far from the side of his head. He had a slightly annoying perhaps, nervous laugh. He didn't look like he was long out of wearing a blazer and cap, with a school satchel dangling from his shoulder. Having completed a few seasons, he thought himself more important than he was and was keen to offer titbits of his knowledge gained from repping. I'm sure he meant well.

A timetable was handed out to us for the next eight days, starting with, in military style, 15.00 that same day; "distribution of uniforms by syndicate group in Sonnenalp bar". The timetable also advised us that "Breakfast will be served in the Sonnenalp & Abendruh between 7.30 & 8.30am every day and 7 & 8am on Tuesday". As yet, we trainee reps were blissfully unaware of why breakfast was earlier on Tuesday. The timetable went on to confirm "The seminar will take place in the Optimum Centre every day. Both chalets are non-smoking". And then this particular day, Saturday, finished up with what was supposed to be a motivational quote, "Success depends on where intention is". As I scanned through the timetable for the week ahead, I saw there were helpful suggestions to get motivated after each day's listed activities. It didn't bode well, for I and, as it turned out, most of the other trainee reps, had a particular aversion to such banal statements. Sunday's was, "See every difficulty as a challenge, a stepping stone, and never be defeated by anything or anyone". *Yeah, right.* I turned the page over and went straight to Monday's thought for the day: "Be realistic, plan for a miracle". *What?!* I was reminded of a piece of advice given to us at school when I was about fourteen.

It was delivered to us by the history master, who was quite old and whom I think must have been with the school since its foundation in 948 AD, so he knew a thing or two about life. His advice, which has stuck with me and cuts through all this motivational crap, was, "Don't go expecting life to be fair, boy, cos it ain't!" Not very motivational, I will admit, but infinitely more memorable than this drivel and probably more use long term.

The queue for the uniforms turned into a bit of a scrum when it became apparent that there were actually two types. One (last year's version) was quite a stylish blue and red with a fleece lining inside to the collar. The other was a rather garish ensemble of very bright blue, yellow, a bit of purple across the shoulders (or was it sun-faded dark blue?) and orange, which used to be red when new, some six or seven seasons ago. Dapper Bob was overseeing the distribution of kit, including navy blue tee shirts, polo shirts, lined fleeces and bright red logo-emblazoned baseball caps and, when he saw that I had got one of the old models, he reassured me that, as I was destined for Scandinavia where it could get down to minus thirty five, I would be able to swap my old one for one of the newer style. It never happened but, you know, bearing in mind all the hype surrounding ski clothing regarding brand names and *Gore-Tex* technology and material that wicks away rivers of sweat from your body etc, layers being what you need, it performed admirably. I had never heard of the brand *House Colours*, and I doubt you have either, but apart from the very uncool garishness of something designed in that fashion nadir that was the late 80s, it did the job – and that's saying something when enduring a winter in northern Sweden.

The first evening meal went well for the chalet staff and the old seasoned "seasoners" in our chalet entertained us with tales of their past seasons and tried to fend off questions about what will happen during the week. The best advice they gave was to remember we were being observed all the time as to how we interacted with other people, dealt with authority, behaved in public, managed our time-keeping, coped with stress and presented ourselves.

On Sunday morning, at 9am, we were all sat in the Optimum Centre, Kaprun's Sports Centre, a short walk from the Sonnenalp chalet. A beautiful sunny morning, it was one of those ski days that lifts your spirits in the gloom of winter that permeates the UK winter. The snow was already quite thick and adorned all the roof tops and roughly cut post and rail fencing surrounding a nearby field, as if someone had dabbed a thick white paint brush on every flat surface like some obsessive doodler during a boring meeting.

It was a lovely day to start our week but we were inside listening to another opening speech from the Marketing Director, somewhat incongruously still dressed in a suit and tie and looking like a heavy weight Freddie Mercury. He displayed Freddie's teeth when he smiled too. He was the corporate side of things, making his presence known. His speech only lasted for half an hour and then we were straight into learning about important stuff that we needed to take notes on.

The St Johann office was the title of the next talk by a bloke called Karl, who had a habit of turning up everywhere during the week when he wasn't making important corporate phone calls on his mobile from within his Chrysler Voyager people carrier with blacked out windows. The St Johann office was the nerve centre of the entire Austrian, Swiss, Norwegian, Swedish, and Bulgarian winter ski season operation. It was where the money was sent to and from, where we got paid, so we needed to pay careful attention to its procedures. As important as it was, it was only given fifteen minutes' air time.

It was followed by Karl's wife talking about the cabaret we were all going to have to perform. The idea behind that was an exercise in time management, I think, rather than entertaining skills. Along with learning all the procedures and memorising where the important legal bits are in the brochure, we were required to take part in all the excursions to give us an idea of what we could arrange for our guests. We also had to find time to put together a cabaret act, which would be performed towards the end of the week to the rest of the entire group of reps. Mercifully, Dapper Bob had told us that we wouldn't bother with all that nonsense in Sweden or Norway – it's just for the Austrian and Swiss reps – but we still had to take part and do a show, just to prove our suitability to entertain guests. At the first coffee break this was, not unsurprisingly, the topic of conversation amongst the Scandies and it was quickly decided, as one of us had an ABBA CD and another was a native Swede, we would do a performance of *Money Money Money*… in Abba fancy dress. That showed good rep skills if anyone was watching us – quick and decisive.

The morning continued with a long presentation, accompanied by copious printed notes on rooming lists, self-billing, extra beds, avoiding over-booking, late bookings, superdeals, and the Freesale System for administration. After lunch, we learned about insurance and communication skills – a vital part of the rep's job indeed. By dinner time at 6.30pm, we had a sense of information overload, as it was all new terminology to most of us, but we had a fun evening of Alpine Bowling. This went some way to relax me until I noticed that some of the senior staff were standing at the back of the bowling alley drinking their beers but not talking to each other, just watching us. I had forgotten about The Observers, or Camp Guards as we had named them. *Had I been ebullient and sociable enough with my fellow reps? Had I drunk enough, but not too much?* I quickly downed another couple of free beers to liven me up just in case. We continued bowling and drinking through the evening and got progressively worse at the former and better at the latter. Before we left the bowling alley at about 2am, Bob called for quiet to announce that we all had to be on parade in our chalets at 5.45am the following morning, fully kitted out in our uniforms, looking sharpish and ready to go out on the Treasure Hunt at 6am. That meant setting the alarm for 5.15am. *Why had I not read that in the timetable? Why did I have so many extra beers on top of the two needed to perk me up?*

The week's printed timetable confirmed it was true. A 6am start for a two hour treasure hunt, that began in the dark in a snow covered meadow, was followed at 9am by two hours of accounts, with a hangover. The handy one liner motto at the end of the previous day's activities was the rather Churchillian: "*See every difficulty as a challenge, a stepping stone and never be defeated by anything or anyone*". The purpose of the previous night and early morning was to test our ability to stay out socialising with guests and still be able to make an early morning transfer to the airport.

If the early romp around the snowy meadow and adjacent streets hadn't cured the hangover, there was a sobering sight that greeted us on arrival in the Opium Centre, as it was referred to. We were partaking in a reverse or perhaps perverse game of musical chairs as we realised there were now more chairs than reps this morning. Had people overslept? Or were they too hung-over? No. The Camp Guards had struck at their prey and removed them already. Bloody Hell, they weren't messing around. Three people had already been singled out and sent home. One of them, we found out later, had to go home because he was ill, but it was a stark warning none the less.

Accounts were followed by a coffee break and then more accounts. It is crucial as a rep to get your accounting done correctly. In the large resorts, where you may get a hundred or more people arrive in a week, you could be handling a lot of money (dealing with currency exchange, booking ski school, ski hire, lift passes, and all the excursions you were hoping to sell) and the money starts coming in to you the moment you pick up the guests from the airport as you do your transfer.

Most of the people broke again for German lessons, but the Scandies and Bulges (Bulgarian reps) had a civilised cup of coffee. Accounts dragged on in the afternoon but we were rescued from it at 14.30 by First Aid, appropriately, for an hour and a half. There was the necessary basic first aid instruction for those that were looking after guests in a chalet, but this was followed by mountain first aid directed at reps who were going to be ski escorting. It was a major responsibility taking a group of people out around the mountains and if anything went wrong we, as ski guides, had to know what to do. We were frightened into paying attention by accounts of one skier who had an arm amputated whilst skiing at speed past a metal gate, outstretching her arms just at the wrong moment, and another story of a family who got lost when the weather closed in too quickly. They got disorientated in the woods and decided to split up. One half of the family made it back to the resort, the other two weren't found until the spring when the snow melted and their bodies were revealed.

We were told that the most common injuries we would have to deal with were to the knee and thumb and the main reason for that was bad equipment. Rented skis would not be adjusted fully to account for weight, height or experience and the release binding mechanism could not always do its job.

Our essential procedure in the case of an accident, which is good advice for anyone skiing, was:

1. Form a X with the skis twenty paces or so uphill to secure the area.
2. Check where the injury is.
3. Remove skis.
4. Do NOT remove boots.
5. Place injured person in most comfortable position.
6. i) Is injured person able to move by him / herself?
   ii) Do you need ski patrol to take him down the mountain?
7. Ask another skier to report the accident and exact location to ski patrol.

As the lectures and seminars progressed, I amassed more and more paperwork in the form of instructions and operations manuals (one running to over a hundred pages) as well as examples of form filling, ledgers and a copious amount of my own notes on just about everything I heard. I was beginning to feel swamped, but Bob reassured me that perhaps 20% of what I was listening to might only apply to Austrian resorts and things were a little different in Sweden – more, low key. For anyone who thinks the rep's job is easy, there is a tremendous amount of work going on behind the scenes and if your ski week goes smoothly then you have a good rep. It was like being back at university carrying around A4 bundles of paper from lecture to lecture. There was a mass of important information to absorb in a short space of time and so much new terminology, such as: Arrival and Departure Lists (details of your arriving and departing guests), Rooming Lists, Release Dates (when the rooms are released back to the hotels). For example, you would receive by fax a long sheet of names, which detailed each family or group as follows:

Arriving 28 Dec 96 at KAPRUN ORGLER HTL (accommodation code no.1473)

Mrs A Smith	142997 (CS) HB	BY557A MAN/SZB	arr.10:55
Mr J Smith	7 days	28 Dec–96 07:55	Sat 28 Dec
	10 Batn WC	BY 6573 SZG/MAN	dep. 11:55
	Balcony (7x1Q)	04 Jan–97	Saturday
Mstr M Smith	age 6		
Miss R Smith	age 8		

	Extras:	6 Day: 2 Adults: Lift Pass
		6 Day: 2 Adults: Skis & Sticks
		6 Day: 2 Adults: Boots
		6 Day: Adults: Tuition

And it would go on for pages and pages, depending on how big the resort was. You could generally tell what kind of week ahead you were going to have by scanning through these arrival lists; whether there was any chance of making some money by selling excursions or because they hadn't pre-booked passes, equipment and lessons. I remember getting a bit annoyed on receiving one week's list where they had pre-booked nearly everything – miserable buggers. Other schedules could bring a smile to your face if they listed a group of arrivals as:

Miss ....

Miss ....

Miss ....

Miss ....

Miss ....

Miss ....

And even better if they hadn't pre-booked a thing!

In the Operations Manual, they had fortunately listed a 'Jargon and Reminder Summary':

Section One listed all the airport and airline codes with contact telephone numbers. Section Two listed the other tour companies operating in the same resort. Section Three listed everything else as:

Amendment Form	Form that you send to Tom or Reinhardt with corrections from the first set of transfer figures.
Arrival List	A list of arrivals for your resort, received in company mail seven days in advance.
CAS	Client and Agent Services.
Coach Splits	Tom's figures that have been reformatted so that you can see exactly who is going on which coach.
Company Mail	Mail that comes from the UK containing rooming lists, arrival and departure lists.
Cover Sheets	A list of guests per flight produced by each rep (one for each flight).
Departure Lists	A list of departures for your resort, received in company mail seven days in advance.
Evening	A day or night time event organised by the rep for which he pays the supplier direct.
Feeder	A taxi that drives to or picks up from a central pick up point to meet the coach.
Flight Schedule	List of flights scheduled for winter with local landing and take-off times.
Information books	Red folders to be out in each hotel or chalet.

Late booking	A booking for a hotel after the release date has passed.
Manifest	A list of arrivals by flight (you will only see this at the airport).
Notice Boards	Four, two or one page boards to be put up in hotels and chalets ASAP.
OPS	Operations or anything to do with bookings or flights.
PAX	Passengers.
QC	Quality Control.
Release Date	When the rooms are released back to the hotels.
Ski Packs	Ski school, ski and boot hire, and lift passes.
Superdeal	Late booking that has not booked a particular accommodation.
Tom's figures	Transfer figures that you receive from Tom.
Transfer Grids	The grids you complete for your own reference.
Welcome get together	Meeting held on Sunday afternoon / evening to tell guests of events through the week.
Welcome pack	Eight page information for the guests.

It went on further with references to brochure updates / marketing ideas and where we should send them (this was pre-email days), along with hotel self-billing forms, quality control, report forms, client complaints, rooming list problems, discrepancies between rooming lists and manifests, no shows, curtailments, hotel changes, flight changes, queries about whether clients had paid for facilities (e.g., balconies or ski packs), lost property (we were advised not to send anything back to the UK!). The Operations Manual stretched to some twenty-six pages of A4, followed by almost forty pages of appendices showing examples of Late Booking forms, manifests, coach splits, transfer correction forms, free room reports, snow reports, and finally, the questionnaire. Additionally, we had been supplied with a ninety page Overseas Representatives Information Manual. I was impressed by the detail and thoroughness of this ski company, that's for sure.

So... not all skiing, drinking and sleeping then... and a surprising amount of training given to reps of this particular company, which must be reassuring, although apparently the Austrian training week is tougher than the French and Italian, a fact confirmed by some of the other reps that had done a season in Italy. Our Monday, the day to *"Be realistic, plan for a miracle"*, was to culminate in a pub crawl through Kaprun at 8pm.

We have some odd archaic traditions and customs in the UK but nothing quite like the Krampus. Most tourists aren't in Austria at this time of year, and that's probably just as well.

If you were as tired and stressed and really wanting to crawl into your bed as we all were, you really don't need another night out drinking and socialising, but the Camp Guards were pushing us to our limits again. What you certainly don't need is to come out of a bar feeling a little bit shabby only to be confronted full on by a large wild and angry furry goat-like man with a deathly-white face, long fangs and claws, and two foot long horns protruding from his skull.

If that's not enough, there wasn't just one of them, the streets were full of them. If you didn't move out of the way quickly enough – only having had a few hours' sleep the night before, a few too many lagers and shots of *Jägermeister*, whilst trying to bang a four inch nail into a tree stump with the wrong end of a hammer head – they would beat you savagely with their chains and ring their bells demonically. They too had been drinking and had lost all sense of what was an acceptable level of force to use when beating members of the public.

Dating back to the Seventeenth Century, the Krampus are part of Alpine folklore, although I haven't ever seen them in France or Italy, and come out at this time of year to punish children that have been bad during the year. Resembling half bear and half goat like creatures, they were supposed to carry off naughty children and take them to their lairs, but this is not allowed any more for obvious reasons and perhaps because there aren't many children staggering out of bars in the centre of places like Kaprun at ten o'clock in the evening.

I think we caught the tail end of this odd Yuletide celebration. These monsters had been drinking copious amount of schnapps and beer, after rounding up random kids and scaring the crap out of them, and it was now their turn to pick on the adults. It was a wonder the infamous child catcher of Vulgaria was not involved in the evening's event. He still scares me all these years later when I watch *Chitty Chitty Bang Bang*. With their full head gear, most of them stood well over seven feet tall and were standing in the middle of the street roaring at the pedestrians and thwacking their chains on the ground, glaring threateningly at anyone that dared to step closer.

The locals were equally enthralled and scared at the spectacle, as they packed the pavements to get a closer look and then reeled back en mass when one of the monsters lurched towards them. Things could easily get out of hand and, indeed, I saw one of them down a side street being bundled into a police van resisting arrest, shouting and trying to shake them off. They were truly terrifying, particularly as they all appeared to be very drunk and very violent. I always thought circus clowns were scary enough for children; the Krampus were likely to have very long lasting effects on a child.

As much fun as it was being chain whipped by an inebriated oversized goat, we soon tired of it and headed back to the chalet, running away down one street as fast as we could on the snow when one of them roared at us when it caught sight of us. It would have been very unfortunate, if not a little irritating, to have to pull out of the training because of a Krampus inflicted injury.

The following day began at a more leisurely 9am, where we met at the Sonnenalp chalet for what was described as a "Fun day skiing and ski guide training". If all was to go wrong at the end of the week and I wouldn't make the grade, at least I would have had a day's skiing in Austria and a few interesting days away from grey London. I was a little apprehensive about today as I had only done seven weeks' skiing and the entry form had said a minimum ten weeks was required. This was the day I could be found out as a fraud if I wasn't careful. As it turned out, I had nothing to worry about and the day was indeed a fun day, mainly because we could escape from the constant observation of the camp guards and we could yawn without punishment. In the lectures and seminars, if we were seen to yawn, slouch, or worse – nod off, they would call out and you would lose points for your team. We would need all the points we could muster as we had only snatched a spare hour to run through our Abba cabaret routine and had yet to source the costumes and props, even though show time was tonight.

The skiing test was carried out on an easy red run and we just had to follow other reps around in small groups and then do a basic slalom course under observation. We learned from the experienced reps about the dos and don'ts of ski leading; essentially, to keep the group together and not lose anyone on your way around the mountains. It was stressed, rightly so, on the importance of leading a group sensibly and being aware of everyone's skiing abilities. It only dawned on me then properly that it was going to be a huge responsibility taking a group of tourists out and about on the pistes and the buck would stop with me. The rep would be responsible for their enjoyment of the day and their safety. It was important, therefore, to note how many you had in a group, allocate a backmarker so you know when they arrived at a point on the slopes that you had your entire group together as one. It was their job to ensure they were last down a slope. We were instructed to always stop the group at the side of the run and not in the middle, as well as remembering to stop reasonably frequently to make sure everyone knew where you were going. We as reps also had to take the decision to exclude any guest from skiing if we felt they were not up to it and this, we were told, could cause problems so it had to be done with tact. This is why we were encouraged to offer two ski escorting days during a week, the first one covering blue and red runs, the second one, reds and blacks. I hoped the blacks weren't going to be too steep in Sweden or I might be following my guests down, embarrassingly. I reassured myself that I could pick some easy blacks to do with the guests and would make finding those a priority in the week I had in the resort before any guests arrived.

The Information Manual was keen to stress that the ski escort was not there to teach the guests to ski but we were to accompany the clients whilst skiing, rather than leading or guiding them. The role was described as one that required organisation, patience, dedication and, above all, a professional attitude. Fair enough.

In the late afternoon my team, the Scandies, met in a corner of one of the chalet lounges to prepare our Cabaret for the evening. It revolved around the Abba song *Money, Money, Money* and was no more than us miming to the lyrics, acting out different parts wearing ski gear, with the finale being two of us throwing lots of money (newspapers cut up into five pound note sized pieces). Our *pièce de résistance* was that one of our team, Ulrika, was actually Swedish, although she sang all her lines in English. Suffice it to say, we didn't win the reps competition later that night, but we scored enough points to ensure we were still all in the running for our respective resort jobs. We were all very relieved that, as Scandinavian reps, we would not be required to put on such a show each week for our guests and I pitied the ones working in Austria who would. Was that really what skiers wanted to see? It seemed more of a Benidorm type of thing to me.

Wednesday started with another lecture at 9am – "Transfer figures – Compilation" was the title. I struggled to keep awake and got caught napping by the overseers but my crime did not find its way to our team total. During the coffee break at 10.15am I stepped outside to fill my lungs with some crisp mountain air. As I stood outside the building on the snow and chatted to some others, I noticed that the base of my left foot began to feel cold. I looked around at everyone else's boots. They had all followed the instructions and bought new Timberland boots. I, on the other hand, had convinced myself that my four year old walking boots from Milletts would do the trick, thereby saving me a hundred pound. This was not the time for them to give up their usefulness. If they were starting to wear thin now there was no way they would survive a further five months of the coldest winter I (and they) would ever know on the Norwegian-Swedish border, and that meant my parsimoniousness would in fact backfire on me when I was forced to buy a new pair of boots in Sweden.

Back into the lecture hall and we faced the written Transfer Test for an hour and half, followed immediately by an hour's talk on the actual transfer itself, which included what you do going to and from the airport and selling on the coach. Airport etiquette was also an important topic and that covered wearing the corporate cap at all times, not chewing gum, wearing the correct boots (ahem), the clipboard, the coach board, and the rule not to wear the ski jacket inside the airport building.

We were told that selling on the coach was a crucial skill as it brought in a lot of revenue to the company as well as ourselves. It was a pressured time because the guests were often tired from their early start and flight but excited to be in the snowy landscape. It was your first opportunity to meet them, get to know them, and make a good impression. It was their first chance to ask you often ridiculous questions, but you had to reassure them all was well. The most important thing to tell them was that there was snow in the resort, which usually got a cheer. The most important thing not to mention was anything to do with the return trip to the airport. They had only just arrived – under no circumstances were we to refer to their homeward journey on the airport pick up. We had the opportunity to sell ski packs and earn commission and the beauty was the guests could sort out everything with one payment. Many lift companies don't take credit cards but we do. Skis and boots could be upgraded with us on the coach and we were to stress that these would be new boots which would be more comfortable, with more adjustments; they would look better and therefore the guests would ski better!

On to Ski School and we were encouraged to say that no one was too good for it, which is true. Even the Austrian ski instructors go every two years, which I wasn't sure was true. It was a good way to meet people, true, and they would always learn something and see the mountain, also true. The more days they booked the better value it became and of course the more commission we earned.

Buying the lift pass through us meant that the guests would not have to endure the morning lift pass queues as we would promise to get the passes for them first thing and deliver them to their hotels or chalets. We were to promote the benefits of purchasing an area pass, rather than a local pass, which also boosted our commission.

After another lunch in the Orgler restaurant, we returned to the lecture hall to receive the results of our Transfer Test and then had a two hour Accounts test. This was becoming an endurance test, not only physically but mentally too, and was much more involved than I ever imagined it would be. As we took our seats for the test, I registered more empty seats again, but I had never seen anyone being dragged off to a waiting minibus, so how did they remove people?

The accounts test was in three parts:

Part 1
Prepare the ski pack vouchers (both pre-booked and resort sale) for the clients listed below:

We were given the names of five guest groups and what they had booked and where they were staying – Morecambe x2, Wise x2, Corbett x 2 1/2, Barker 3 2/2 and Hill x2 (presumably Mr B).

Part 2
Complete the ski pack accounts and the day and evening excursion accounts for the resort. Make sure that the paperwork is complete and that all relevant forms are used.

Don't forget a complete set of accounts includes the following documents:

Ski Packs:

- Paying in slip.
- Resort Sales Summary.

- Credit Card Summary plus credit card payment request forms.
- Resort Sales vouchers.
- Pre-booked and learn to ski vouchers.
- Supplier vouchers.

Day and Evening Accounts:

- Day / Evening paying in slip.
- Day excursion summary.
- Evening accounts summary.
- Tax receipt forms.

Part 3

Complete all the relevant amendment forms in relation to the additional queries set out under 'Other Matters'.

Don't forget expense claims will only be processed if all supporting documents are included.

We had to answer questions and fill in forms dealing with different scenarios, such as: if one party wanted to pay by credit card and another by cash, if one person wanted to upgrade what they had booked, or if there was a late booking / arrival. This was all quite taxing, even in the peace and quiet of the lecture hall. It must have been a doddle for the reps who had worked a season previously but quite challenging for the majority of us.

At dinner that evening back in the chalet, we all realised we were more than half way through the week test which was something to celebrate and planned to go out to a bar later. That idea was scrapped when we were told to report to Rudi's Bar for a quiz at 8pm. After that, we were dragged half way up a steep meadow where we waited, in line and in small groups, to jump into an inflated truck inner tube, which was then heaved off the starting line and spun and bounced and almost tipped over as it careered down the snowy field to the bottom corner. Following this, we were herded off to another location and chucked onto toboggans. One of the reps crashed badly and damaged his wrist, which was tough, although he was allowed to stay on the course. It would have been very unfortunate to have got this far and to be sent home through no fault of your own, although it emerged later that perhaps he had been drinking a bit too much.

The purpose of these activities was to demonstrate the variety of evening activities we could organise and sell tickets for. I and a few others managed to sneak off back to our chalet and miss out on the shots that were being lined up at the last bar. We worried that we might be docked some points for this but it was not the case and, if we had been, we had prepared an argument that we had used our rep's judgement of when it was right to call it a day.

Thursday morning brought us the Transfer Training session, where we all had to assemble outside the Sonnenalp at 9am with our passports and in full uniform. Three coaches were parked across the road and we were soon allocated to one for the journey to Salzburg airport. We were each called up to the front of the coach in turn and asked to talk over the microphone about something while they assessed you. This was quite daunting, talking to fifty other colleagues about "something". In the heat of the moment, my mind went blank as I took up my position at the front of the coach in the jump seat. I've no idea why but, before I could stop myself, I had announced that I was going to talk about… olives; green ones, black ones, oil, soap and trees. Well it filled a couple of minutes and that's all that mattered.

When we arrived at Salzburg airport, we had a very interesting tour behind the scenes and some of us were offered a go on the tannoy system. It was not a busy time in the airport day but the few passengers that were there must have been confused at a string of announcements that included "Arsenal 2, Liverpool 1", "You plonker, Rodney", and "the 10.27 train for Bristol Temple Meads calling at Slough, Reading, Didcot, Swindon… has just departed".

On the return trip to Kaprun, a few of us were called up again to practise the "leaving the airport speech", the "mid-journey speech", the "arriving into resort speech" and the "drop off at your hotel speech."

After lunch, we listened to even more talks on hotel visits, office hours, preparation of information books and boards, welcome meetings, quality control paperwork, and diplomacy in dealing with awkward clients (with role play situations to enact). *How much more was there to learn?* I wondered as, indeed, probably you are wondering too.

Another late evening ensued, as it was Party Night at Café Nindl, and then another day dawned. Only one more to get through after this one, but there was still more information to take in. We had a brochure knowledge and booking conditions test, then a coffee break, then a talk on health and safety, a talk entitled "Taking the stigma out of selling; how, when and what to sell. Special offers and costings". Lunch was followed by three more hours of talks on: selling tactics, cross selling, sourcing features and benefits and putting these into a sales pitch, target setting, and troubleshooting. It was quite clear that the company needed us to push sales as much as possible to boost revenues. Although our accommodation and food, season lift pass, and ski hire was all paid for, we were being paid only £80 a week, so it was in our own interest to push the sales as much as possible. However, as the week had progressed, it became clear that many of the seasoned reps had details of scams that could be run to boost our earnings and, naturally, we were keen to learn more. Huddled conversations were being had in corners of chalets and bars.

The evening's extravagantly titled Gala Dinner signalled that we must be nearing the end of our test and Saturday morning's assembly at 9am produced the Accounts test results, where I was pleased to learn I had scored nine out of ten, but less pleased to read the comment "A bit messy". I felt like a school child again, a very, very tired one. After the coffee break, we broke into smaller groups, where the Scandies had an informal chat with Dapper Bob, resplendent in full Sherlock Holmes style tweeds, who gave us a run down on the immediate things to be done in the resort. Did this mean that we had passed? There were two resorts in Sweden; Åre and Sälen, and two in Norway; Geilo and Hemsedal. There were seven of us in our group and I knew that Åre required two reps, being the largest in Scandinavia. It looked as though I had got a job, but where?

We had an unreasonably long wait to find out. We sat with a large group of the Austrian contingent in one of the bars, playing cards, drinking coffee, chatting and waiting nervously to be called out of the room to be told our fate. After two hours, we still hadn't found out so we went outside for a snowball fight to relieve the pressure. We watched other reps step out of the consulting office and head off to collect their belongings. Some were elated and whooped as they left the building and didn't object to a well-aimed snowball. Others were quieter and some were very down. No one who had got this far was to be rejected, as the no hopers had been wheedled out previously, but there were good and bad resorts to be allocated to. Some of them were very lucrative. With hundreds of guests arriving each week, there was a huge opportunity for the experienced reps to earn big commissions, which meant they could take the summer off and just work the winter season.

We had moved back inside by the time I was called into the office. *Why me ahead of anyone else?!* I was apprehensive as I entered the room, but they quickly told me the good news that I had passed and was being sent to the resort of my choice, Åre. A Contract for Services of Overseas Representatives was produced for me to sign, informing me I would be paid £80 a week towards subsistence expenses, but only £60 of which would be paid at the end of every two weeks, the balance at the end of the season (assuming I went the distance).

The commission was to be based on 10% of the company's profits on sales of ski equipment hire, ski school and lift passes and 20% on evening activities. There would be no contribution to accommodation expenses but I was told that we would be staying at Sporthotellet (The Sport Hotel), a *former* grand hotel – stronger emphasis on the word former should have been used – along with other Swedish resort staff, and all meals would be provided for us at the Hotel Åregården, which was the best hotel in the village. We'd be eating in the basement with the hotel staff. That all sounded fine to me. I would be working alongside "schoolboy" John, with whom I had been sharing a room this week. He had worked there before, which was good to learn, although I expected much more imparting of knowledge from him and that might become irritating.

The third member of the Swedish team would be Ulrika, who spoke impeccable English. She was a healthy looking Swede with shoulder length white-blonde hair, blue grey eyes and a smattering of freckles. She would be based in Sälen, where her family owned a chalet and would help us out when required. I was too exhausted to whoop for joy as I left, but I still got a celebratory snowball in the left shoulder from one of the Austrian reps.

A great wave of relief came over me and I began to look forward to what the next five months had in store for me. It was going to be an adventure of a different kind.

Super Trouper

The next morning our little group was up early. We were breakfasted, packed and ready to go by 9.30am. We waited in the entrance hall of the chalet for our minibus to appear. It didn't. And for quite a long time it didn't appear. For a holiday company that had spent the last week preaching to us about efficiency and promptness of service, this was ironic to say the least. After an hour of waiting it became mildly irritating and, after a further thirty minutes, we began to wonder if they had just forgotten about us, being the minor group compared to the vast number of reps and chalet staff working the Austrian and Swiss resorts, who had had coaches a plenty laid on for them.

Dapper Bob appeared through the entrance door and announced the good news that our chariot awaited and apologised for the wait. They had had to requisition the vehicle from the Austrian head office in St Johann – and more form filling had been demanded. We gathered up our luggage and headed out into the bright sunshine. The other good news was that the minibus was reasonably new and therefore we would be riding in relative comfort. The bad news was that this minibus would be taking us all the way.

"Whaaat???"

"Yes, it will be needed in Norway for the season," Bob confirmed.

"OK... what about those going to Sweden?" I asked, hesitantly, not knowing what to expect but assuming a tour company such as the one I had just signed an employment contract with had the resources to stick us on a plane. That would be the quickest way to get to our resort. After all, we had our first guests arriving in a little over a week. We would be driven to Salzburg airport and board an airplane to Stockholm or somewhere.

Bob drew a deep breath. "The plan is we shall all be going in the minibus to Kiel in northern Germany, where we will board an overnight ferry to Oslo. The minibus will then head on to Geilo with the Norwegian reps and me. The three Swedish reps will get a bus from Oslo down the coast to Gothenburg and then get a train to Åre… err… via Stockholm"

The Norwegian reps started to chuckle, particularly my new mate Simon, with whom I had bonded during the training week.

Bob had shown he had a great sense of humour and I knew he was now joking with us.

"Funny, Bob, very funny. What are we really doing?" I demanded, hoping he was winding us up.

"No I'm afraid it's true," he replied. He looked at John, who looked at me and nodded uncomfortably.

"You could have told us all that before we signed our contracts!" I joked, sort of.

"That's why we are telling you all now," he said, adding, "Look, I am coming with you. It will be a laugh. John has his guitar and the Norwegian ferry is like a floating hotel."

"Oh, great. How long is the train ride from Gothenburg then?" I enquired.

"It's about twelve hours," answered John.

"How long have you known about this?" I asked him.

"For a few days now"

"Come on, Mr Grumpy," encouraged Simon, "We're all in it together, mate." And he gave me a dig in the ribs with his elbow. *Why was I the only one voicing my alarm?* There was one couple who were going to be joint reps in one of the Norwegian resorts who were so lovey dovey I doubt they had even taken in what was about to happen.

"Baggsie front seat for the twisty mountain roads then," I exclaimed and we all began lifting our luggage up to be packed into any spare space we could find.

Within half an hour, we were off, John at the wheel. Dapper Bob had some paperwork to finish off and said he would join us at head office in St Johann, which is where we needed to be heading now to pick up stationery and other stuff for our reports. We hadn't gone more than three kilometres down the road before Simon let one go; a big strong early morning one. The couple didn't notice but everyone else reached for the window winders quickly. This was going to be a long journey.

Heading out of Kaprun, my spirits lifted somewhat as I took in the beautiful mountain scenery. The fields at the side of the road were covered in deep fresh snow that made the day seem even brighter under the blue skies, as they reflected the sun's light back at us. The road sides were lined with tall black marker poles at regular intervals, behind which stood steep cliffs of snow. The snow ploughs had already been busy. The black tarmac glistened in places with the water residue of melted snow, but the strong sun had dried most of the road and, unlike England with only 2cms of snow, the traffic moved freely.

Loaded to the gunnels, we made our way through villages and hamlets, passing farm buildings with steaming cattle secured at ground floor level, under the human accommodation; natural under floor heating. The ski industry so dominates the landscape here it was often hard to see how different the scenery would look in the summer under this thick white blanket. The road took us alongside the Salzach River in the valley floor for about 30 kms until, about an hour into our journey, we arrived in St Johann in Pongau. John had been to the Austrian HQ many times before and so it was odd that he couldn't find the office building in Kaierstrasse. Up and down the main street he drove us, but the building he was searching for was nowhere to be seen. He stopped by the side of the road and phoned Bob.

"Ah... no we're in St Johann im Pongau," he confessed.

"Right…" It didn't sound promising and he grabbed a road map from the door pocket and spread it out across the steering wheel, holding the phone in the crook of his neck.

"Oh… yes I see now," he continued, somewhat embarrassed as he was the type of person who claimed he knew it all and was never wrong about anything. He laughed it off; we didn't and gave him some well deserved abuse. He had driven us an hour in the wrong direction and we should have been in St Johann in Tirol but there was no point in making a big deal out of it as we all had a long way to travel together. It was even longer now. The map showed a narrow mountain road a little further ahead beyond our St Johann that looked like it would take us to Saalfelden, so we took that and weaved our now less than merry way towards the proper St Johann, where it was very easy to find the office in Kaiserstrasse.

After a brief stop to load up with stationery and Bob and his luggage, we set off again for Salzburg with everyone being very helpful to John, shouting out signs to Salzburg when they saw them. We stopped at a service station near on the outskirts of Salzburg for a coffee and a sandwich and then swapped around seats. I packed myself into a seat, rearranging some luggage and jackets to make my journey as comfortable as possible and to enable me to get some much needed sleep, and we headed off towards Germany in a northerly direction and along busy main roads. I was grateful someone else was doing the driving and settled into a deep sleep.

The next thing I knew, we had stopped in another service station car park and everyone was piling out. It was dark now and cold. I followed the rest of them to the café, not wanting to wake up properly, and we grabbed another light bite. We had made reasonable progress and I was looking forward to getting back into my seat but was told it was my turn to drive. We were on the southern outskirts of Munich. It was dark and had just started to rain as I pulled out onto the autobahn. My stint also happened to coincide with Munich's rush hour, so that woke me up properly.

We swapped driver stints every two hours and, about eight hours later, we pulled off into another service station car park for the night. Not in an hotel, or even a cheap roadside motel, but in the bloody minibus. All the Austrian reps would be safely ensconced in their warm chalets by now, having had an opportunity to familiarise themselves with their resort a bit and had a hot meal inside their bellies. We were stuffed into a freezing minibus and were woken every few hours during the night with either big trucks manoeuvring close to us, their headlights illuminating the interior, or the engine being switched on and running for ten minutes so the heater could take the edge of the freezing temperature and melt the ice that our breathing had created on the inside of the windows.

I felt I was fully justified in being Mr Grumpy again the following morning. It was so cold at 6am that no one was sleeping so we decided to press on and, after an hour on the road, we arrived in the port of Kiel. We pulled into a car park and stretched our legs around the town. Nothing was open, apart from a few cafés and a McDonalds, so we pressed Bob into coughing up for a Big Mac Breakfast for us all and sat there for a while after having coffees and warming up.

Our ferry to Oslo was not open for boarding until 2.30pm so we spent the time in various cafés and wandering around the dock area. The temperature was hovering around zero degrees but compared to the minus ten it was in the Alps, it felt so much colder. The damp air of the docks penetrated our clothing and went right through to the bone. It was miserable and the leaden grey sky did nothing to lighten our mood. We were the first on board the ferry and it felt good to be in the dry and warmth of our cabins. We joked with Bob that we were amazed to find ourselves in a proper cabin. We'd expected to have to sleep overnight on seats. We were all tired and grateful to be able to stretch out on a proper bed, so an early night was called after a full evening meal.

The next morning greeted us with the same grey skies but a much lower temperature. At ten o'clock, after our breakfast, we all went out on deck to watch the small wooded islands come and go as the huge ferry made its way through the outer archipelago. At first, there were just the odd pine covered islands scattered among the water and then they appeared with more frequency, as if someone was loading different sized broccoli onto a conveyor belt, only we were the ones passing by.

As we progressed further up the fjord, the land became continuous and covered with trees, no longer broken up by patches of dark cold water. We expected we were nearing the city of Oslo, so stayed out in the cold to observe our progress but, after two hours of this slowly changing landscape, we were still heading up the Oslo fjord. Some of the islands we passed were splashed with reddish brown square blobs of colour, the summer homes of the city dwellers, contrasting with the grey rock and dark green of the foliage, but the islands were such an appropriate earthy colour. Nature's colours finally succumbed to the urban beige of man's sprawl and we finally eased our way into Norway's capital city and came to a rest in the port.

The minibus dropped us, the three Swedish reps, at the bus station and we said goodbye to the Norwegian team. It was quite a sad moment as we had all got to know each other quite well and were then going our separate ways. John, Ulrika and I caught a coach, which took us down the west coast of Sweden to Gothenburg as we call it – or Göteborg, as they spell it, and Yertibori, as they pronounce it. *Borg* means 'castle' and the city sits on the mouth of the Göta älv. Bjorn Borg translates somewhat quaintly as 'Bear Castle'. It was a mere three hour coach journey to Gothenburg and I had given up keeping tally of how many hours we had been travelling since leaving Kaprun. Our first guests had probably begun packing their bags ahead of their holiday and all the Austrian reps had recce'd their resorts, prepared their welcome packs, and were kicking back waiting for the first arrivals list to come through.

The final leg of our journey, the overnight train directly to Åre (well, via Stockholm on the other side of the country), was not due to depart the train station until 8.45pm so we had another few hours to kill. Fortunately, Gothenburg rail station is very pleasant place to while away the hours. It's all big expanses of glass, mixed with strips of fine cut timber, dark stone and slate and crisp metal. There are restaurants and shops and a relaxed atmosphere. Good looking, well dressed people with smart luggage move about with ease knowing that their train will definitely not be cancelled and will certainly leave on time. That creates a relaxed air and I could sense that in these travellers. What's more they hadn't been fleeced by the rail company for the price of their tickets. For the price of a single ticket from London to Brighton, a journey of fifty miles, the Swedish rail company, SJ, would take you well over seven hundred miles and give you a bed in a smooth, clean and tastefully decorated carriage (with water cartons supplied free of charge).

The journey to Stockholm took us almost horizontally across the country to its capital city but it was a further three hundred miles up to the ski resort in the region of Jämtland (pronounced *Yemtland*). From there, you could travel almost another seven hundred miles north before you would enter another country, Finland. If you were to swing it round on its axis a hundred and eighty degrees, it would stretch right across mainland Europe as far south as Tunisia.

That's one of the incredible facts about Sweden; it is a vast country. It is so big that it has its own measure of distance, as if expressing distances in mere kilometres would be too silly. The

Swedes have adopted our mile as a measure of great distance only their Swedish Mile is the equivalent of 10 kilometres. It is not the longest country in Europe, Norway is, but Sweden from its most northerly point to its most southerly is twenty two miles short of a thousand miles. It's three hundred and ten miles across and is Europe's fifth largest country in geographical area, but has a population of just nine and a half million. The Metropolitan area of London's population is thirteen million.

And that's the thing about Sweden: it is relatively unknown and unvisited, although everyone seems to have an opinion about it, which usually includes Abba, they are all blondes, it's dark and cold… and the beer is expensive. However, it has made a far greater contribution to the world but has been, in true Swedish style, a little understated. We have all heard of Volvo and Saab, two of Sweden's most well known exports, but there are many other Swedish companies that many people don't know are Swedish: Electrolux, Swedish Match (OK, that might now be a bit obvious but it's a huge company), 3H Biomedical, Abba Seafood (nothing to do with the group), Astra Zeneca, Atlas Copco, Ericsson, Filippa K, H&M, Hasselblad, Handelsbanken, Hestra, Husqvarna, IKEA, J.Lindberg, Kopparbergs Brewery, Koenisegg, Nudie Jeans, Orrefors glassworks, Peak Performance, SAS Group, Securitas, Scania, Skandia, SEB, Skanska, SKF, Spotify, Stora Enso, Tetra Pak, Thule.

The USA and the UK have contributed most to the world of music over the last half century, but would you ever have credited Sweden with third place? Consider the following: Abba, Roxette, Europe, Ace of Base, Kent, Neneh, Eagle-Eye Cherry, The Cardigans (to name a few). Ireland might actually compete for third place, depending on how the contribution is determined, but it's very close. Anyway, the point is that, compared to other more globally identifiable countries, in terms of world contribution and influence, Sweden is way up there.

We boarded the train at 8.15pm and found our way to our sleeper cabin. For once, it was a pleasure to be on a train. The couchette was well appointed and tastefully decorated, using generous sculpted cuts of birch ply. The train staff welcomed us warmly and genuinely. It was more like boarding a plane. Before we settled in for the night, we had a drink in the restaurant carriage and, as I watched the second hand on the oversized platform clock sweep towards the number twelve, the train hissed and moved off effortlessly.

As we began the final leg of our journey at 8.45pm and one second, I began my first Swedish lesson with Ulrika. "Swedish in twelve hours," she called it. I had visited Sweden a few times before and so I had a limited knowledge of the language, but it was very limited. Although most Swedes, especially the younger ones, speak almost perfect English (perfection would be without American accent), she decided I needed to learn some basics:

- *Jag heter* Andrew – My name is Andrew (useful just to show a willingness to speak the language).
- *Jag är från* England – I am from England (when I am spoken to by someone who thinks I'm a local).
- *God morgon* – Good morning (or, Good Moron, as it sounded, rather amusingly).
- *God kväll* – good evening.
- *God natt* – good night.
- *Sov gott* – sleep well
- *Jag pratar inte Svenska* – I do not speak Swedish (I so wanted to learn to say that without any trace of an English accent).

She continued with:

- *Och* – and.
- *Med* – with.

- *På* – on.
- *Var så god* – You're welcome.

And then we moved onto words relevant to where we were going to be:

- *Lift kort* – lift pass.
- Öppet – open.
- *Stängt* – closed.
- *Backe* – piste.
- *Lavin fara* – Avalanche danger.
- *Skit* – shit (not sure why she threw that one in. Had she been watching my skiing on the test? She was a qualified ski instructor after all). It is pronounced *Hhquid* – I just know you want to know how to say that in Swedish.
- *En stor öl* – a large beer
- *Vad är klockan?* – What's the time?

The Swedes always use the twenty four hour clock so that's easy when you have learned the numbers and I could already count to twenty but "a quarter past three" for example is "*kvart over tre*", quarter to nine is "*kvart i nio*" but five thirty is "*halv sex*" – half six. That quirkiness could cause real problems on timings as you could find yourself an hour late if not careful.

Weirdly, I felt compelled to impress her by telling her that in Norwegian Supercalifragilisticexpealidocious was *Superoptikjempefantafenomenalistisk*. She looked at me blankly for quite a while. Unsurprisingly, she was not impressed as she had never seen the film nor wanted or had any need to know what it was in Norwegian. With hindsight, I am not sure how many people on the planet would be impressed with that knowledge, other than the rest of the school class of my Norwegian friends' eleven year old daughter, Madeleine, who taught me to say it a couple of years previously, but I had never had the chance to use it and, right then, it seemed like it could have been a good opportunity. Even though Ulrika wasn't impressed, I convinced myself it would come in handy at some stage in the next five months, so determined to keep it logged in the memory banks. Surely a Norwegian girl would be bowled over?

The couchette was cosy to say the least, especially as it was supposed to accommodate six people. There were three narrow bunks on each side that had been folded down in place of the seating and a small table by the window with six cartons of "SJ" branded fresh water. The dinky little blue/grey curtains that you could pull across to give a bit of privacy were also SJ branded, as were the blankets folded so tightly over the crisp white sheets that, when you got in, your feet were forced into pointing downwards and you could hardly move your legs without a lot of kicking about to loosen it all. There was a little reading light and, once settled in the bed, it would be a cosy place to spend the night.

I had a middle bunk and hoped no one else would be above or below me. No one did and it was just the three of us occupying our compartment. I read for a short while but the gentle rhythmic motion of the train was making me read the same line over and over again and I placed the book on the little side table, pulled the curtain, and switched off the reading light.

I awoke several hours later and realised the train had stopped. I wondered where we were, but if someone had named the town I would have been none the wiser as my geographical knowledge of Sweden outside the main areas was non-existent. I reached for the curtain beside my head and pulled it back a little. Someone had pulled the curtains to the compartment window and I had to stretch out to lift up a corner in order to see out. It took me a while to focus but, in the darkness outside, I could make out a neat pile of railway sleepers stacked five or six high and the top one had a thick line of snow on it. Scanning the area left and right, there was a covering of snow across the ground as far as I could see, which wasn't far as there was no light but the snow appeared to give out a soft glow. I allowed myself a contented smile. Everything was so still and it felt like I was the only one awake for miles around.

As my eyes became more accustomed to the darkness, I saw that we were in a siding and there was a short low platform further ahead. I suddenly had an image come to mind of the Krampus and swiftly let the curtain drop for fear of one of those hideous faces appearing outside glaring at me looking out, as they usually do in horror movies. I guessed we had stopped because the train drivers had to get some rest too on this long journey.

I snuggled back down, pulling my curtain shut and heaving the sheet and blanket well up over my shoulders, trying my best not to focus on the image of the Krampus that was now embedded on my mind. *Think Caribbean beach, think bright warm sand and azure blue sea, blue sky and green palm trees*, I willed myself. It must have worked as the next thing I knew we had stopped again and the train was straining to get going again. What's more we were being shunted about and, after moving for about fifteen seconds, we stopped and then there was another jolt and we started off again.

The swaying carriage sent me off to sleep once more only to be woken much later as I sensed movement in the compartment as someone surfaced and clambered out of their bed. I looked at my watch through one half open eye and registered it was now 7.40am. Lifting the corner of the curtain to the window again revealed it was still very dark outside but also revealed to Ulrika that I was awake.

"*God Morgon,*" she greeted me from the other side of our tiny room.

"Urrghh," I groaned. It was too early for another Swedish lesson. Conscious of the fact that we would be arriving at our final destination in an hour's time, I yawned, shook my head, massaged my face, and threw back the bedding; my first positive moves to actually get out of bed and prepare for the day ahead. Some of the other passengers were stirring too and heading to use the facilities. We did the same before moving through to the restaurant carriage to grab a coffee.

"When does it start to get light around here?" I asked Ulrika.

"Oh, about nine thirty this time of year," she replied.

"Hmmm," was all I could muster, still rubbing the sleep out of my eyes. "And sunset?"

"About two thirty is when the sun goes down behind the hills on the other side of the lake," offered John.

I was too tired to calculate how many hours of daylight that was, but it didn't seem like it was many. The coffee helped to revive me and I took another look out of the window by our table squinting to focus on the outside world rather than the reflection of the bright lights of the restaurant carriage.

It was very dark. The ground was dark too. I didn't feel the elation that I did on seeing the blanket of snow earlier in the middle of the night.

"Where's the snow gone?!" I exclaimed. Both Ulrika and John leaned towards the window to peer out into the gloom. They confirmed my fears.

"There was a full covering of snow a few hours ago when we were much further south but now, when we're almost three hundred kilometres from the Arctic Circle, there's nothing!"

The train passed through a station called Brunflo and on towards Östersund, a reasonable size town by the look of it, and where "our" airport was located. Quite a few people left the train here but even more boarded. I saw a sign that welcomed us to

Krokom Kommune before we rolled through Krokom town, then we swung westwards over a river and skirted a large lake, Storsjön. The gloom outside was ever so slowly lifting and I could make out more station signs slipping by the window, the black letters on long white boards illuminated by small bright spotlights and, now and again, further away car headlights appeared then disappeared behind thick forests. Of course, the reason I couldn't see more whiteness out there was that this was a very heavily forested area, the roads cutting a swathe through the trees.

Most of the buildings I could see away from the towns were timber farmhouses and barns, a few painted in a rich mustard yellow but most in a dark rusty red. Their gable ends were edged contrastingly in white as were the window frames. The paint originated from the copper mines in Falun, in the region of Dalarna, mid-Sweden. Traditionally used on country houses and farms which were constructed in timber, it was supposed to represent more expensive brick construction.

The wide expanse of Åresjön (Are's lake) eventually came into view on our left and was a much lighter grey tone than the blackness of the trees that covered the hillside on its far side. The top metre or so was frozen solid, of course, and gave me some reassurance. We were now descending to the level of the lake, the tracks running along its edge, and I sensed the train beginning to slow before the screech of the brakes confirmed they were being applied. A great wave of anticipation and excitement came over me and I began to absorb my surroundings more keenly. I could see fewer red sheds and more concrete commercial buildings, a couple of houses, a line of trees, a railway shed and then very suddenly the two storey station building clad in painted yellow timber under a dark grey pitched roof. It was the sort of station that wouldn't have looked out of place in a Western. The horses would have been tied up to a hook on the end of the station house. Our carriage stopped just short of it, by a wooden bench with a light blue steel porter's trolley leaning up against it.

I stepped down from the train and my excitement was quickly crushed as my boot made contact with the buttery mud. My other boot mocked me by repeating a disappointing squelch and, as I turned around to lift my luggage out of the open doorway, all I could think was, "Was this still part of the test? Were the camp guards waiting for us close by to see if we reacted in a bad way?" If I threw my toys out of the pram now, I would risk being sent home, so I muttered to myself under my breath.

"I can't believe it. All this way and we get mud".

Ulrika sensed my disappointment and disbelief. "Don't worry, Andrew. It will be alright," she said in her excellent English and cheerful sing-songy voice.

I said nothing but followed them both as we trudged up towards a collection of large multi-storey buildings, which I took to be the centre of town. We picked up a pathway that lead us up over several grassy levels and into a large courtyard garden alongside a white timber clad hotel called the Diplomat Ski Lodge; the large black swirly numbers "1913" were fixed to a wall, announcing the date of its construction. Beyond that, we crossed a car park lined with tall birch trees and up over a bank that did have a fine layer of snow still lying on what must be its shady side. We stepped onto a road that ran up hill and then levelled off as it reached the town square – *torget*. Turning sharp left, we dragged our bags along a narrow pavement and approached an imposing, dark, wooden three storey building that dominated the town square. The entrance porch protruded from the main wall of the hotel and was supported at the front by four sturdy timber beams. Large grey flagstones bore scars of skis and boots being scuffed across them over the years and, in the back right corner of the porch, logs were stacked up high ready to be thrown on the fire. At each side of the heavy entrance, door candles burned in big decorated tins, which unnervingly was to ward off the wolves.

John pulled on the wide front door and beckoned us to enter the lobby. All the external doors here opened outwards to prevent snow being pushed inside. The dark brown wood featured inside too with the tables and chairs and the reception bar, and the grey flagstone floor continued into the building. Dozens of framed photographs of skiers adorned the white painted walls and the purest white candles burned all around. The large log fire was already lit. It was such a warm and welcoming place to be after our epic journey.

We were soon greeted by the manager of the hotel, Madeleine or "Maga" as she was known as; an elegant, charming and wholesome lady with bright blue eyes and a healthily tanned face. For someone who must have been in her late fifties, she was strikingly attractive with thick long blonde hair that caught the light of the candles. We introduced ourselves and she ushered us into the breakfast room to the side of the reception lobby.

The walls of the breakfast – *frukost* – room were covered with the same dark wood but in square panels and a large stone fireplace stood proud along the middle of one wall – the log fire still in rude health, kicking out some heat. The hotel guests had already breakfasted. Above the mantelpiece was a large stuffed elk head with antlers that spanned almost a couple of metres and a tall Christmas tree stood in one corner with its white lights sparkling at us. The oil paintings that dotted the room, and the blue tartan curtains that hung heavily guarding the windows, gave it the air of a Scottish hunting lodge. The breakfast however was very Swedish. The oversized wooden table at our end of the room was covered with several blue and white gingham table cloths on top of which was arranged a tremendous spread of food. Four ornately carved wooden candlestick holders with the same white candles lit the scene to give the effect of a huge birthday cake covered with *hundreds and thousands.*

I didn't know quite where to start. Large oval white plates carried a variety of cheeses, meats, salmon, herring, dry krisp bread biscuits – *knäckerbröd* – in a range of shades and textures and shapes and a host of different breads. Wicker baskets, containing warm hard boiled eggs wrapped in crisp white cotton napkins, jostled for position with bowls of fruit, red and green peppers, cucumbers and china tubs of cereals, glass jugs of fruit juices, pots of jam, honey, lingon berries, marmalade, loaves of bread for toasting, tall glass coffee pots on metal warming plates, boiling hot water and wooden boxes of tea bags.

"Andrew…" John was urging to get my attention. "Maga asked 'is this your first time to Sweden?'" I realised they had been busy chatting to each other whilst I had been surveying the scene and salivating at the prospect of a proper breakfast.

"I'm sorry," I replied, turning to her. "I was just overwhelmed by the sight of the breakfast. Yes, I mean, no. I mean no to Sweden, yes to here. Sorry, I'm still tired and we've had a long journey from Austria."

"Well, you are very welcome here, please help yourself," and she gestured with her hand that we should tuck in. "I can tell you want to get started. This is our typical Swedish breakfast, or *frukost* as we call it. You will have to learn some Swedish while you are here, Andrew."

"Yes, I want to and Ulrika has already given me my first lesson on the train," I replied enthusiastically as I reached for the largest spare plate I could see.

"Andrew, that's a serving plate," interrupted Ulrika, taking it out of my hands and replacing it with a smaller one.

"Go on, I will leave you to enjoy it," Maga said graciously. "If there's anything else you need, please ask." With a gentle squeeze of my elbow and her warm smile she left us.

Breakfast by candle light seemed such a civilised way of waking up on a dark winter's morning and it must have had some impact on me as, to this day, I still light a white candle on the breakfast table during the months of December and January.

We tucked into the fabulous spread set before us enthusiastically.

"Don't expect you're going to be getting this breakfast every day now," John warned. "We'll be eating with the hotel staff in the basement."

I nodded my acknowledgement with a piece of krisp bread lodged in my mouth and tried to work out what was contained in the jugs labelled *apelsinjuice* (orange juice) and *äppeljuice* (apple juice). The jugs marked *mjölk* were easier to figure out, being sub labelled *varm* and *kall*. It's the best way to learn a language, being immersed in it, although most Swedes speak excellent English and actually enjoy speaking it. I determined then and there to make the most of this opportunity. Words I had seen in location on the train and the station had lodged in my memory and what had started as an unfathomable language was already becoming clearer. It is, after all, a Germanic language, like English, and in fact we derive many of our words directly from the Nordic languages. Many Nordics settled and built their lives in the British Isles, their presence contributing to our language. In the county of Yorkshire there is a well known seaside town called Whitby. The word *by* (pron. *Bew*) means village. *Vit* is white. Street names such as Coppergate, High Ousegate, Feasgate and Fossgate in York don't relate to gates but the word for street in Swedish, *gata*.

After we had stuffed our bellies, we waddled off to the Sporthotellet, which was to be our home for the next five months. We headed along the side of the main village square and I noticed the wonderful old timber *Bergbanan* station building on the opposite side of the square, a cog railway that ran up part of the mountain to link into the lift system. A row of white flag poles edged the far corner of the square above a bank of concrete steps, the flags of Sweden, Åre Lift Company and Åre tourist office all hanging limply. We passed a light grey timber slat-walled office, where the tourist office was located, and then a red barn-shaped building, which housed the Peak Performance store, a brand that now has presence across the world but was started here in Åre. Beyond this, the variety of buildings continued with a modern structure on the corner of the square, which contained apartments above a smart ski hire shop we were going to use on the ground floor; Hanson.

As we continued walking, there was an old dark wood building with its contrasting ornate white lettering announcing it was called Läbands Krog, a restaurant. We crossed the road and headed up a rough path to a well-used run of timber steps that lead us up to the side of a large five storey off-white timber building. With its red tiled, pitched roof, pointed gable ends and a further gabled structure standing proud in the middle of long lines of windows at each level, it dominated the immediate surroundings. The three gables stood like huge upended rowing boats stacked up against the main body of the building. It was built at the turn of the century as a grand hotel nestling at the base of a ski run and looking far out over the lake. It was now used solely to accommodate a panoply of resort workers, which included mainly those of the Hotel Åregården and the Diplomat Ski Lodge, but also "randoms" like us: DJs working for the local radio station, Radio Rix; band members who were here for the season, playing every night at the after-ski parties; ski instructors; parapente flight operators; and some husky dog excursion leaders.

On entering the spacious hallway, we were greeted by an enormous wrought iron chandelier hanging from the centre of the ceiling. The main thick circular band that held it all together was punctured at regular intervals with swastikas. During World War Two, neutral Sweden, had allowed the Germans to occupy their country; their steel industry had even benefitted from increased orders for ammunition and weaponry. The German Army was able to base themselves here, which made it easier to launch attacks on the fiercely independent and much smaller neighbour, Norway. The Norwegians, understandably have never forgiven them for that. On a more welcoming and brighter note, the corner of the hallway was filled with a grand fireplace marked with the date 1904 emblazoned on the shroud.

The fire door to the corridor swung shut with a loud bang, a sound that would be a constant for the duration of my stay and we wandered along to our assigned rooms, past the communal shower and loos room. I was pleasantly surprised to be on the ground floor, in a good-sized room of about three metres by five metres, with its own basin, a single bed, wardrobe, low table and an armchair and, most impressively, overlooking the lake. The pine clad walls and ceiling gave the room the look of a sauna and outside, just below the triple glazed window, there was a narrow shelf, presumably for potted plants in the summer and a small thermometer fixed to the outer glass. It read plus two degrees but I noted it could read minus fifty. I shivered involuntarily and went to rest my hand on the industrial sized radiator, like the ones we used to have at school. Unlike those, this one worked. It was very hot and I lifted my hand off quickly.

I had an hour to unpack and sort my stuff out before John and Ulrika called for me and we headed down to the Diplomat Ski Lodge, a short walk down the hill towards the lake where our office was located. John was anxious to know when our first guests were due to arrive, so we detoured via the Hotel Åregården's fax machine. John felt it necessary for only him to collect the fax and not show us where we would need to go, so Ulrika and I waited in lobby.

He returned a few minutes later walking briskly in a bit of flap, brandishing some papers and announced that our first guests would be arriving on Sunday. We had three days to prepare all the welcome packs, notice boards, check all the hotel reservations, ski hire contracts, ski school lessons, ski passes and, on top of which, I had to get to know where everything was and get some skiing in so I could talk knowledgably about the resort.

"How many do we have coming in?" I asked.

"One party of four, one of two, a group of six and a one on… *his* own," he replied, checking the list again. Thankfully not a large number at all, as it was early in the season, but we still had to get everything ready and the "one on his own" was going to be a worry, he warned, they always are.

I spent the next few days working not in our office, as that had no computer, but in the relative comfort of the ground floor office behind the reception desk of the Hotel Åregården. The resort itself had only been receiving British guests for a couple of years and only one other UK tour company was bringing skiers here, so they were keen to offer support and help us out as much as possible. It seemed that pretty much everyone, from the local bus and taxi drivers to the tourist office and hotel owners, had all been briefed by someone to do whatever they could to assist us. We were very well looked after throughout our time in the resort. This made things a lot easier than they could have been, and certainly better than in some French resorts that was for sure. The Swedes like us Brits a lot and were delighted, if not a little bemused, that we would want to ski in their resort. They mostly wanted to ski in Europe, where the sun was warm and stayed out for more hours of the day. I would say that most of the guests that travelled to this resort were tourists wanting a new experience rather than hard core skiers, although the resort has hosted some major ski races and a lot of the top international and Olympic Swedish skiers – and they are numerous – had begun their skiing here.

I set to work on the computer creating and updating the written information we needed to provide to the guests, whilst John and Ulrika did the rounds of renewing contact with the suppliers. As the property industry at that time still relied heavily on phone calls and personal contact and computers were just used for storing mailing lists, I had minimal computing skills so I was in at the deep end. This was particularly so as the language was set to Swedish, naturally. I learned some new important words such as *spara* (save), *sida* (page) and *söka* (search) and was very dependent on the help of the girls in reception who were also trying to do their jobs.

However, what was more of a concern to me was the lack of snow but, when I stirred from my slumber after the first night in my new quarters, I sensed a distinct quietness outside. Apprehensively, I slowly pulled back a corner of the curtains, but my spirits lifted on seeing white fluffy flakes drifting down onto an already snow-covered ground. The temperature gauge read minus five and the village now looked like the ski resort it was purporting to be.

I donned salopettes in celebration and pulled on my new corporate fleece and jacket. The boots soon shed their offending mud as we traipsed across to the Åregården for breakfast with the hotel staff down in the basement kitchens. More introductions were made as John knew most of them, but I immediately forgot everyone's names. Fortunately, all the reception staff were smartly dressed in dark trousers with black waistcoats or skirts and navy blue cardigans, with metal name badges pinned to their chests, and the kitchen staff, dressed in white, also had their nameplates on display. Still, they weren't all called Bjorn, Benny or Ulrika and there was between twenty and thirty of them.

My second morning was much more productive and I continued to update the documents we needed, although I felt the pressure building as we moved towards D-Day and the first arrivals. I had suggested drawing a village map to accompany the welcome pack and that gave me the chance to get out and about and get my bearings. Logically, I started with the tourist office, moving on to the ski hire shop, the main cable car station, and the start of the World Cup Lift, the ski school, a couple of supermarkets, and taking a closer look at the Bergbanan in the village square. I finished with the post office, System Bolaget (government controlled off licence), and bakery – *bageri* (pronounced "*buggery*" or so it sounded).

John had decided he would do the first transfer and, with so few guests due, we only needed to order a minivan from Stefan who ran the imaginatively named Stefan's Taxis. John also decided I should be responsible for the Hotel Renen in Duved, a small hamlet about five miles away along the shore of the lake. At first, I thought he was being kind because there was only one family of four staying there in our first group but, as the season progressed, it became a chore to haul myself over there four times or more each week.

Most days the free ski bus ran back and forth, linking the two parts of the resort. The buses broadcasted the local radio station, Radio Rix's, playlist all day, although every time I caught the bus it would be playing Toni Braxton's *Un-Break My Heart*. "Rardio Rix" as it sounded, was what I woke up to each morning and they seemed to play Toni Braxton every half hour. As a result, I would have it in my head most mornings, which was slightly embarrassing when I unconsciously started to whistle it out loud in the office. Damn – it's just popped into my head now as I write this.

Before my clock radio alarm woke me each morning, I would be aware of the door across the corridor from me opening and closing as Mariha left for work as the Radio Rix weather girl. Noise travelled easily in the spartan corridor. I kept meaning to request them not to play Toni Braxton but, whenever I saw Mariah later in the day, I either forgot about it or thought it was a bit mean. Now and again, at the end of her weather bit, she added, "Sorry I banged the door this morning, Andrew," or "C'mon, wake up Andrew! It's a nice day for skiing!" which was sweet and a little strange hearing your name mentioned on the radio on a regular basis.

If I didn't take the bus, I had to blag a lift off anyone who might be going there, which was usually no one or, when I had to be over there first thing in the morning to hand the new arrivals their lift passes, I had to drive "the mean machine" as John called it. It wasn't mean at all, in fact it was rather tame, so I don't know what he was used to driving back home in England. The old Toyota Hiace van belonged to the ski shop, Hanson. It had studded tyres, which were essential here as the roads were never cleared of snow and ice. There was no point because it would snow so much and under the snow was hard compacted ice. Everyone just got on with it; none of the wild panicking that happens in England when we get an inch of snow on the roads. Although the bus drivers were kind enough to pick me up from the side of the road when they saw me, even if I hadn't reached the bus stops, and often dropped me right at the front door of the Hotel Renen, I was very grateful for the use of the van. I was even more grateful for the confidence the four wheel drive gave me in these conditions, as there hadn't been many opportunities to perfect my skills on the snow and ice in the mild winters of south east England.

The road out west of the village of Åre was in fact the E14 and if you look on a map of the country you will see that it is a green road, which means it is one of the main roads that straddles the country all the way from the Baltic Sea in the East at Sundsvall to the Norwegian border in the west. Now I am sure that, in places, it actually looks like a main road but, up here in the wilderness, it was nothing more than a two lane highway and by that I mean one lane in each direction, often surrounded on both sides by dense forest. It was early one morning that I was mightily appreciative of this fact as I headed along the E14 in the van.

I was on my way to meet some new guests, having collected their lift passes from the lift company, which was all part of the service, and travelling at about 60 kph. It was early in the season, so my mind was running through the stuff I had to tell them about when, all of a sudden, I realised I had just driven past the ninety-degree left turn off the main road leading to the hotel. My instinctive reaction was to stand on the brakes, but a little too forcefully. The studded tyres lost their grip and locked up and I slid along the road for 20 metres or so, the back end of the van slowly coming around to meet me, wanting to swap ends. I held my breath and watched it all happen in slow motion, remembering to steer into the skid.

"Ffffffffffff...!!!" was all I managed to hiss as I finally came to a halt about a metre from a ditch at the edge of the road. A hot flush came over me and I blew the air out of my lungs, lifting my gloved hands to grip the sides of my face in relief. I looked ahead of me up the road but could see no cars coming from the other direction. In the rear view mirror, all I could see was dark green trees as the van had slewed sideways like a skiing hockey stop. I don't know why, but I applied the handbrake, got out and looked back to where I had come from. Panic over and I was now quite pleased with my tell-tale tyre tracks and the divergent course they had etched on the hard packed snow and ice.

"Cool..!" I uttered to no one in particular, nodding my head as I tried to get something positive out of the situation. What struck me as really odd was that, considering this was the main road through this part of the country, there were no other cars around and, thankfully, no one to witness my carelessness. Nothing at all. Just silence as I had stalled the engine. I was truly on the edge of the wilderness. One of the guys in the tourist office had told me if you walked in one direction from the resort you wouldn't find any signs of man for a day and in the other direction walking across the lake – which you could do during the winter – it would be two days before you reached any habitation.

The welcome pack was quickly taking shape and the Information sheet we would use at the Welcome Meetings listed the excitement that we could offer our guests. There was not a cabaret in sight and some very alternative activities and excursions, which I was looking forward to experiencing myself, let alone the guests. They were enticingly described as:

SNOW SCOOTER SAFARI

Simply the best and most exhilarating way to travel in the Swedish wilderness, but definitely not for the faint hearted. Drive your own scooter across the frozen lake and through the forests on prepared tracks. Turn off the engines and take in the stillness and peace of the Swedish mountains.

Dress warmly, though protective gear and clothing is supplied.

I was continually amazed how many guests turned up for this excursion without wearing their ski gear. One family held up the whole group whilst I suggested they might be advised to return to their hotel and get their gloves. The snow scooters could do 75 mph – at that speed the air is extremely cold. At the Welcome Meetings, we did stress what clothing would be required, but you just can't tell some people.

TÄNNFORSEN SPECTACULAR FLOODLIT FROZEN WATERFALL

This is an ideal excursion to do after a day's skiing. Wrap up warm and marvel at the winter wonderland of the frozen waterfall (120 ft high) lit up by powerful flood lamps. Then return to the warm hut where there will be a hot drink and Swedish waffle waiting for you.

This was by definition a night time activity and the advice to wrap up warm was heeded by most but, inevitably, some of our Brits-abroad thought better of it. There was a temperature gauge that all passengers could see on board the coaches we used and the coldest trip I accompanied the guests on was minus thirty three degrees. I remember arriving at the location grabbing the microphone to announce we were about to leave the warmth of the coach and, "Yes, the temperature gauge you see at the front of the coach is accurate".

SKI TASTER EVENING

Have you ever wanted to try out the top test skis, racing skis, the new carving ones (it was 1996–7) or be a hero and try Telemark (Tuition can be arranged).

On Friday evenings, it's your chance to ski on the amazing floodlit Gästrappet run (1.6 kms long) between 18.00 and 21.00 using the Olympialiften. Please let us know at least 24 hours in advance what you would like to try.

If only Mr B from Sutton Coldfield had read AND understood before he turned up at the ski hire shop at 17.30 on the evening he wanted to ski. He threw all his toys out the pram in the shop when not all the skis were available and frankly embarrassed himself and our country by his subsequent rant. He was still in full flow when I arrived in the shop to try and solve the problem. The poor staff and other holidaying Swedes had, I am sure, widened their already extensive English vocabulary thanks to him. He complained bitterly to us and then sent a vitriolic letter to HQ when he returned home. Later on, during his week's stay he turned up for ski escorting one morning with the long suffering Mrs B from Sutton Coldfield and I wondered why he felt the need to test skis as he could barely master the skis he had hired from the shop. We, as reps, had to report any complaints to head office, but John also kept his own diary of complaints which, interestingly and for the most part, correlated directly with the cheaper weeks and any special offers the ski company were making.

HUSKY DOG SLED RIDES

The adorable husky dogs just love to pull and pull, so sit back and be whisked through the snow covered forests into the wilderness experiencing fantastic views of the Swedish mountains and frozen lakes. This is an ideal trip for both children and the romantic at heart.

Very true, but only if you book the afternoon ride as the one that goes off not long after the dogs have eaten their mainly meat-based breakfast will have you burying your nose in your jacket collar as you try to block out the overpowering smell of dog farts as they pull you along through their wake.

SNOWBOARD TRIAL

Snowboarding has been tipped by some to outgrow traditional alpine skiing, so this is your opportunity to get to grips with "riding" the pistes. The ski school offers special trial sessions where they provide specially adapted snowboards for your normal ski boots to simply – click in and go.

Again, it was a time when snowboarding was only just making it onto the pistes.

ICELANDIC HORSEBACK RIDING

Icelandic horses are known for their good nature, dependability and hardiness. This is your chance to meet them, groom them and then let them take you out into the Swedish mountains, through snow covered forests and on to fantastic frozen lake and mountain views. Extra value for money is the free pick up and drop off to all your hotels.

This was a lovely idea but in the entire season not one guest decided to go on this excursion, in spite of the free taxi service; I am not sure that, if you decide to go on a ski holiday, you really want to ride a horse through fields of snow.

ICE KARTING

Challenge your friends on a ploughed ice track, driving motorised go-karts fitted with special studded tyres.

Another great idea and fantastic fun, although it relied on the ice circuit not being covered in thick snow on the only two mornings of the week the operator was prepared to open it. That and the questionable reliability of the karts which, when we trialled them on three separate occasions, didn't last for more than a maximum of seven or eight minutes before conking out. The experience was supposed to last fifteen minutes and was consequently dropped from the list.

TOBOGGANING EVENINGS

A traditional alpine pursuit, the illuminated toboggan run goes from the Hotel Fjällgården down to Åre square. The Bergbanan mountain railway takes you up to the top of the run and is open on Monday and Thursday evenings from 18.00 to 21.00 from 27/12. Toboggans and helmets are hired at the Hotel end of the railway line and you can make as many runs as you wish.

We hoped this would be a safer pursuit than the one we had experienced in Austria as the form filling required by us after any mishap would be very tedious.

TAXI RIDES

This was not on the list of activities and excursions but it absolutely should have been and we both highly recommended it at our welcome meetings, although we couldn't make any commission on it. We suggested the guests staying in Åre should consider visiting the smaller village of Duved for an evening meal in the Hotel Renen's restaurant, where they could get the best reindeer steak in the resort in a beautiful restaurant that showcased modern Swedish architecture and interior design. The resort was secondary to Åre and the skiing much less challenging, apart from some great off piste snowboarding areas, and so the hotel had to offer so much more to tempt bookings; hence the restaurant. The rooms were also spectacularly large, verging on apartments, and each had its own *bastu* (sauna). Likewise, I encouraged the guests staying there to make a trip into Åre by taxi, not the free ski bus, just for the sheer exhilaration.

As snow continued to fall and got compacted on the roads, it froze over night so, over a short time, you couldn't see the tarmac and it was pointless trying to clear the road of the ice. All vehicles had to be fitted with winter tyres that had small metal studs the size of large nail heads protruding from the tread. Most of the non airport taxis were Volvo, Saab or Audi saloons or estates and were not four wheel drive. The first time I had need for one was a morning when I had to get to Duved quickly and had no time to wait for the next ski bus and the mean machine was unavailable.

I was walking along the edge of a road that connected the

two main roads that ran parallel to the lake at the top and bottom of the village. The yellow taxi was heading uphill away from the lake when I stuck out my arm to hail it. The driver acknowledged me with a raised hand and promptly spun his car round a hundred and eighty degrees on a pinpoint in the middle of the road and pulled up alongside me. I hopped into the back seat and told him where I needed to go. He didn't know I was late for a meeting, having been delayed getting the morning's lift passes, and so it took me by surprise when he sunk the accelerator to the floor and we headed off at an indecent speed towards the lake to connect with the lake side road. For a moment, I thought he was drunk; we careered around the T junction in a full on four wheel drift as he deftly adjusted the steering wheel, correcting the direction of travel and it was clear he was anything but.

On the road out of the village, the last few houses flashed by with ever increasing speed and we were out onto a straight bit of open road. Trees with their branches heavily laden with fresh snow became a blur on my right whilst intermittent lines of small boats moored up on the edge of the water in those dark late days of autumn (and were now in the grip of the frozen surface of the lake), flitted by on my left.

I pushed myself up off the back seat to steal a surreptitious look at the speedometer, trying not to let the driver catch my concerned expression in his rear view mirror. I blinked, trying to focus harder at the delicate white numbers on the black background where the red needle was hovering between a hundred and fifteen and a hundred and twenty kph already (about seventy five mph... on snow and ice, let's not forget). He barely lifted the accelerator as we approached what I thought was quite a tight left / right kink in the road, guarded by thick tree trunks and a high snow bank on the right. I tensed up my leg muscles and clenched other parts as the back of the car twitched one way then another in response to his quick tug on the handbrake and flick of the steering wheel. The car came back into line and we slithered through and onto a straight section again. We appeared to be floating over the road surface and he continued to make little adjustments to the wheel as we skirted round more bends.

A journey that took twenty minutes on the ski bus took barely five and no sooner had we set off we were pulling up outside the hotel reception. Only then did I realise I had apparently been holding my breath all the way and exhaled loudly. I tried to gather my composure as I fumbled for my wallet for what should have been about a £20 fare but he waved his hand in dismissal.

"Ah, don't worry about it. You guys are bringing us business. Have a nice day."

"Really?" I questioned in too high a pitch. "Well, thank you very much. That's kind," I added in a deeper, more manly voice.

"*Tack så mycket,*" I ventured in my best Swedish, although how I remembered to say "thank you very much" in his language I have no idea. I think I was just relieved we weren't upside down in a field and wondered why Stig Blomqvist hadn't made enough money by now to retire. Perhaps it was because he didn't charge for taxi rides?

Knowing Me, Knowing You

The preparations for our first guests were almost finished and a neat row of welcome packs were laid out in our office. I was resting on my bed one evening, two days before the first guests were due to arrive feeling exhausted with all the organisation we had done, when I realised I hadn't yet taken the opportunity to ski around the resort and familiarise myself with a few of the runs. I also hadn't phoned home. So I pulled on my jacket, boots, gloves and hat and headed along the corridor. A few more doors were open as further season workers had arrived and were unpacking their things. Music was being played from a number of portable CD players and there was a general buzz of activity in the building as people were coming and going and chatting in the corridor.

Right across from my room two girls were chatting and laughing and as I locked my door they called out:

"*Hejsan!*" (Hi there!)

"Hello" I answered in a very English way and went across to introduce myself.

"Oh, are you the British guy?" asked Mariha, whose room it was.

"Yes, I'm one of them. There's two of us"

"Coool…!" they both cooed together and Lena then introduced herself with a big white toothed smile and beaming blue eyes. They both worked for the local radio station and Mariha, my new neighbour, a very petite, slim girl with doe eyes and her blonde hair tied up in plaits around the top of her head, was the weather girl. They were both very naturally pretty in that healthy Swedish way, very friendly, and most bizarrely thought it was "Coool…" being a British guy. We chatted for a while and then, feeling re-energised, I headed outside. The heavy swing door creaked open and slammed shut on its closer as I let it go, forgetting to hold onto it as it closed. Sorry everyone…

It had been snowing most of the day and all evening and only now was beginning to ease off. I stepped out onto the timber platform at the top of the steps and promptly slid right across to the top of the first step only just managing to grab the hand rail with both hands as my legs and body continued on, slipping over the edge. I was reminded of a Pink Floyd lyric that aptly described my predicament, being English and quietly, desperately, hanging on. With both boots scrabbling for grip like a desperate Disney character I found myself hanging onto the handrail with both hands, arms and even elbows for what seemed like almost a full minute trying to prevent myself from sliding right off the side and onto the steep bank below which would have pitched me into a roll down a small hill onto the road. *My God, it had turned cold*. The night felt like it was burning my throat as I inhaled. The snow had been trampled smooth and flat by the feet of those going in and out of the building and was now sheet ice. Whilst I could have usefully done with a helping hand to pull me back in over the edge, I prayed that my lovely new neighbour and her friend weren't about to head out, for the "Coool" British guy image would have been very short lived.

After gathering myself together, I proceeded down the steps very gingerly. There was only one set of vehicle tracks on the street that led into the village square and no footprints apart from mine. All was quiet and still. No matter how many times I see fresh snow it will always delight me how beautiful it makes everything look. The last few snowflakes still gently fluttering down were illuminated in triangles of light from a couple of street lamps and one shop sign. A little further up the street I could see what now looked like the wide expanse of the village square, the snow cover having blended the car park, street, pavements and steps under the one pale blanket. As I reached the corner of the square next to Hanson's ski hire shop I turned left and headed out diagonally across the fresh blanket. I began to step delicately not wanting to ruin any more than I had to of the pristine smooth covering. After twenty paces, I told myself not to be so ridiculous, it was only a bloody car park and of course there would be plenty more snow. Two parallel skis draw beautiful lines on fresh morning snow; footprints are like graffiti on a clean wall.

On the far side of the square there was a small ICA supermarket store and just outside it was a phone box. An old Chevrolet pick-up truck had pulled up the same distance from the phone box and was parked in the darkness out of the range of any streetlights. The tyre tracks I had seen earlier had drawn a big arc around the square to the vehicle. I detected some movement in the cab and then the driver's door opened; the inside light momentarily illuminating its occupant. I was edging closer, flinching once or twice as I felt the cold snow penetrate the sole of my left boot. I promised myself I must be brave enough to look in the window of the ski hire shop on the way back to check out the prices of new boots. It wasn't going to be cheap in a ski resort in Sweden where they all stock the best quality equipment. Even with my 10% rep's discount, it would still probably cost me a week's wages.

The occupant of the Chevy was striding out towards the phone box too. As we converged it was clear that we were both heading for the box and we were going to reach it at the same time. Both of us wanted to get there first and not stand around in the freezing night waiting for the other to finish their call, but neither of us wanted to break into a run. It would have been churlish to do that so I just took more purposeful strides.

As we got closer, I realised the person was dressed head to toe in light tan animal skin decorated with a diagonal patterned front. Small baubles of snow had attached themselves to the errant strands of long black hair that protruded from the heavy hood and I saw the face of a Sami woman.

We stopped equidistant from the box and looked at each other before I motioned with a gloved hand for her to go ahead. She mumbled something in Swedish, incomprehensible to me, which I took to mean "thank you very much" and gave me a little bow, nodding her head. It was as strange moment but here we were, just the two of us with no one else around, the snow still gently falling in the middle of the village in the middle of nowhere. Our lives had converged at one point in time; she from Lapland, me from South West London.

Whilst she dialled a number, I turned around to face the other way and, for the first time, it dawned on me why this village felt vaguely familiar. It was a Swedish version of Cicely, Alaska, the setting for a sitcom I loved watching; *Northern Exposure*. This lady was the equivalent of Marilyn Whirlwind, the gentle Native American woman. I had already met the local DJ, there was bound to be a bar with a moose head on the wall and I had heard that later in the season light aircraft would be flying in to land on the frozen lake. All that was missing right at this point was a solitary moose wandering up the main street. Little did I know that I was soon going to experience the wonderful but rare sight of a moose close up. The theme music popped into my head just then and I whistled it quietly, moving my feet to the beat as I tried to keep warm.

Eventually, I heard the door of the phone box open as it swished against the snow and "Marilyn" stood there holding it for me. I smiled as I took it from her, saying "thank you" before correcting myself with a *"tack"*. She wished me a good evening, or something, although it sounded like she said "washing machine" and she headed off to the warmth of her truck cabin.

Inside the phone box wasn't any warmer than the outside – I don't know why I thought it would be – and I had to take off my right glove to accurately dial the numbers. After a few rings, I heard the familiar voice of my mother and I pictured where she would be in the corner of the dining room of my parents' house.

"Hello it's me," I said in response to her friendly and informal "Hello?" If it been my Dad, he would have picked up the phone and announced the town followed by the telephone number in a time-honoured fashion, like he had done ever since the beginning of the fifties when he started to answer his parents' own home phone.

"I was just saying to your father 'I wonder how Andrew is doing' and then the phone rang," she continued following by, "Is it really cold there? Are you warm enough?" It was a typical caring mother to son line of questions, even though I had left home well over a decade ago, but she stopped at suggesting sending me a food parcel.

I brought her up to date with most of what had happened and confirmed I was warm enough, although I was calling from an outside phone box and it was minus fifteen out here. Yes, I was wrapped up and no I hadn't started the Christmas cake she had kindly made for me. It was good to hear her voice all the same and, after a quick chat with my Dad, I said I was beginning to freeze standing so still, so had better go, and I would write soon with a more detailed update.

The run up to Christmas proceeded at reasonable pace and I managed to steal a few hours' skiing to familiarise myself with some of the runs so that at least when the first guests arrived I could sound fairly knowledgeable about part of the resort and know how the runs linked up and where the good restaurants were. Fortunately for me, at this time of year, the entire resort was not open as it was just too windy up at the top of the mountain, so I only had to memorise a part of the skiable area. The wind was one thing but that had an effect on the temperature and, at times, the *köldeffekt* at the top of the mountain, Åreskutan, dragged the temperature way down. In fact, on 15th February I would note on the lift company's weather forecast for the day that the high zone was officially closed because it was minus fifty one degrees at the top of the mountain. That was the coldest it would get all season, but clearly far too cold to ski in.

On my recce of the resort, I called in at the best mountain restaurant, Hummelstugan. Everyone always asks the rep "Where's the best place to go?" so it was important to have the answer to that. It was perched imperiously on the "knee" of Åreskutan, the highest mountain. The wooden terrace overhung the red run, Rydbergs Väg, which dropped down from the top station, although it was closed this early in the season. It had a fast paced switchback that wrapped around the restaurant. All the restaurants offered a free refill if you had purchased a coffee or a tea; in fact, as many refills as you wanted. Cries of "*Sacre Bleu!... Gott im Himmel!... Mamma Mia!*" would be echoing across the Alps at the very thought of it.

Taking the easy run down to link up with the Gästrappet run and then riding the four man lift up to Café Olympia, I skied across to the Olympia gondola and took flight up over what looked like the surface of the moon. When the top of the resort opened up, the longest run was 6.5 kms, if you had the legs for it. There was one run leading back into the village that was declared too steep for the World Cup. John had told me that, to get to the very top of the mountain, skiers have to be towed by a snow cat up to the extreme peak for a small charge. From there, a run called Störtloppet, a steep and often icy red run, led back down to Café Olympia. I headed down Rodkullevägen, an easy but fast blue that was good for a long tuck, through the trees and under bridges, down to Fairisvägen, making a sharp left turn winding though more trees down to the base of the Olympia lift. The view of the lake and village appeared and disappeared as I switched back and forth through the trees. That was about all

I had time for. The rest I would have to play by ear and during some overtime when I had the chance. That's if skiing really could be considered as overtime?

Our first guests arrived without any dramas, my welcome speeches went off without any problems and the guests spent their week enjoying all that the resort had to offer. It is a quirk of the ski business that the peak time for numbers of guests and the highest cost of the holiday coincide with a period of time when you as a rep are just getting into the swing of things. It is also a time when we had some of the most demanding guests. They had forked out a lot of money to bring their family on a Christmas ski holiday to remember and they expected everything to be absolutely right. That included having the entire resort open, even though it stated very clearly the whole area (mainly very high up the mountain) was not open for skiing until early February. This did not stop Mr F from Crawley having a big whinge at us. He was an important banker in the City and worked very hard, he informed us. "The resort is not fully open and what were we going to do about it?" he demanded to know. He also demanded compensation. We politely pointed out what it said in the brochure but he wouldn't have it. We arranged for a bottle of wine to be delivered to his table at dinner that night, but it wasn't a good enough quality wine; in fact, he was insulted by it. The only thing he, John and I could agree on was that he was indeed a banker. If only he was staying in a chalet, we thought, for we could have asked our chalet staff to make sure they cleaned his toilet with his own tooth brush but, alas, we had no chalets.

Christmas in Sweden is a very special occasion. Because of the short days and long nights at this time of year, the houses, offices, shops, restaurants and hotels are festooned with white lights and candles. White painted furniture is prevalent in Sweden as are white painted walls and floors. It all helps to alleviate Seasonal Affective Disorder as does a regular blast from a Light Therapy Lamp or even a half hour on a sun bed, which was being recommended to us to help us get through the season.

To mark the time of the shortest winter days, Swedes celebrate with vigour the festival of light that is Sankta Lucia. It is quite a remarkable festival that I just could not see happening in the UK. My first experience of it was as I stood in the queue at the tiny local branch of Handelsbanken just off the town square. There I was, minding my own business, when there was a shuffling noise of people trying to get in through the doors to take up their position at the back of the room. I turned around to see what was going on only to be amazed to see six beautiful blonde Swedish girls all dressed in white robes with red sashes and a framework of Lingonberry branches supporting burning white candles in their hair. They carried bread rolls and *pepparkakor* (ginger biscuits) – heaven! No sooner had they assembled themselves in a neat little line than they broke into harmonious song. Bank staff and customers alike stopped what they were doing and watched in wonder and respect.

It was December 13th; Saint Lucy's Day. The day used to coincide with the winter solstice but, as the calendar changed over the years, the feast day became a festival of light. The original saint had to fix the candles in her hair so that left her hands free to distribute the food. This would account for the saffron-flavoured raisin buns at breakfast time I had scoffed greedily in blissful ignorance and without thanking my new favourite saint.

They sang the song to the well-known Italian melody about a place near Naples, but the Swedish words described the girl rather than the place:

The night goes with weighty step
Round yard and stove
Round earth, the sun departs
Leave the woods brooding.
There in our dark house,
Appears with lighted candles
Sankta Lucia, Sankta Lucia.
The night goes great and mute
Now hear it swings
In every silent room
Murmurs as if from wings.
Look at our threshold stands
White-clad with lights in her hair
Sankta Lucia, Sankta Lucia
The darkness shall soon depart
From the earth's valleys
Thus she speaks
A wonderful word to us
The day shall rise anew
From the rosy sky
Sankta Lucia, Sankta Lucia.

So overwhelmed was I with the spectacle and the sound of these girls that, when one of them broke ranks and circulated amongst the dozen or so customers and staff proffering a healthy smile and a collecting tin, I found myself giving more money that I wanted to or should have done. I was at the bank, after all, to open my Swedish bank account with a few kronors and I think I ended up giving more to whatever charity they were collecting for than I was about to put into my account. Not only were the girls charming, angelic, beautiful, tuneful and offering free biscuits, they were very cunning targeting us folks in the bank holding our cash. The girls were calling into all the public buildings in the village and the ritual was being re-enacted across the country in buildings, town squares and churches and cathedrals. Not all girls had lighted candles, though, and apparently, girls under twelve years of age were not permitted to have burning candles on their heads, so had electric ones, although I am not sure whether it was an actual law.

With all the excitement of Christmas, the hotels were busy organising extra events and wanted to appeal to their British guests, which required us providing some translation work. Most Swedes speak very good English, better than most English people in fact, although some have an American accent that they have picked up through travelling and working in the US or from films and TV shown in Sweden, which is never dubbed, only subtitled. The hotel staff were diligent enough to really want to get their words reading correctly in English and we were happy to help translate form what we referred to as Swenglish. The lovely Anna from the Hotel Renen in Duved called me up one morning to ask me if I could help her with some translation she had done for their Christmas programme next time I was at the hotel. I got her to fax over a copy of what she had done and, after reading it through and seeing her message to me ("I've done my best. Please send me a correct copy"), I didn't have the heart to make as many amendments as I should have done.

I called her up and said, "I've read it through and it's fine, really."

"Fine? I want it to be perfect English, not just fine," she replied.

"Well I think it looks quite... charming... the way you have written it. I would leave it like that as it is perfectly understandable and it is almost more impressive that it reads like a Swedish person has written it in very good English rather than a 100% correct English version."

"I don't understand you," she said, slightly frustrated, I could tell.

"In England, we love the way French people speak English. It has a certain appeal and charm and it's nicer that they have an accent and don't get all the words right. You said to me the other day you love the way I say good morning in Swedish, with a British accent. It's the same only in reverse."

"Oh, OK. I get it. Well, as long as your guests don't think it sounds like it was written by a stupid person."

"Anna, they won't. I promise you. They will be very impressed that you have written it in English. The only thing I would suggest you change is the bit about killing dogs and eating hotdogs for the children."

"What?" she exclaimed. "Oh my God, what are you talking about, Andrew?"

"On December 26th, you have written about dog slaying and then you have typed 'followed by hot dogs for the children'. I think that might scare them and ruin their Christmas…"

We both began to laugh as she realised the error.

The *Christmasprogram* as she had described it was presented in a very Scandinavian, organised way; it seemed churlish to change it:

DEC 22:d   *12.00 Christmas market in Duved. Santa Claus arrives at 15.00.*
16.00 Torch-caravan to Duved's church and Maria devine service.
18.00 Welcome information at the bar.
21.00 Wine testing at "Loften" (Notify your interest at the reception)

DEC 23:d   *08.00 Breakfast*
Outdoor-day with skiing and sledging. Christmas decorations at the hotel and "stay-up-night" by the fireplace.

DEC 24:th   *08.00 Breakfast.*
Make a skiing trip to the Christmas market at Tegefjäll.
The children may go by horse and sleigh.
12.00 Traditional Swedish Christmas-lunch at "Armfelds krog".
15.00 Donald Duck on TV at the bar.
16.00 Santa Claus arrives with horse and sleigh.
17.30 Traditional Swedish Christmas-buffé at "Armfelds krog".

DEC 25:th   *06.00 Early morning-coffee by the fireplace before Christmas devine service.*
07.00 Christmas devine service at Duved's church.
15.00 Snow-race competition at Hamre. Price-distributing at Renen 17.00.
15.45 Torch-caravan at Hamre, both for children and adults.
17.00 Dinner at "Armfelds krog".

DEC 26:th   *08.00 Breakfast.*
16.00 Hotdogs and dogsleighing for the children by the tipi.
16.30 Pizza-buffé at the bar. Eat as much as you can for 89 SEK.
17.00 Dinner at "Armfelds krog".

DEC 27:th   *08.00 Breakfast.*
13.00 Skistar-competition at Hamre, both for adults and children.
17.00 Dinner at "Armfelds krog".
18.00 Shrimp and cheesbuffé at the bar. Eat as much as you can for 99SEK

After-ski every day by the open fire at the bar. Good food and drinks. Nice prices! Play room for the children, WELCOME!

A couple of things may have stood out to you on reading this. One is that 06.00 is an awfully early start time for what is our Christmas Day – their big day is the 24th when presents are exchanged – but even for their equivalent of Boxing Day it was an extraordinarily early start and a full three hours or more before faintest glimmer of daylight. Two – why is Donald Duck on TV at the bar highlighted as an *event*? Well, it seems that since the early sixties at 3pm the Swedes have traditionally gathered round the TV to watch the Disney production of *From All of Us to All of You* hosted by Jiminy Cricket and Mickey Mouse. With the Swedish re-titling, it became *Donald Duck and his friends wish you a Merry Christmas*. The same show every year and it wasn't really that amusing, but I made a mental note to remember to see for myself.

"*Christmas in Sweden is magical*" as it is in most ski resorts, if I am honest, but that's what it says in all their brochures. They also say "*Summer time in Sweden is magical*", which is undeniably true too. However, snow on the ground at this time of year helps a lot with the visual imagery and magical-ness, as does the tasteful (but often simple) decorations; the myriad white lights and bright – whiter than our white – candles burning in windows, on tables and in doorways; and the very lovely Swedish girls flitting about the place, being friendly and cheerful. It is a dark time of year but wherever I went they all appeared to be chirpy, contrary to the popular belief that it's so dark and miserable in winter that they all want to jump off their IKEA wardrobes.

In the run up to Christmas we continued to busy ourselves visiting all the hotels to check brochure accuracy, meeting suppliers and negotiating prices (e.g., ski hire shop, excursion operators, airport transfer operators, meeting all the hotel staff etc). I was continually amazed and heartened by how well we were being looked after. They were so proud to have a British tour operator here and were keen and enthusiastic to help out, which made our job so much easier. In the space of a few days, I think I had met about fifty or sixty people who we were going to be working with. They all knew who we were because we stood out in our bright uniforms and they would call out to us as we crossed the street, but I couldn't remember all their names. They weren't all very Swedish sounding names either; so far, I could count five Cillas, three Ulrikas, three Mats, two Maxs, three Annas as well as a Helen and an Elizabeth, plus one crazy but very friendly Finn called Kai. They were so keen to get everything just right and asked us if we could translate their menus from "Swenglish" to English. It was almost unkind to translate their already very good written English. I had seen menus and signs written by English people that were far worse.

"Naaaay," they would say in disbelief *Nej* (No), "That can't be true. We can't write better than English people."

"Oh yes you can, I promise you. And most of you speak much better, more correct than many English people." They didn't believe me of course, but when you live in a country of nine million people and no one else on the planet speaks your language, you have no option really. They learn it in schools to a high standard and, of course, they hear it in movies, TV and music.

I was lucky to have had the benefit of a good private school education where classes were small but (when I was about fourteen, I think) our French teacher, Mr Buck, an ex-RAF war pilot who smoked a pipe constantly, taught us just enough of the language so we could get by if ever we were shot down over France. I was forced to take Latin "O" level to my irritation, as I believed it to be pointless and consequently never revised for it… and subsequently failed. I had learned it for my Common Entrance exams to get me into the next school, which was acceptable in my book or *liber* as they say in Rome, but I wasn't allowed to study German or Spanish, unlike all the other boys who had joined the school at the age of eleven. The new bugs, all twelve of us, had to endure two years of Latin. In fact, the more I think about it, we didn't have that many good teachers at all; ones who could really teach rather than just spout facts and shout at us a lot.

We had a Mr Walker who taught us to shoot in the school range with .22 rifles and how to handle a gun. That was more use to me than most of the other stuff the teachers had to pass on. He must have taught something else apart from shooting, but I can't remember what. We also had an ex-Sgt Major, who was a lovely Scottish chap with a large belly and very ruddy cheeks, who taught us how to dismantle and reassemble a Bren gun after a liquid lunch (his, not in the event of…). Anyhow, I have digressed, quite a bit.

Christmas Eve arrived, bringing a gloriously sunny day, and the temperature hovered at a balmy zero degrees. Outside each of our rooms, we found a Christmas goodie bag from the manager of the Hotel Åregården, which was a lovely touch and made me feel part of a big team rather than just the two of us. Ulrika had left for her resort, Sälen, a few days ago, as she had a few guests to prepare for. The brown paper bag had a hand written note stapled to the side saying in big letters "*GOD JUL*", literally "Good Yule", and then in smaller writing "*Från oss all till se alla*", which I deduced rightly or wrongly to be "From all of us to all of you". Inside was a bag of sweeties and a bluish, purple hyacinth in a pot with a tiny Father Christmas standing in amongst the moss and sprigs of lingonberry.

As it was not the big day for our guests yet, we had ski escorting duties to perform so John and I met some of the guests in the town square and headed up the mountain as far as we could in one group for a quick whizz about. After all the long hours in front of a computer or meeting all the staff at different hotels and trying to absorb and retain all the new information in preparation for the guests' arrival, it was a relief to be actually out in the fresh air and doing some free skiing. We were all feeling in a buoyant mood because it was Christmas Eve, the sun was shining and we were out skiing – something of a rarity for us Brits.

During a quick coffee stop at the Olympia restaurant, I made a hasty and exhausting run up the slope in ski boots to grab a photo opportunity before the sun started its downward trajectory. Somewhat depressingly, it was only 12.30pm and before 2.30pm it would have disappeared behind the hills on the other side of the frozen lake at this time of year. But, with a clear blue sky, it still remained light for another hour after that.

However, we had an important rendez-vous in the town square that we had to make; Father Christmas was coming to town at one o'clock… the real one!

What would make this arrival so much better than a sleigh on wheels being pushed around a dark grey damp town centre in England was that a) the sleigh was actually drawn by a team of reindeer and b) the reindeer trotted along on the hard-packed snow. What slightly took the edge of it was that Roy Wood's 1973 hit, *I Wish It Could Be Christmas Every Day,* was being played through speakers mounted in all four corners of the square.

As we stood waiting for his arrival, I turned to look up at where we had been skiing just minutes earlier. I could make out the tiny dots of skiers as they traversed the slopes. It looked much sunnier up there and had felt much warmer, but perhaps that was because we were being active rather than just standing around. I discovered later that, in fact, there was indeed a temperature inversion thing going on here and, although it was explained to me in some detail, I failed to fully understand the cause.

I was surprised to see so many people waiting lined up,

four or five deep, around the perimeter of the square. Across the other side of the square from me, there was a gap near the tourist office where people wearing dark green Åre Fjällen ski jackets were marshalling others, keeping them apart. There was a sense of anticipation and the kids that stood about the place were getting very excited indeed. I didn't know what to expect but stood in the crowd and waited, listening to the gentle sing-songy chitter-chatter all around me (of which I understood not a word) and the swish, swish, swish, swish sound of ski trousers being walked here and there accompanied by the crunch of fresh snow under ski boots. After a while, there was a murmur and several people pointed their gloved hands towards the dark wood building that was the Hotel Åregården. The music was, thankfully, stopped abruptly and a man's voice enthusiastically announced the fat man's arrival. People started to clap, the sound muffled by their ski wear. My eyes moved around searching for a red cloak.

"I can't see him!" I exclaimed to John in a more panicky voice than I had intended. I sounded like a desperate five year old. An old white Volvo estate car with a roof box drove slowly but purposefully across the other side of the square. "Surely not..?" I wondered, a little dismayed. Then I saw some movement and the 'marshalls' became more agitated, trying to keep the gateway open to the square as the crowd surged forward a few steps. I spotted the antlers first, as they passed through a gap in the crowd, then two ropes leading to the fur-gloved hands of a man dressed head to toe in animal fur (not surprisingly, the same fur as the reindeer), who stood on the front of a large wooden sleigh, then Father Christmas. When he pulled up into the clear space I could see he was wearing the same bulky reindeer fur jacket, but with red trousers and the traditional red and white hat, his long white curly beard splayed extravagantly across his expansive furry chest.

Two reindeer were tethered to the back of the sleigh and trotted along behind and another 'reindeer man' walked with a couple more reindeer on ropes, one of them stamping his feet and feverishly shaking his head to and fro to make the bell tied around his neck ring out. Clearly, he had wanted to pull the sleigh that day and was now trying to grab all the attention.

With all the bulky reindeer fur around him, or perhaps quite a bit of over-eating, Father Christmas heaved himself up out of his seat, onto his feet and waved to the crowd. It was the real Father Christmas or, *Tompten* as they call him in Swedish, with jingling bells and a sack of presents for the children. All the kids charged forward, dragging their parents with them, their hands outstretched wanting to catch whatever it was he was about to throw them from his sack. He disappeared from view under a mass of ski helmeted children and cloth-capped adults – only a concentrated rising steam of breath identified his whereabouts.

His gifts were fresh fruit, which was a nice touch rather than Mars bars or crap toys, and he had a lot of them. As he busied himself reaching into his sacks and throwing out the gifts close to him and further afield, his hood began to slip backwards and he had to keep pulling it back over his head. On one occasion, it slipped right back to reveal his true identity. I knew I recognised those distinctive glasses – it was the bloke who ran the village off licence, *Systembolaget,* next to that "buggery" place. The kids were so focussed on where the next present was going to be thrown they did not notice.

After such excitement, I needed a hot coffee and a warm pastry so headed up to the tiny café that we had on the second floor of our old hotel and just caught it before it closed. It was run by a couple of girls who worked for the hotel and just catered for us resort workers. I am not sure how much money it really made, as it was more of a place for the hotel staff to meet up and the café staff to play music at full volume. As I ascended the stairs, I could hear something at full crank and when I went through the door Alanis Morisette was screeching angrily something at me about the mess someone left. The café girls were too busy miming at each other and dancing in the window bay that looked out across the frozen lake to notice me as they were clearing up the area. I could not be heard so I waited a bit for the song to finish, which it did very abruptly, and then said in what felt like a very posh English voice, "Err...hello... any chance of some coffee and a pastry?"

They looked shocked to hear such an accent and then started laughing with embarrassment at their dancing but smiled and one of them replied, "Yes, of course, Andrew, anything for you, Mr Englishman". I hadn't yet got used to everybody knowing my name yet but they weren't taking the mickey. Everyone here was genuinely happy to serve and amazed that they had British guests coming to stay in town. It was more like my school tuck shop in size, but it did sell some splendid cakes and pastries and strong dark coffee.

One of the peculiarities of the Swedish pastry scene at the time was small round balls of chocolate, about an inch or so in diameter, rolled in shredded coconut. They were called *Negerbollar*, although I think they have renamed them now in most cosmopolitan places in Sweden as *Chokladbollar*. I once tried eating a pair of them with my coffee but they were far too sweet and I felt a bit sick afterwards.

"So, you like our buns?" she enquired innocently.

"Yes, I like your buns", I answered. If my mates had been with me there would have been chortling, but I resisted any attempt to explain the alternative meaning as they both smiled at me, standing the other side of the counter, arms akimbo in their tight white tee shirts.

The TV lounge bar in the Hotel Åregården beckoned next for the three o'clock showing of Donald Duck. It was packed out with families and there was standing room only at the back for me. Three generations of families crammed into the room; babies held in their mother's arms for their first indoctrination, kids perched on the cushioned arms of large sofas and rows of children lying on the floor, their heads resting on their upturned hands. Grandparents who had experienced many pre-Donald Duck Christmases dutifully turned up and waited with anticipation for the show to begin. It has become one of the most watched shows on Swedish television and in some years as much as 50% of the population sat down to look at it. I watched it, as well as the scene in front of me, rather bemused.

I walked back through the hotel via the main dining room to see the remnants of what had been a festive feast being cleared away by Elin and Anna, the *frukost flickor* (breakfast girls).

"Aha…!" I said, in a very Alan Partridge sort of way, "a genuine Swedish *smörgåsbord*…?"

"Yes… Well, actually it's a *Julbord*," replied Elin.

I lingered, casting my eyes back and forth across what was left of the spread of food set out on the long table, hoping to be asked if I would like to try something, but trying not to make it too obvious.

"Would you like to try some traditional Swedish food?" she asked.

"Mmmm, yes please."

"OK, but don't tell Maga as this was supposed to be *yust* for the guests." I found it quite endearing the way the Swedes could say all the difficult words like "supposed" and "traditional" perfectly but persisted with the "y" instead of a hard "j" for a word such as "just."

She proceeded to tell me what was on offer whilst Anna stopped clearing away and stood smiling as I was introduced to the range of dishes.

"We have some herring. Of course, you know we Swedes

love our herring. And we have *gravlax*, which is sal-mon (not pronouncing it "sammon"), which has been cured in sugar salt and dill and we have smoked sal-mon as well as other cold meats like turkey, beef and a special Christmas ham that we call *julskinka*. We have also some "sheeses" (they don't do "ch" either), liver pate, salads, pickles and lots of bread and sweet bread and savoury krispbreads, and here we have some meatballs," and she spread her hands across the table, "some *prinskorv* (sausages), *koldomar* (meat stuffed cabbage rolls), jellied pigs' feet, *lutfisk* (dried cod served with thick white sauce) and *revbenspjäll* (oven–roasted pork ribs)."

There were also potatoes and red cabbage and *dopp i grytan* (bread dipped in the broth and juices that are left over after boiling the ham). For dessert, there was a selection of sweet pastries, saffron buns, *pepparkarkor* (ginger snaps) and some homemade sweets. And, to wash it all down, there were large glass jugs of *glögg* – sweet mulled wine and strong Swedish coffee. Oversized red and white striped peppermint sticks called *polkagris* were also scattered around the table. I had a small plate of odds and sods, stuffed a couple of rolls into my pockets and headed off for my room in the Sporthotellet.

It was still a full working day for us, so I returned to our little office in the Diplomat Ski Lodge Hotel to find John on the phone dealing with an irate customer who had booked a hotel that was way out of the town centre and wasn't happy with it. In the brochure it had been accurately described as an "Apart-Hotel… comprising three buildings with skiing virtually to/ from the door… and is surrounded by its own Scandinavian wood cabins." It went on to say "Åre village centre is a short ten minute bus ride away by the regular ski bus (FREE with lift pass) or the evening shuttle bus (small local charge)". From that, I would have deduced that it wasn't in the village centre but it was apparent from the half of the conversation I could hear, from what John was saying, that Mr E had not. And he was not happy, not happy at all. To make matters worse this was the first year they had not brought their nanny on the ski holiday – more likely she had declined a free ski holiday with them – and they simply couldn't be with their children all the time, could they?

John was dealing with the complaint very well and sympathised with Mr E about spending *every evening in with the kids*, after all it was Christmas time and wholly reasonable to expect them to be left inside while Mr & Mrs E went about town from bar to bar drinking themselves silly. Mr E had chosen the most expensive week to go skiing but had also chosen the cheapest accommodation in the resort as it was a) self-catering and b) right out on the edge of the resort, as it implied in the brochure.

There was a knock at the door and, before I could get to it, in came Daniel and Mellissa from our competitors, Ski Scandinavia. They quickly realised John was having a difficult conversation so did the only thing they could do in the situation, and that was sit down, noisily open a couple of cans of coke and watch him at work. My video camera was sat on my desk so I switched on and filmed him, suggesting it would make a good training video, which on reflection probably wasn't very helpful. John had done a couple of seasons and, although I'm sure he meant well, he was a bit of a know-it-all, so we three were relishing the awkward conversation he was having with his guest.

He also believed he could ski better than Daniel and would bang on about his Austrian style of skiing. Let's ponder that... Daniel, a Swede who had been skiing ever since he was two years old, or John from Kent, who had learnt to ski in Austria (keeping his legs too close together) when he was sixteen? Fortunately, my guests were all behaving themselves so, after we had tired of our amusement, Daniel, Mellissa and I left him with the plastic trout that travelled everywhere with him, apparently (and spent the entire season resting on the pen shelf at the base of our white board). We headed off to the Diplomat Ski Lodge bar for a couple of beers beneath the giant stuffed moose head, mounted high up onto the wall under a pair of old wooden crossed skis that looked out over the main bar.

When I awoke the next morning, our Christmas Day, I felt like I had been hit by a... I was going to say steam roller but snowplough is more apt. I had, over the last week or so, been fighting off a cold and, with the long hours and stress of this new business, I had finally succumbed to *mannen influensa* as they say in Sweden. I spent the whole day in bed feeling awful and a little depressed. My mother's Christmas cake went unwrapped and uneaten and I didn't even make it to the phone to ring home.

John called to wish me Happy Christmas and said he was off skiing if I felt like it later, but I just groaned and slept for most of the day. I had rallied a little by the time darkness had fallen but didn't feel well enough to get all togged up to walk outside to go to get an evening meal from the Hotel Åregården, so tucked into a stale bread roll I had scavenged from the *Julbord* the day before, with some Marmite as the main course, followed by a few too many *Japp* bars – chocolate filled with nougat and caramel for pudding – from my *God Jul* bag. This was washed down with what was left in a large Coke bottle – warmed to room temperature, of course. I remembered a bit late in the day that I had brought with me some Christmas presents from home so, after rummaging around in my bags, I found my Grandmother's sensible pair of gloves present and a super Maglite torch from my parents.

A rather unusual Christmas day, for sure, but I was feeling better at the end of it than the beginning. Naturally after such a strong dose of *mannen influensa* it took me a few days to recover fully and I learned that you cannot be ill in this job as the guests keep coming – damn them!

Things quietened down a lot during the week after Christmas – I only had a family of three and one couple to look after at the Renen Hotel – and that gave us the opportunity to sample one of the activities that we were going to encourage our guests to take part in – the Snow Scooter safari. Our friend Mats ran the imaginatively named *Skotersafari* company, which was based in a collection of portacabins on the edge of the lake just a little way out of the village; too far to walk to but just far enough so that the guests had to go by taxi.

We used Stefan's taxis as he had a couple of VW minibuses. He would charge us the equivalent of £30 for the round trip from the pick up outside the Hotel Åregården in the town square and we could pack up to ten people into the minibus and charge them £10 each for the ride, so any trip with more than three people in it and we were making a nice profit, which was cash in our grubby-gloved paws.

The ski company would make money on the sales of the snow scooter safari, and pay us our commission, and Mats would also make money so "Everyone's a winner, Rodney", as Del Boy would have said. It was a great scam and one excursion that we heavily promoted at our Welcome Meetings. The added bonus was that it wasn't a hard sell either as pretty much everyone who came to the resort wanted to do that, and the husky dog sleigh rides more than any other excursion. The husky dog adventure was even further out of the village so the taxi fare was more, of course.

A group of twelve of us (two taxis' worth) assembled at the *Skotersafari* base, wearing full ski gear with gloves and goggles, and Mats took us inside one of the portacabins to explain things. It was rather spartan inside and reminded me of a local town football club's changing room with a row of benches with wire mesh holders underneath for shoes and boots and a framework running along the back with a row of hooks. We got kitted out with thick dry suits that were either small, medium. large or XXXL and fitted cumbersomely over our own ski clothing before being told to choose the right size winter boots from a line up along the outer wall. Next, we were paired up with the right sized helmet and gathered around a map on the wall.

Mats was a six foot something strapping Swede with a healthily weathered and tanned face edged with a grizzly blonde beard and wild hair, usually contained in a hat of some kind. His ice blue eyes shone out above high cheekbones – the ladies liked him but I think he was oblivious to the effect he had on them. He could have been aged anything between twenty five and forty five years old, I really had no idea.

He explained the general operation of the snowmobiles and the route we were going to take, pointing out the half way hut where we would stop for a coffee. At this time of year, we would be returning in the dark, so we would get the full experience, but we had to be very, very careful on the return journey as we wouldn't be able to see the cracks in the ice when we were on the lake. There was a palpable shift in mood at that moment, from excited nervousness to nervous excitement, quickly followed by mild terror as he finished up with "…and if anyone falls off on the way back we won't be able to see you in the dark so the wolves will get you." He laughed. No one else did. If I was a guest, I'd be thinking one week in Meribel would have been very nice, thank you.

Once outside, we clumped around like a sleuth of bears at a honey-fest and waddled down to the lake side. It was 1.45pm and still light enough for us to see the blue ice of the lake water where the snow had been blown away in big patches like bruised skin. Following Mats's lead, we each in turn stepped gingerly onto the frozen water, half-expecting it to collapse and be drawn under. It was an odd sensation, stepping from what was clearly a wooden jetty onto the lake – a bit like stepping out onto a glass floor in a tall building – even though we couldn't see through the ice, as most of it in this immediate area was still covered by snow. The three old wooden boats, moored up with their ropes disappearing into the snow about twenty metres away, served to remind us of what we were walking on.

Mats waited patiently for us all to gather round his collection of snowmobiles for the final briefing on the controls. We were about to take control of a Ski-Doo Touring LE which could travel up to seventy five miles per hour. They were two seaters (kids under fourteen could not drive them) and had an engine capacity of 400cc. Mats started one up by pressing the starter button. It was as loud as starting a chain saw in your bathroom. Mrs F, from Wakefield, who was standing too close, chatting to her daughter and not listening to the instructions, jumped a foot in the air and fell down on her backside. I wondered whether the wolves would be devouring her later.

Being an avid fan of motorbikes and fast cars myself, I thought it sounded great.

Mats left the engine popping and banging to warm it up and the guests either buddied up or grabbed their own scooter. I had spied a rather racy looking green one with a blue and yellow swish down the sides and saddled up. Like a jet ski, you have a cord around your wrist linked to a kill switch so if you do fall off the engine cuts out and the scooter comes to a halt, in theory giving you sufficient time, assuming you have no broken bones or knocked yourself unconscious, to scrabble across the ice or through the deep snow and clamber back on again before those beady eyes and long teeth have you on the menu.

I sat on my scooter, feeling quite at home being not too dissimilar to a motorbike, although the thin caterpillar tracks beneath my seat and the short dainty skis out front were a novelty. I looked out across the surface of the frozen lake towards the other side, which was bounded by a dark line of forestation that rose gradually upwards for a few hundred metres before it stopped, revealing a row of snow covered hills.

Mats checked we were all OK and had started our machines and then, with a wave of his arm, we were off at what I thought was quite a fast pace for novices. It was bumpier than I had expected and there were some alarmingly large areas of bare ice with crack lines running through them. As we spread out in a line, I became more acutely aware of the sheer scale of the lake. It felt as if we were shrinking into the landscape and we Lilliputians were snowmobiling across the top of a large Christmas cake.

Even with a full set of warm ski underwear on, ski jacket and trousers *and* the big over-suit, I could tell how bitterly cold it was with the wind speed as we raced across the lake. The heated handlebar grips were very welcome too and I could feel the warmth through my ski gloves. The thumb throttle could have done with its own little heat booster, though. Mats slowed a bit and waved people by him, so he could check we were all together, and we passed like a wild west cavalry charge across the plains. Then he accelerated at a tremendous speed, his snowmobile jumping around on the lumps of snow and ice, and took the lead again, this time not slowing down but maintaining his pace so we all had to speed up. We were probably only doing about 50 mph but, because it was such a new sensation for us, it felt like we were doing 100 mph. It was exhilarating but after fifteen minutes of this we were happy to slow down as we reached the far end of the lake and maintained what seemed like a walking pace.

We were brought to halt and Mats checked if we were all OK before announcing the next stage of the ride would be off into the country into some fairly deep snow and through the thick dark forest. We must follow in his tracks, no overtaking, watch out for low branches and shift our weight to help the machines along where we could – oh, and if we felt the scooter turning over on top of us then make sure we jump clear.

The next twenty minutes or so provided us with a different challenge – that of keeping the thing upright and heading in the right direction. The fresh snow fall had not been compacted yet, so we were ploughing a new course through the trees, our headlight beams bouncing off the snow banks and sturdy trunks of the dense pines and reflecting off the lighter silver birch tree trunks. Up and up we dragged our snowmobiles, through twists and turns of a route Mats must have known like the back of his hand, pausing every now and again when someone in the line got into a bit of difficulty.

Finally, we popped out above the cover of the trees and onto a clear piece of snowy wasteland and Mats pushed on ahead, picking up the pace a little. Dutifully we followed him in a line, feeling quite pleased with ourselves that no one had fallen off yet. After five minutes of relatively easy riding, we pulled up near a tiny wooden hut and Mats leaped off his machine and guided each of us into the parking area before ushering us inside.

To our astonishment there was a log fire in full blaze and a man busying himself with preparing a dozen coffees in an old black pot. We sat down on wooden benches covered with reindeer skins and huddled around the fire whilst Mats passed around a wooden tray of buns. We were all full of the excitement of the adventure and chatted excitedly, me momentarily forgetting that I was actually working and not on holiday with these people. No sooner had we warmed ourselves up properly than we were zipping up and pulling on our gloves and head gear and saying goodbye and thank you to our host.

Stepping outside, we were hit by the dark of night. It had been a cloudy day and now the sun had disappeared and we were out in the wilderness; it was very dark indeed. We couldn't see the twinkling lights of the resort from here, but the snow cover on the ground contrasted sufficiently with the dark of the trees to help give us some awareness of our surroundings. Mats checked again that we were all OK and warned us about the dangers of going downhill on these machines. Then we were back in the saddle and heading off beyond the hut for a while along a ridge, before plunging down into a small valley and back into the trees for a bumpy, twisty route down to the shore line about half a kilometre along from where we had left it earlier.

Stopping briefly to check numbers again and to give us a breather after what had been quite a strenuous ride down, we set off at full chat along the edge of the lake, our headlights picking out the scooters in front and clumps of snow on the frozen surface. We sped along like a line of ants with miners' lamps, if that were possible, eventually peeling off right and heading diagonally across the blue grey expanse of night time snow cover finally reaching the cluster of portacabins. Seeing the lights of the village beyond and the moving headlights of passing cars up on the road ahead made me appreciate how close I was to the real wilderness just the other side of the lake – apart from the little hut with coffee and buns, of course. I was also excited by the prospect of being able to do this excursion every week if I wanted.

New Year's Eve came around quickly and all the UK reps, namely John and I and what was now two girls from Ski Scandinavia, Mellissa and Katrina (whom John always mistakenly called Natasha, much to her annoyance), got together with three English guests we got along with and joined the Swedes in the Diplomat Ski Lodge bar. Fireworks had been going off since it got dark across the town and, at about 8pm, there raged a pitched battle from one side to the other with sporadic explosions letting rip into the night sky overhead. We counted in the Swedish New Year and then, after an hour's more drinking, we counted in the proper GMT New Year, receiving some strange looks from those immediately around us in the very noisy crowded bar, but by that time we didn't care as the beer and vodka had taken full effect. We missed the fireworks in the square but partied well into the early hours of the morning with a couple of hundred like-minded Swedes.

3

JANUARI

Happy New Year

What better way to start a new year than to go skiing? The answer is to be paid to go skiing. That answer is fine as long as you haven't been up until 5.30am and had a skinful of beer and vodka and you are on ski escort duty at 9.30am in the morning. It would have been an earlier bed time but, after leaving the Diplomat bar, we headed into the Country Club night club or as they call it rather amusingly a *nattklubb*. We danced (bobbed around) and sang (shouted) to a load of UK, US and Euro hits and with just as much verve and vigour as we did with the Swedish ones, although we'd never heard any of them before (apart from the Abba ones, of course), particularly their Happy New Year song; even now, it brings back very happy memories whenever I hear it. I can actually say I enjoyed New Year's Eve for once, and not because I must have hugged and kissed more than thirty lovely Swedish girls in one night, although that would be a hard tally to beat.

On the way back from the Country Club, we diverted across

the town square to get a pizza from the tiny takeaway joint that did phenomenal business between the hours of 12.30 and 5am. I staggered back to my room with my pizza but don't recall eating it all and I don't think I dropped it en route.

It was drilled into us in the training week in Austria that whatever happens, wherever you end up the night before, you must always be there on time for ski escorting duties and the transfer to the airport. As I was feeling so rough on Christmas Day, John had done the honours in exchange for me doing New Year's Day. I considered it a good trade at the time we struck the deal. Not so now, as I struggled to rouse myself from a warm bed and staggered about unsteadily trying to find my ski gear. My head thumped and ached as I forced my feet into the ski boots, feeling a little queasy. I downed a glass of water, brushed my teeth and searched around for all the paraphernalia I needed before opening the door with one hand, propping it open with one leg and a boot, reaching for my skis and sticks, which were leant up against the wall with the other hand. I really didn't feel up for this at all and couldn't recall if I was doing blues and reds today or reds and blacks.

God help me if I was doing black runs. Maybe the guests wouldn't want to do that? I thought.

It was only a five minute walk along a piste that ran right into the town square along the back of the Sporthotellet. The swing door slammed shut with its usual bang and I was out in the freezing air again, which helped rouse me a little. I trudged along the empty piste before stacking my skis and poles carefully against the sign post that was our nominated meeting point. I was five minutes early and I took a few deep breaths of the cold sharp air. It was only minus eight degrees so it didn't sting your insides like it would do when it got really cold. I started to feel better, but after another ten minutes of waiting it began to dawn on me that I might be the only one for ski escorting this morning. Annoyingly, that proved to be the case and, at 9.50am, I took the decision that no one was coming. My bed was still warm but I was up and out now so I decided I might as well go for a ski and get to know some more runs to see how they linked up. I had an invigorating two hour ski and felt so much better for it; I was after all being paid to ski, much to my continued amusement.

We had a couple of excursions booked up for New Year's Day and it was crucial that I went along to experience them both. The first one was a trip to Njarka Sami Camp, some 30 kms north west of Åre, close to Lake Häggsjön, as John called it. Even at this early stage of my Swedish I had worked out that a *sjön* was a lake but, in the same he way he persisted calling Katrina Natasha, he called all the named lakes Lake something or other. So Åresjön, according to John, became Lake Åre Lake and this one became Lake Hägg Lake. He was annoying me more and more each day. And we had another five months to go.

The Svenssons' coach we used was operated by a local guy called Svensson. His first name was Sven and he spoke no English whatsoever, so you couldn't even have a bit of fun with him about his name. For the entire six month season, he wore the same black trousers, black boots, black shirt and black leather jacket from the early eighties, which went well with his Kevin Keegan perm of black hair. He was, however, very friendly and, most importantly, very reliable.

Whatever the weather threw at us, he would be there and his luxury Van Hool coaches were always immaculately turned out, apart from the slightly worrying massive crack right across his windscreen, which he didn't seem to care about. In a way, it was good that he spoke no English because I had to learn to speak Swedish to him to tell him how many guests were staying at which hotels. The occasions when I had to ride the jump seat in an empty coach for an hour with him to the airport to do a collection did drag on a bit in an awkward silence though as I quickly ran out of things to say and his Swedish questions went uncomfortably unanswered. He never came in to our office to deal with our payments to him but always sent his wife. She had left the eighties and progressed to the nineties and was always very charming, if not a little too flirty: she always finished our meetings with an invitation to go snowmobiling with her.

We pulled out of the town square at 2pm with a few of our guests and did the rounds to various hotels and apartments picking up others as we went and then headed off to Duved to collect my guests at 2.10pm. John was doing the chat on the microphone and entertaining the guests (he thought) with his (not very) amusing stories and anecdotes. I was supposed to be learning what to say from him but decided when I did this trip I would be saying a lot less and just let the guests relax. Most of them were staring out the window anyhow, watching the unfamiliar snowy landscape pass by. Forty five minutes from Duved, we arrived at the camp, filed off the coach and ambled up a gentle incline to the camp.

Since we were so far north, we were very fortunate to have this camp as an option for people to visit. The land of the Sami people spans Arctic Sweden, Norway, Finland and Russia. They are one of the world's indigenous people with their own language, culture and customs. What we know as Lapland is only part of the vast Sami area. They have lived off the land here before anyone else, as hunters and fishermen and gathering wild plants and berries. There are over 80,000 of them, 20,000 of whom live in Sweden. Central to their existence is the reindeer. Traditionally they have moved with the reindeer on their ancient migration routes and seasonal foraging grounds. Of course, the reindeer do not recognise modern day country borders and nor do the Sami people. I hadn't seen any reindeer around the resort yet, other than Santa's, but I had been told to expect some and was looking forward to seeing herds of them on the edge of the ski area.

Our visit to this camp was a chance to learn about the reindeer and "get up close and personal" with them by feeding them and even lassoing them as well as learning about the Sami culture and people. The camp was only open for two weeks in the winter, oddly, so we weren't able to add it into our Welcome Pack as a regular excursion. It consisted of three *goahtis*, tipis (not to be confused with a *lavvu*, which is the smaller more mobile tent) were set up in a clearing about five to ten metres apart in a semi circle. Pathways had been created out of the snow by people trudging back and forth spanning out from a central area to each tent.

The tents themselves stood maybe four or five metres high and, at the base, were perhaps four metres in diameter. They were open at the top, with the poles of the structure protruding, and were covered in snow which presumably acted as insulation. Each had a light wooden front door, which lifted upwards and outwards, and were thick with snow. Some way off behind these tents were a group of small dark red timbered houses set amongst the pine and birch trees. And behind those I spied a Chevy pick-up truck and a Volvo estate car. I think our guests chose not to see that, suspending their belief and telling themselves what they were about to experience was genuine.

There was no doubt that we were meeting true Sami people, the reindeers were real and this was their way of life, but they had adapted to modern day living. The elevated camp looked out over a sea of dark green trees as far as you could see and in the distance the hazy snow covered hills merged with the sky.

The reindeer were not corralled and moved freely about the area and a series of logs were strategically placed around the perimeter, each one supporting a pair of lit candles in tins to ward off the wolves. The leaden skies slowly began to release a light fall of snowflakes as one of our hosts, an intelligent looking man with a dark skinned, weather-beaten but cheery face, dressed in full Sami regalia with a brightly coloured sweater and head gear, brought out a bag of lichen, introduced himself and welcomed us to the camp. A few of us reached in to grab a handful of the shrub to feed to the reindeer. The grey and white soft furred animals moved slowly and calmly towards us and began to nibble delicately while the man told us about the Sami way of life, their antlers occasionally clattering against another's as they jostled for position. More and more reindeer began to edge towards me and my outstretched clump of lichen and the mood began to get a little energised. I could see that, before too long, I would be completely surrounded with an empty upturned hand, so gave up my lichen to the chap with the largest pair of antlers and hopped out of the herd before it became a melee.

Re-joining our group, I caught the end of an interesting fact that our host was telling us – that reindeer do actually have red noses. Apparently scientists in Norway have used nasal video microscopy and infrared imaging to investigate why reindeers' noses glow so red. *Really…?* I wondered to myself. I looked around to see if our guests were taking this in – they were all focussed intently on him, like small children being told a captivating story. He went on to confirm they found that the red glow helps reindeer control their body temperature during strenuous exercise. They have hairpin shaped radiator-like blood vessels.

"Rudolph's nose is red because it is richly supplied with red blood cells," he continued. "It acts like a radiator in a car and is specially adapted for reindeers to carry out their flying duties for Santa Claus". He sounded very convincing but there was a ripple of laughter when he finished. "No, it's true," he said with a very serious face now, slightly insulted that we thought he was lying. He was so convincing I believed him, and do you know what?

I have since discovered it is absolutely true. Not the flying bit though, well I don't think so, but maybe that is too?

John had positioned himself by one of the entrance hatches and lifted it up to reveal a blazing fire inside and a pot of hot coffee resting on a circular metal structure above the fire pit. We filed in walking across a thick bed of pine leaves spread across the floor and took a seat on large logs covered with reindeer rugs arranged around the circumference of the *goahti*. At the far corner was another older Sami man, who I presumed to be our guide's father. He was squat, slightly plump and not so elaborately dressed, but sported a rather splendid reindeer fur hat. John announced we were all *Engelsmen* and we didn't speak Swedish. He looked as if he found this all a bit tedious and couldn't wait to get back into his house to check up on the latest football scores on his satellite TV. He perked up a bit when a couple of Swedes entered the tent and he realised he could have a conversation. He busied himself with the coffee pot, his gnarled blackened hands seemingly impervious to the heat of the kettle he had just lifted off the fire and then offered us all some coffee. To his left on a low table was arranged some sweet pitta bread for us all to try with our coffee. It was surprisingly warm in the tent, even with the roof open at the top where all the timber boarding almost met at a point.

The door squeaked shut as the son came in to help pour out the coffee whilst explaining how they farmed the reindeer using every bit of the reindeer body to help them survive. Obviously, the meat kept them fed, the fur kept them warm and the horn could be used for tools and knife handles. A pair of shoes could be crafted from just the fur around the four legs and even the tendons from the legs were used by children to floss their teeth. In true touristy style, we were shown a range of Sami handicraft, all decorated beautifully, the materials used being reindeer horn, birch roots and protuberances growing on birch trunks. They produced spoons of reindeer horn, knives, a range of sizes of bags, from reindeer leather, cups of birch and jewellery bags. After we had finished our coffee and breads and some of the guests had made some purchases, we tramped back through the snow to our waiting coach. I promptly fell asleep for the entire journey back to Åre, not even waking up at Duved to say goodbye to the guests I was looking after. I figured they had had a good excursion; I had chatted to them at the camp and, besides, they were not the sort of guests that were going to cause any trouble, so I considered it safe to get some much needed sleep and the warm environment of the coach was too soporific to resist.

It was, of course, pitch black by the time we got back to our office to do some paperwork and check on the incoming guest lists that had been faxed to us via the Åregården Hotel (and in case you have been mispronouncing that all this time, it's the *Aura Gordon* Hotel).

We headed down to the basement kitchens to take our early supper at 5pm with the hotel staff and I was extremely grateful to load up a plate of boiled potatoes, salmon and peas, accompanied by a couple of krispbreads and a glass of *apelsinjuice* which, when I saw the labels on the china jugs always made me stop and think because it was orange juice, not apple juice. We lined up in a school-like fashion as the hotel's chefs and kitchen staff dished out the food to us all and then we sat at tables in the extensive basement area with whoever was there. I was so tired I had picked up a serving plate rather than a proper dinner plate but easily managed to wolf down the extra quantity of potato and peas. I was in need of some fruit and made a mental note to stock up at the ICA supermarket the next day, if I could.

We had begun to get into a regular rhythm of work and I was getting used to where I needed to be at what time and how long it was going to take me to get there. It was still early in the season and we had been warned about the bargain hunters; those guests who had booked at the cheapest time of the year and were feeling pleased about the amount of money they had saved by coming in the low season. They were the ones who would complain bitterly if anything at all went wrong and demand to be compensated further. The next week we had a great young bunch of people who were a huge amount of fun and wanted to do as many excursions as possible, ski with us at every opportunity, and party every night. That may sound great and it was, in part, although I had to keep reminding myself that I was not on holiday with them and still had my "behind the scenes" job to do, and that they weren't the only guests in resort. However, while it was still fairly quiet, I was happy to oblige and particularly as they would insist on buying me lunch and coffee every time I went skiing. In exchange for taking them to all the best after-ski places and getting them into the night clubs ahead of the queues, I would get free beer all night. So much for a quiet week ahead.

One of the best, arguably *the* best, after-ski venues to go to in the resort was at the Sunwing Hotel, a huge grey battleship sort of a structure wedged into the side of the mountain with two different sized red timber Air Traffic Control-like towers mounted on top; the larger one in the middle and the smaller one jutting out over the end of the building that over-looked the ski pistes below. Tacked on to this end was a creamy yellow more traditional building, which could have perhaps been the original hotel.

The main accommodation comprised hundreds of rooms and apartments and, because of the keen pricing, the location right on the pistes and the fact that you could cram more than half a dozen people into a tiny apartment (with the use of pull-out beds etc) it was very popular with the 'youth'. That and the, as described in the brochure, "large after-ski bar, featuring frequent live music". Frequent? It was daily and had quite a reputation.

For most of the season, it was a covers band called Angeline and they really knew how to entertain a crowd and get them revved up. The great thing about this venue was you could ski down to it and park your skis and poles outside and have a drink and then ski down to the village centre. The tight and twisty blue didn't really test you at all until it straightened up and sent you barrelling down a fast shute under a road which would have you slipping and sliding up one side then down and up the other side after firing you out of a sharp bend. It would then spit you out the other end onto the final short run back into the village square. Most times you just had to go with the flow and let it have its fun with you after you had had one too many beers. It was best not to head off at the same time as everyone else as it was a bit of a funnel and collisions were common.

When approaching the Sunwing Hotel on an afternoon's skiing, you would be able to swing casually down through a few turns and along a bit of snow-covered road and then pop out of your skis, carrying them the final five metres across the main entrance way to the hotel, careful to avoid any coaches that were manoeuvring about. There was ample space to leave your skis and then head in through the main doors to turn left towards the bar area. What confronted you next was the rather odd sight of a massive pile of ski boots dripping with melting snow in the warmth of the hotel. After the obligatory removal of ski boots, you would pass through the double doors in your socked feet and head on in, walking across the slate floor of the bar area and into a part of the building that overhung the slope. An unusual Swedish custom, you ask? No. The hotel had had a bar in this location for many years and as it became more and more popular with its own guests as well as skiers staying elsewhere in the resort, it had to expand to accommodate all the extra bodies so they extended out into the air over-hanging the drop. That was all fine for a while but the previous timber floor was getting all chewed up from the thousands of booted skiers walking about and jumping around to the music so they decide to recover the floor with something more durable: slates. All was looking good and they opened for trade the next season. The skiers continued to dance and jump around only this time when they all jumped up and down together to certain songs that encouraged mass jumping, the floor started bouncing up and down and the entire end of the hotel was at risk of breaking off and sliding down the mountain into the village square.

Somebody had got their calculations wrong and, although they had taken into consideration the extra weight of the slates and the human bodies, they had forgotten those two hundred bodies would also be wearing ski boots and that's what quite literally could have tipped it all over the edge. So then the solution was to de-boot before entering the bar area.

Whether it was co-incidence or just that the band, Angeline, played it so well or that it was the perfect after-ski song, but Van Halen's *Jump* certainly got everyone onto their socked feet and up into the air. They played it every night to a rousing reception. They strung out the opening keyboard and drums anthem to great effect and on many occasions, if I was sitting in the main bar having a beer with some guests, I would hear the beginning of the song and suggest to them "This is worth watching" before picking up my beer and dragging them all through to the dance area. There's nothing quite like a live band; a DJ playing it would just not have worked. The band, a sort of Bon Jovi, Iron Maiden, Europe, Van Halen cocktail that had been going for ten years, seemed to lift the spirits of everyone there. Spirits that had been out in the fresh mountain air all day, getting exercise, away from their day to day routines and fuelled with alcohol.

The dance area was darker than the bar but spotlights circled the crowd and the band itself was lit up. Most people were still in ski gear and lifting their arms up as they jumped. Others had clambered up onto the tables alone or in small groups and were precariously holding each other together as they jumped around screaming and hollering and raising glasses. The band knew exactly which songs to get them all going. Another one they regularly played a much heavier rockier version of was a song that the Swedes loved (in fact it sent them nuts) – the equally crowd pleasing and jump inducing, *Just Nu* by Tomas Ledin.

It was Sweden's 1980 Eurovision entry and, during the performance, his microphone lead *famously,* according to the Swedes, became unplugged, although he did manage to reconnect before he had to sing the second verse. No, I had never heard of him either and knew nothing of his lead detachment incident. This band played every night for weeks on end and put the same energy and enthusiasm into each performance. It was no wonder this venue was classed as *Scandinaviens bästa after-ski.* It could easily rival anything I have ever seen in Austria and there was always the added thrill that the whole venue might break off and slide down the mountain.

There were other bars to go to for after-ski, of course, but none quite like the Sunwing, partly because of its setting and partly because of the music, but once you had finished there you could ski down into the village and visit Broken Dreams in the town square, an American style diner complete with red leather diner-style booths and a burger-filled menu. Alternatively, you could try the rather sedate golf club-style Åregården bar and, if you headed further downhill to its sister hotel, the Diplomat Ski Lodge, the Diplomat bar or, *Dippan,* as it was known locally as, you never knew who would be there. It could be stacked full of Swedish celebrities, the equivalent of our Lorraine Kelly, Graham Norton or a Nordic Laurence Llewelyn-Bowen, and I hadn't a clue who they were – but soap stars, singers, TV presenters were regular visitors. They mixed with the wealthy Stockholmers who, according to the locals, referred to it as *Diplomaat*.

I discovered that the Stockholmers were generally disliked in the resort as a lot of them behaved like they owned the place. Many of them probably did, in fact, own large parts of the place. I was reminded how far north I was in the country when the locals I was working alongside of talked disparagingly about The Stockholmers. It's no different to most countries really, and was comparable with a load of wealthy Londoners descending on a small town in Yorkshire, for example, or New Yorkers partying out of their immediate habitat. However, I did witness a shocking display of wealth one evening in *Dippan* where a group of about twenty revellers had lined up a row of tables and chairs right in the middle of the bar area so everyone could see them. They had already drunk quite a lot and were being fairly rowdy, shouting at one another and singing loudly, amusing themselves but irritating everyone else. Then one of them came back from the bar accompanied by two barmen loaded down with champagne. There must have been twenty bottles of champagne, one for each of them. They began handing them out along the table, each recipient scraping away the foil and releasing the pressure on the wire muselets. They had a team count down before they all shook their bottles, popped the corks and sprayed each other or guzzled the contents.

The look on the other drinkers in the bar was one of disgust. The Swedes may have a higher standard of living than most in Europe but they frown upon those that flaunt their wealth. This was a very obscene and ostentatious display of wealth. They didn't care for it at all and we weren't even in the dreaded week nine of the holiday season, which is when all the skiers from the Stockholm area took their half term holiday. That was the week when all the BMWs would be parked up on the pavements.

With a population of some nine million people and only a few home ski resorts, they very sensibly divided up the country so not everyone took their half term ski holiday at once.

It was the week when there would be a tangible amount of pushing and shoving in the bars. So far there had been none, not even in a busy bar, which was a refreshing change from England where if you happened to knock someone's drink you would risk some idiot getting over aggressive. Here they accepted that if you were in a busy bar, your drink might get knocked and some spillage might ensue.

The days ahead became more regulated with weekly events and a typical seven days ahead in my diary I would show notations such as Duved (my hotel visits) with a note in red saying RTN BUS 19:00 to remind me not to stay chatting for too long as that was the last free ski bus pick up to get back to Åre, welcome meetings, free skiing (without guests), airport (reminding me it was my turn to do the transfer), names of guests (which hotels they had booked and what they had pre-booked) and ski escorting. In bright orange marker pen ink, I would write HUSKY DOGS, SNOW SCOOTER, TANNFORSEN (frozen waterfall) and TOBOGGANING. This was in stark contrast to the previous year's January diary, which would have had things like: Monday morning meeting, shopping centre leasing meeting, beers with Pete & John – Duke's Head, lunch with lawyers, squash match, Sainsbury's big shop, renew tube pass, client meeting. I thought often about what my friends would be doing back in London round about the same times of the day.

The Husky Dogs excursion proved to be my favourite trip, which was odd really having had a fear of dogs most of my life, owing to a couple of frightening early experiences of Alsatians. Just to put you in the picture, the first of these happened when I was aged about six. I was following my mother and brother diagonally across a yard behind a pub that sat on the corner of a crossroads. Everyone used the cut through to go from one row of shops to another and we had done it many times before. We had got about half way across when there was a lot of barking coming from the back of the building behind some crates and bins and then this wolf charged at us – more specifically, me. It still sends a shiver down my spine when I remember looking into his wild eyes and gnashing teeth – my head height must have almost at the same level as his so for me it was like standing next to a horse would be for an adult. He grabbed the shoulder and hood of my jacket in his jaws and started shaking me violently. My screams must have got him even more revved up. My mother turned around in horror to see me being shaken about and a moment later a bloke came running out of the back of the pub and quickly separated me from *Prince* or *Brutus* or *Armageddon* or whatever the bloody thing was called. Incredibly there was no damage done to my body, just my favourite blue jacket and, so it transpired, my mind.

My second Alsatian moment occurred only some six years later at Prep school. We had, for one term only, a temporary PE teacher who was freshly ex-RAF Police. I remember him being a squat, stocky little man with a big, aggressive attitude. Not able to leave the forces experience behind him, he drove a squat, stocky little grey mini-van with a tiny roof vent that contained a big Alsatian with an aggressive attitude. One lesson, he lined all of us twelve year olds up along the edge of one of the football pitches. Walking up and down in front of the line of anxious boys, he barked his instructions at us. Each one of us, in turn, would be required to sprint as fast as we could across the pitch on the first blow of his whistle. We were to have our right arm strapped into a thick leather arm cut from an Irvine flying jacket that was bound up tightly by leather straps.

On the second blow of his whistle, five seconds later, the Alsatian would set off after us. When he had bitten into the leather arm we were to stop immediately. Whoever had covered the most distance was the declared the fastest runner and would win the "event", as he termed it. I still feel sick thinking about it now. At the time, waiting in line for my turn, all my insides were in turmoil. You might have thought I would have been able to run my fastest ever fifty metres but when the whistle went for my run I sprinted off and then wanted to get it over with as soon as possible. I distinctly remember hearing the second whistle blow and then felt myself slowing down so the dog would catch me quickly. The thundering sound of his padded feet as he charged towards me from behind getting ever closer to me followed by a sudden violent tug on my arm still haunts me. I know I wanted to cry but couldn't in front of the other boys. I was twelve years old, for God's sake – almost a man. We all had to stand on the pitch where we were caught, like pathetic sad statues of wretched orphan boys. No one looked at any one else. I am sure most of us felt sick and tearful. I cannot imagine that sort of thing happening at a school nowadays. It was utterly preposterous.

So it was with some trepidation that I headed off for my first experience of dog sledging in the wild. I guess it was the authenticity of the excursion that made it so popular with our guests. They were real husky dogs, you were taken out on a real handmade wooden sledge and you could actually drive the thing yourself if you wanted to, though most people, when offered, shied away from it, leaving either John or me to step on to the back of the thing and take up the 'reins' as it were. The very first time I did it, I was, much to my surprise, totally captivated. Each excursion began with a taxi ride or a (*lots-of-profit-for-us*) Stefan's Taxi ride for a group of guests out of the village to our chosen supplier. In this case, it was Åre Sled Dog Adventures, run by our genial host, Tommy Bernhardsson.

Tommy had grown up in the mountains of Jämtland (the

province in which Åre sat almost bang in the middle of). The province covers about 8% of the total area of Sweden – about 13,000 square miles (about half the size of Scotland) – and has been a strategic county throughout the years, being part of Norway for four hundred and fifty years and then Sweden for three hundred and seventy years. Its coat of arms, which I had seen displayed in many places by the road side or on the edge of towns, rather alarmingly, shows a moose being attacked on both sides by what looks like an eagle and, you've guessed it, a dog, although not an Alsatian, more of a small greyhound or a large whippet. Despite the somewhat violent imagery on its county shield, it nominates as its county symbols an orchid for its flower, a moose as its animal, a hawk owl as its bird and a brown trout as its fish. I thought these symbols were both very appropriate for the area and also quite cool. They compare favourably with, for example, Närke, that nominates cowslip, a hazel dormouse, yellow bunting and a pike, and Småland which chose the twinflower, an otter and a song thrush, but just couldn't be arsed to choose a fish.

The blurb in Tommy's handouts that we gave out to the guests at the welcome talk in their hotels described him as having a:

"Natural interest in life in the wilds. Hunting, fishing, skiing and walking expeditions have led him to work as a guide and, since 1981, as a professional dogmusher, offering trips for tourists.
"Tommy is the Swedish Champion in middledistance races and he also competes in longdistance races with his dogs".

Tommy was, therefore, our man. His leaflet tempted us with:

"travelling through quiet and unspoilt nature with the chance to see reindeer, lynx, wolverine and arctic fox. Through the night you can also have the chance to see the northern light!"

To me, that all sounded wonderfully tempting and exciting, and so it did to virtually all of our guests. My only real problem was the final paragraph of his flyer, written in Swenglish as:

"Your dogteam consists of 4–5 Alaskan Huskies and you self are standing on a nomesled."

I didn't care what a *nomesled* was but I did have concerns about the four to five huskies, particularly as when I first read it quickly I thought it said *Alsatian Huskies*.

Within twenty minutes of the village centre, the taxi turned off the main road and headed down a narrow track to a clearing in the woods, which was where Tommy and his wife's small holding was located. The small holding could be best described as a compound surrounded, as it was, by timber posts and high wire fencing. As we pulled up at the gates and slowed to a halt, the dogs started to bark. I couldn't see any but could hear lots of them, the echoes of their barking bounced back at us off the trees so the volume and number of barks was amplified. I sensed my heart rate increase as I anticipated the gates being opened and being driven in, just like Daniel entering the lion's den – although he wouldn't have been in the safety of a VW taxi van of course.

Tommy soon attended to the gates, swinging one of them open so that we could drive in. He closed it quickly behind us, I noticed. John took great pleasure in winding me up now, knowing I was trapped inside the compound whilst the guests we had with us did their best to reassure me. After all, we wouldn't be doing this if the dogs were dangerous, would we?

The taxi drove on towards the main house and now I could see kennels full of dogs running around yelping, and yet more dogs dotted here and there out in the open tied with chains to tree stumps or wooden kennels. The little wooden boxes were elevated about a foot off the snow on stilts. The dogs were jumping up and down and barking their heads off, all wanting to have a piece of me. Once we had stopped, Tommy pulled back the sliding door, motioning for us to get out, and welcomed each one of us with a big smile through his grizzly ragged beard. *He seemed friendly enough*, I thought, as I jumped down onto the snow. Kerstin, a friend of ours, had come with us for the experience. She worked in the resort teaching disabled people to ski on specially adapted frames with hand skis and, although she had worked for a few seasons and even owned a husky herself, she had never done any dog sledding.

Whilst we stood by the side of the minibus, Tommy formally introduced himself whilst his wife, Ulla, dragged four basic-looking wooden sleds into position. Each seating area was covered with three reindeer skins for comfort and some degree of warmth.

Tommy and his wife were in their mid-thirties, I guessed both clad in a mix of modern North Face gear, accessorised with more traditional Sami clothing.

Thankfully, the dogs had quietened down a bit now our vehicle had come to a halt and we remained stationary. Just the occasional bark or howl interrupted his welcome chat, explaining what we were going to do and where we were going to go.

Tommy gave a barely perceptible nod to Ulla, which every single dog must have been waiting for because absolute pandemonium broke out. They all went completely berserk. Ulla smiled at us and explained that every dog wanted to go out for a run and they were all crying out, "Pick me! Pick Me! Oh pleeease... pick me!" The dogs were running up and down their cages with great excitement, barking and howling as she went about them, searching for a particular dog whilst the ones tied up were leaping up to stand on their back legs, as if to make themselves taller and more noticeable than the next one.

Tommy explained that they had to select certain dogs to lead up at the front of the team and others to follow. Some of the dogs didn't work well with others and didn't like being alongside others. He explained further that the dogs were bred to do this and simply lived for this moment; they absolutely loved pulling the sleds. The Alaskan Husky is slightly larger and leaner than the Siberian Husky. Having greater stamina than the Siberian, they were the preferred dog of choice for pulling sleds. On the big races, his best dogs can cover a hundred miles a day in sub-zero temperatures for seven days in a row. I was staggered by this and instantly developed a big respect for them, no longer regarding them as potential attack dogs. Tommy reassured us that they were actually very friendly as a breed. These were happy, excited dogs, desperate to go out on a long run, eager to please their master. We learned that when they retire from racing and can no longer pull the sled, they often die quite quickly as they no longer possess the will to carry on with life.

One by one, they selected the teams and led each dog to its place in the harness. There must have been over forty dogs here but Tommy and Ulla knew each dog by their distinctive individual black and white markings across their heads. I was surprised at the variety of the dogs' colouring. Some were black and white; others black and tan, there were all white ones and many were a mix of everything. Once fastened, the dogs calmly stood very still in their positions, looking quite pleased with themselves, honoured almost, to have been picked. We got a chance to make a closer inspection, John of course pointing out one of them which had his eyes fixed on me. Feeling brave, since the dog was securely tethered in his position, I returned his gaze looking directly into his iridescent pale blue unblinking eyes. He turned his head on one side as he inspected me. These creatures were truly beautiful. Kerstin fell immediately in love with all of them.

Every now and again, one of the dogs not selected would give out a loud howl or bark, the sound echoing back from the surrounding trees before fading into the forest.

Ulla joined the presentation and asked us to divide up into four groups. As we shuffled about in the snow, she said, "Now who wants to drive?"

There was a stony silence and we looked around at each other. She encouraged us by adding: "You don't have to say left or right because Tommy will be in the lead and the dogs will follow him, but someone needs to be standing on the back of the sled to help steer and to brake."

John, having done it before put his hand up and stepped forward.

"Good. Any more?" and she looked my way.

"OK, yes" and for some reason I stepped forward too, as if bravely volunteering to go on some dangerous mission. No one else wanted to take command of a sled so Ulla selected one man to steer the fourth one and the remaining guests breathed an audible sigh of relief.

Ulla stepped onto the back of a sled, one foot on a runner on each side and held onto the rear bar with both hands. "You stand like this and you never, never, never get off."

Looking down at a large metal cheese grater about the size and shape of a brick that was fixed between the runners, she added, placing one booted foot firmly on it, bringing it down into contact with the snow: "And this is the brake and you have to brake very hard in the beginning, especially in the start, because the dogs are very strong. And also, you have to brake because you need to have distance between the sleds and always the dogs will want to run up to the next team in front of them. And also, when you have to go downhill you need to brake because you have to keep it tight," and she pointed to all the connecting leads. "It's like to tow a car, it's the same kind of thing, and you can't go too fast then because his legs can't keep up," and she pointed to the dog closest to her at the back of one of the lines.

I missed the rest of the instruction as one of the selected dogs cried out and that set a few of the others off again, as if they were being taunted for not being picked.

"And that's about it really," she concluded, I heard as the din died down. "Just when we go off, as the snow is quite soft, we may have to push like this…" She demonstrated pushing along with one foot whilst the other was on the runner and then she encouraged us all to have a go standing on the back and pulling the brake down with one foot.

Tommy had moved up the entrance and the moment he pulled open one of the gates the barking and howling started again. One of the dogs on the last sled began a repetitive bark that sounded like a horn on an old veteran car. It was more like a honk, honk, honk, honk, honk, honk. He was a very excited boy.

We all clambered aboard our respective sleds and I took up position on the back of one of them with Kerstin sat directly in front of me and two guests ahead of her. One of the sleds had only two guests and just four dogs to pull them. With a final check on us from Tommy, and Ulla making some final adjustments and telling a couple of people to keep their feet up, he waved his arm in the air and we took off out of the compound, gaining speed remarkably quickly. *No need for a push off, then*, I thought, and I watched the harnesses and leads tighten and relax and flap about under the pulling efforts of the team of dogs.

Ahead of me were ten dogs running fast, ten fluffy tails waving about in the air, ten dark bottom holes bobbing up and down, contrasting with ten lightly coloured pairs of furry buttocks. With all those bouncing bottoms, we were fortunate it was a morning's sled ride. Our noses were at the exact same height as the dogs' bottoms and we had learned that enjoyment of the post lunch-rides was slightly tainted by following closely behind the ten bouncing bottoms of ten farting hounds.

As soon as we were clear of the gates and on our way, all the dogs were quiet again, happy to be pulling us along and saving all their energy and strength for the job in hand or, more accurately, paw. Every now and again, one of them would dart its head out to one side and take a bite out of the snow. We headed along a stretch of open ground before pitching off to the left in front of a large, straggly-branched bush. Descending down a bank, the dogs dragging us over some smaller branches poking out of the snow as they ran through the gap, the sled was forced to cut the corner. We executed a sharp right turn, really having to lean our bodies over to one side to keep the sled from tipping over, and headed up a slight incline to where Tommy had stopped on the ridge. I hastily jammed on the cheese grater brake to prevent us crashing into the sled team ahead of us and brought the sled to a halt.

Tommy checked we were all OK and all still aboard our respective sleds, and then we headed across a track and joined another that lead us further up hill, levelling out into a sparsely forested area. Dainty timber poles, with red painted diagonal crosses about two metres high, marked our route through the snow at intervals of five hundred metres or so. The dogs probably knew where they were headed anyhow as previous sled tracks were still visible.

After a while we popped out onto a wide open flat plain. The dogs really dug their feet into the snow, heaving their shoulders hard against the restraining harnesses as they accelerated across the big white expanse with obvious enthusiasm. After taking in the new surroundings and noticing the "plain" area was edged with dark low-lying tree covered hills flecked with whiteness, I realised we were riding across another frozen lake. Tommy brought his team to a halt in the middle of the lake and signalled for the following teams to do the same. The dogs wanted to run on so, holding onto the back of his sled, he called out and motioned with his free arm, "*Höger, höger!* (right, right!)" and they obeyed him, coming to a stop almost parallel to his sled so that all the teams lined up in a vague fan shape.

This halt brought me to my senses, as I had begun to ignore the brightly coloured ski jackets dotted about the sleds and had been imagining that I was racing across the tundra in an epic adventure; just my team of trusty huskies and me in sub-zero temperatures. I was manfully hanging onto the back of my sled, guiding it around deep crevasses by standing all my weight on one of the rear runners and calling out to my dogs.

Once we had stopped, all that could be heard was the dogs' panting. Tommy moved away a little to re-position his sled and then they all started barking again but held their positions. I felt that, at any moment, they could just charge off if they really felt like it. Suddenly, amongst the barking, I heard what sounded spookily like many human voices crying out and shrieking from the trees surrounding the lake's perimeter. It was very eerie but then Kerstin reassured me; it was just the echoes from the dogs' barking.

We got going again, soon heading for the shoreline, which we hugged for a while before making a big arc around the lake and got a glimpse of a distant grey Åreskutan on the horizon, returning to the gap in the trees where we had arrived. The dogs pulled us back to the compound just as eagerly and as swiftly as they had on the outward leg, and I wondered how fast they would go with just me as a passenger, rather than four of us. Tommy said he usually had twelve dogs to pull him when he was competing so the answer was very fast. The hour ride was over too soon and, having enjoyed it so much, I vowed to try to sell this excursion as best I could and to accompany guests as often as I could.

In the middle of January, I did a regular transfer of forty or so guests to the airport at Östersund and was asked to drive a Volkswagen Golf all the way back to the village. This made a pleasant change from sitting in an empty coach or doing another arrival transfer. It was a hire car that had to be returned. The only channel I could get on the radio was a classical one so I was driving along snowy roads that cut through great swathes of snow-covered pine forests and across frozen rivers under a blue sky thinking, *This is alright... there could be worse places to be on a Thursday afternoon, listening to the Marriage of Figaro and watching the sun go down behind a mountain.* What's more, I was managing to save some money too, since we had received some generous cash tips from the happy guests as well as becoming the recipients of many bottles of unfinished whisky, brandy and especially vodka, which were all gratefully received. The drinks shelf in my room, previously used for gloves, goggles and hats, was actually sagging under the weight of alcohol after only a few weeks.

We were also making instant cash profit on money exchanges, since the banks gave us a favourable rate, which was much better than what we were offering the guests. When a guest asked if it was possible to change some sterling into kronor, I'm sure the kronor signs flashed up in our eyes. We'd also like it when the guests arrived on the coach and had not pre-booked anything at all because that was an instant win for us. If we made sales of ski and boot hire, lift passes and ski school, we were delighted as that was direct commission for us, although it was paid into our accounts a little later when head office in Austria had done the reckoning. I remember doing a few transfers feeling inwardly really irritated that virtually everyone had pre-booked – how were we supposed to make a living? It was then up to us, of course, to encourage them at the welcome meeting or the hotel visits we did to book excursions whilst in resort.

Before I started the job, I was dreading the transfers because, firstly, they could be rather frantic. Secondly, I really didn't like speaking to a whole bunch of people and, thirdly, I was convinced I would throw up on someone as I read and filled in forms and dealt with money exchanges whilst travelling with my back to the direction of travel. As it turned out, although they could be quite pressurised, I began to enjoy them and, before long, I was saying at the prospect of a fifty or sixty seater coach being full... "Bring it on!" It was far easier to give the chat to a load of people you didn't know, and when you were in possession of the knowledge, than talking to your peers, as we had practised to and from Salzburg airport in the training week.

Dancing Queen

Östersund was the airport we used for transfers to Åre, which at the time, appeared to have more military traffic than tourist traffic. It was a very small airport about six miles outside of Östersund town, on the banks of the extensive Lake Storsjön (Lake Big Lake as John would call it), and was just over an hour by road to the resort. There was always quite a high military presence in the airport buildings, which I thought added a frisson of excitement to the arrivals hall: people in military uniforms with kit bags and machine guns mingling with the tourists and their ski bags. There was a look of surprise and shock on quite a number of our arrivals when they popped through the doors.

Östersund became a garrison town when the fear of a Russian attack was at its highest at the end of the 19th century and, in the late 1920s, the Jämtland Air Force Wing F4 came to establish itself on the nearby island of Frösön. The military presence has gone now but the airport hard standing areas always had an impressive line-up of Saab Viggens, with their attendant trucks and fuel hoses, which since childhood had always been my favourite fighter jet. Apart from looking very cool and purposeful with its *tre kronor* (three crowns), yellow on blue roundels proudly positioned beneath the cockpit, it must have been a strong Top Trump card to get, which is why it won favour with me. However I recall the Airfix model tested my patience when it came to lining up the water transfer decals of the crown roundels perfectly horizontally.

Usually, after I had dropped off the guests in a morning transfer, the coach drivers all gathered together in the tiny airport café for *fika*, the quaint Swedish word which has no direct translation to English other than to have a coffee, a bit of cake and a chat. Instead of listening but not understanding their talk of ice hockey match results or the latest improvements to snowmobiles, I would grab a steaming mug of coffee and a *Japp* bar and go and sit outside up on the roof deck in the freezing air and wait to see if I could see any Viggens in action. It was worth enduring the sharp cold air as I was often rewarded with the sight and sound of one or two of the jets scorching their way up into the icy blue sky. The downside would be my *Japp* bar freezing solid before I had finished it and the very hot coffee becoming just a luke warm one in a few minutes, then a barely more than cold coffee shortly after. I stopped short of noting down any tail codes and serial numbers though, I promise.

By the time the "incoming", as we referred to them, stepped foot inside the airport building, our guests had already had a long journey, starting their journeys in either Manchester or London and landing at Stockholm where, depending on which flight they were on, either they had a leisurely one hour to kill before connecting with the internal SAS flight up north or they had a mad fifteen minute dash to get off one airplane and onto another. Most of the guests had never been to Sweden before, let alone ventured up to the snowy wastes of northern Sweden. Some were clearly a little apprehensive about what they might find and some had friends that had scoffed at their decision not to go to Meribel for the hundredth time and dare to be different. Skiing in Sweden? Were they mad? "It's dark all year round, there are no mountains, and it's so cold and too expensive," would have been the remarks made by people who had never been here.

We had been told in the training week that the first thing to do when all the guests were safely on the coach would be to give them a warm welcome and reassure them that there was definitely snow in the resort even if the airport car park resembled a Sainsbury's car park, mid-January in England. There would be no doubting the snow factor here in Sweden, as there was always snow piled up around the edge of the car park, if not covering the ground itself. What became apparent was that the guests needed to be reassured that there was daylight, particularly as all the flights arrived very late in the day or early evening. The next thing to say was to confirm the snow conditions were good and tell them the temperature, which they could see from the on-board gauge at the front of the coach above the large expanse of the cracked, windscreen.

Depending on which coach we were in, we would have to make a correction as one of them permanently read minus sixty three degrees and I could see guests thinking that would have been the temperature when we set off from resort and it was so cold that the gauge had frozen solid and still hadn't thawed out enough to be functioning properly again.

It was very easy to spot the Brits as they ambled forward, half of them, no doubt, thinking "I bet the rep is late or too lazy to be here", and not just because they weren't dressed head to toe in military olive green.

As a ski rep, one's first duty of the holiday is to collect the guests from the airport. On any one flight, there might be a couple of hundred arrivals and, although we reps traditionally wear brightly coloured uniforms, topped with a garish coloured baseball cap and a red clip board (so blindingly obvious to most), we still have to keep an eye out for the bleary-eyed guests that wander off aimlessly in the wrong direction.

We then need to use all our *One Man and his Dog* skills to round up the guests and keep them corralled in one area whilst we assemble the entire list of names we have on our Arrivals schedule. Our job is made a lot easier by the average British ski tourist fashion faux pas. In a throng of a couple of hundred ski tourists, I reckoned to be able to spot most of the Brits at a glance by the twenty year old faded Rodeo ski jackets, or worse: the all-in-one suit; the unfit, rotund figures carrying plastic bags of duty free, clinking as they shuffled along; or the smokers desperate to light up after the flight restrictions. Pretty damning, I know, but the differences are so apparent when you see such numbers in one place. Compare us to a typical arrival of Swedes and Norwegians and you would think the two sets of people have flown in from different planets. The Scandinavians stand better, walk better, are clad in quality clothing, carry nicer luggage, and have a confident but friendly air about them – and know their way around an airport. They are, in general, a far more handsome and healthy race of beings.

That's probably enough damning my fellow nationals, especially as they had been good enough to decide to come to Sweden and were going to help finance my sojourn here, especially the ones who hadn't had the foresight to book anything before departure. It was time to switch on the smiley rep face, cheerfully greet them and reassure them they were going to have a good time.

Most were happy to see me. A few were downright grumpy and miserable, and you knew you wouldn't see them all week until you did the transfer back to the airport. They were the ones who wouldn't come to the welcome meeting, wouldn't take part in any ski escorting, and wouldn't book any excursions. You'd not see them out and about on any of the runs either, or the bars. What the hell they did all week was anyone's guess. Did they just sit in their rooms, eating pies they had brought from home and smoking fags on the balcony, moaning about the cold and the lack of football on the TV? I did actually hear one of them complaining about everything being in Swedish and how you couldn't get a decent pint of bitter. He was about fourteen and from Manchester.

Ultimately, it was their holiday and they could choose to spend it as they liked, but what really irked us was that they would be the ones (and we really didn't have many at all) who, when they got home would write stinking letters of complaint about the hotel, the resort and the useless reps and demand money back from our company. They would never discuss things with us so we could try to get things sorted for them.

The other type of troublemaker was the vociferous one who would seek you out as soon as he cleared customs, lock onto you like a guided weapon, and make a bee-line for you. You had to prepare yourself and try to keep the chirpy rep front going, telling yourself: it's nothing personal, it can't be; they've never met you. They would already have a list of complaints as long as your ski pole and the holiday hadn't even begun. Whatever you said would not be met with any reason or understanding and they demanded to know what you were going to do about it. The list of complaints would be getting longer at every opportunity: they had to wait ages for a transfer at Stockholm, there weren't any luggage trolleys; the transfer time was too long, even though they hadn't even begun it. They, too, wouldn't book anything with you on the transfer and would know all about the resort even though they had never visited the country, let alone the resort, as they had read about it somewhere.

As you did the rounds on the coach, collecting any pre-booking forms, the troublemaker would hand you theirs, resisting any eye contact but holding a fixed stare to the front of the coach. It was so tempting to add a note on ski hire form for Hanson, our ski hire shop *"skit förra säsongens skidor vänligen for detta.* (Shit, last season's skis for this one, please)", but of course we didn't and the ski shop wouldn't anyway. We just had to roll with the punches and listen to them go on about the room being too small or even too large, as one couple felt in the Renen Hotel. On one occasion, the quantity of food was apparently "not as much as we had in Turkey last summer"! We did what we could to sort out problems but sometimes it was exasperating.

When I had finally managed to herd my sheep onto the coach, I had to count them all up. We had been given a good tip to start from the rear of the vehicle because if you did it from the front working back a few of them could have clambered on whilst you weren't looking. If you were walking down the aisle no one was going to get past you. There was no "jump seat" in our nice luxurious Van Hools so, to reserve my space, I would always put my rucksack down on the first row of seats on the opposite side to the driver. It was nonetheless surprising how many times someone would sit there oblivious to the internationally-renowned German towel method of reservation. Once the count tallied with the Arrivals Sheet I had been given, I signalled to the driver in fluent Swedish that all was OK. "*OK*," I would say in a slightly non-British way, as if that would help him understand better, and give him the thumbs up just to re-emphasise the "OK".

The big door would hiss shut and seal out the cold air and then, with a shudder, the engine would start up and we would be on our way across the small car park and out onto an extraordinarily wide and straight bit of tarmac.

This was my cue to grab the microphone from the front shelf and, remembering to switch it on, begin my welcome chat, trying my best not to sound like an air steward or a cheesy holiday rep by going up at the end of every sentence. Remembering too that, although I had just over an hour to do all the money exchange, answer questions, taking payments for all the bookings, hand out vouchers for pre-booked ski school, ski hire etc, I also must not rush the chat and appear to be relaxed. After the first couple of transfers, it became a lot easier and slicker, of course, and I didn't forget to mention things and said "err" a lot less, just pausing briefly instead, remembering the instruction from the training week.

I would introduce myself, welcoming them to Sweden and announce our driver's name, which already sounded too Costa del Sol – like, I know, but it had to be done. I would tell them how long the journey was going to take and reassure them, most importantly, that there was good snow in the resort. That usually got a small cheer. Secondly, I would confirm the temperature in resort in the day time. If it was hovering at around minus ten or fifteen, or whatever it was, which got an "ooooh," I told them not to worry because being a dry cold, even minus twenty was actually OK. It wasn't really, but by the time they found out they would be there. The main thing was to relax them and put them in a good mood as it made for an easier transfer.

I continued with: "Now some of you may have noticed the road we are on and are probably thinking we're heading along a runway," which, if they hadn't noticed got them all straining their eyes as they looked out through their windows into the darkness momentarily undermining all my relaxing chat I'd just given them. It ran parallel to the main runway for almost its entire length before skirting the perimeter and heading off towards the twinkling lights of the town.

"Well we are!" I let them ponder that for a moment or two. "You will have noticed all the military personnel in the airport building. That's because this is mainly a military airport. This road we are driving along is actually the emergency runway and it opens up in the event that Sweden suddenly declares war. But since the last time this country was at war was in 1814, I think we're probably fairly safe."

A polite ripple of nervous laughter would usually sweep through the coach. "I'm going to be passing through the coach in a little while with your welcome packs (which were all personalised with their names on to give them that extra special touch) and vouchers, if you have pre-booked and, of course, will answer any questions you may have."

After weaving gently through small forests, we passed modern housing estates and industrial buildings before turning a sharp right across a bridge linking the airport island and we headed towards the mainland and the township of Östersund. The spread of snow and ice either side of the bridge masked the true depth of the cold dark water beneath. I had made a mental note of key waypoints on the transfer as cues for me to do something or say a few words and the bridge crossing was my trigger to put the CD on – *Abba's Gold – Greatest Hits*. What else? When the coach had reached the other end of the bridge, we paused briefly at the junction before it heaved up and across to the other side of the road, turning left in front of an enormous barracks complex.

Time to grab the microphone again: "If you are interested, just take a look on your right if you can as we drive past the barracks and you will see an impressive line up of army trucks, jeeps and some tanks here and there." It would often be quite a sight at night time, those huge olive green hulks standing out in the cold night air lined up in neat rows under high bright arc lights. When the snow was falling, it was as romantic as army trucks could look with *"Dancing Queen"* playing softly in the background.

On the other side of town, we hooked up with the main E14, the road that cut its way across the whole country, which we would follow all the way to the resort. We were soon headed out at what seemed like quite an indecent speed to be travelling at, in something that probably weighed over twenty tonnes. As important a road as it was up here, it was still just a two lane highway, and by that I mean simply one lane in either direction. There was never much traffic out on the road, especially at night time when we were there; just the occasional Volvo or Audi estate that had been on the road already for seven or eight hours, making the long haul up from Stockholm or Gothenburg or somewhere, loaded up with skis on the roof and a family or a group of friends and their kit packed into the back. Inevitably, there were occasions when we would come up behind some slower traffic. The drivers had absolutely no qualms about pulling out across to the other side of the road and burying the loud pedal into the floor. The coach would pick itself up, somewhat lazily, as it was urged forward, kicking up even more mists of swirling snow and crushed ice behind us.

If we had to break suddenly... well, it just didn't bear thinking about, but you just had to trust the fact that the drivers had grown up in this area so knew the roads so well and were totally confident in their driving abilities in these conditions. Only once did the brakes have to be applied rather urgently and we did a spectacular six wheel drift to the other side of the highway to avoid a herd of reindeer out for a night walk. Luckily, I was seated at the time or I might have ended up in the lap of one of the guests. After the vehicle had been skilfully collected, the driver casually turned around to me and blew out his relief through gritted teeth. I acknowledged his actions by an appreciative but restrained nod of the head and I think only the first couple of rows of passengers saw what we had avoided.

The white ribbon of hard compacted snow wound its way through flat open farmland scattered with dark *Falun* red timber farm buildings and isolated dwellings, small villages and now and again the rail line echoed our route. There weren't many landmarks to help prompt me with my tasks and, in the dark, they were hard to see from within the relative light of the coach. Town and village signs, such as Trångsviken and Järpen and the one with all the "Ks" immediately before a low bridge over a frozen river – *Välkommen til Krokum Kommum,* helped mark our progress. After about twenty five minutes we would be plunged into darkness on both sides as we entered a deep cutting and I could feel the coach steadily rising up into a very large pine forest, which accompanied us for a good ten minutes of our journey. Popping out of that, there would be a beautiful church high up on the right side, all lit up with bright white lights, which was my cue to give some more chat about what the resort was like, the excursions we had on offer, and how to buy alcohol in resort (another cheer always went up) via the institution called *Systembolaget.*

Essentially, it was like buying something from Argos. You entered a well-lit shop unit, where there were bottles locked in glass display cabinets, an order catalogue and small order forms, which when completed you would take a numbered ticket from a wall machine and wait your turn to be called to the counter to deal with your order. I am not kidding. For all the advances and innovations Sweden has made in virtually every other sphere of business, it was stuck in the communist era as far as publicly buying your alcohol was concerned.

The Systembolaget AB company, set up in 1955, is a government owned and run chain of stores permitted to sell alcohol over 3.5%, but you have to prove you are over twenty years old to make a purchase. It all goes back to the 18th Century when, after several failed attempts by the king of Sweden to control alcohol consumption, he decided, in his wisdom, to abolish *all* controls, the consequence being that pretty much every household started making and selling their own alcohol based from grain and potatoes and this resulted in stocks of those natural products running low.

It had got out of hand and eventually temperance groups and those of the medical profession started to openly criticise those that were making, selling and drinking their own alcohol. State registered bars and stores began to open up and then things really kicked off at the time of the First World War when alcohol became rationed and stores started actually registering people's purchases. The rationing only stopped in 1955 and people could then buy as much as they wanted to from the government stores, which they did very enthusiastically by all accounts, if they could prove they were a) sober, b) not going to sell it on to anyone else – how? Would they simply promise very earnestly? – and c) were over 21 years old. The government stepped in again by imposing big taxes and reducing the age limit to 20. This brief history of Systembolaget did not form part of the resort talk or I would have missed more of my cues en route.

Approaching the resort at night time was always spectacular because, as we broke through the cover of the final forest, we could see below us the shoreline of the frozen lake stretching out away into the distance ahead of us towards Duved, illuminated by the street lights and those buildings that sat close to the water's edge. From that distance, it looked like a Mediterranean coastal town, the way the lights twinkled picking out where the land met the water, or in this case snow and thick ice. On a Tuesday night, the view was enhanced by the intensely bright floodlights of the Gästrappet run open for night time skiing.

There was a blue-grey haze in the dark sky hovering above the bright white piste and, as we got nearer, we could see little black ant-like figures zig-zagging down the slope. Proof, if proof was needed, that there was snow in the resort. You could now sense the level of excitement and anticipation in the coach heighten and people began to lift their heads up above the seats in front of them and to the side of the head rests to get a better view. Even the grumpy ones were straining to see out the front windscreen, unless I caught their eye and then they would slump back into their seats with clenched jaws and focus on their hard stares at the back of the headrest in front of them.

The story goes that NASA called the Swedish Defence one hour after the very first time they switched one of the floodlights and demanded to know what was going on in northern Sweden. Another rumour about town was that the illumination was so strong it would be visible from the moon. Whatever the truth one thing was for sure, the lights were incredibly strong – 140 lux apparently; good moonlight is 0.5 lux, the lights on a motorway would be about 20 lux. I had read that the maximum capacity would be 950 lux, which must have been strong enough to burn your eyeballs out so it would never be used. The resort had recently invested ten million Swedish kronor in the project to enable visitors to ski day and night in the resort. It would also enable TV companies to show the World Cup competitions on this slope. You could, in theory, lengthen your time on the snow up until 7pm each day and on Fridays up to 9pm. In theory, yes. In practice, no. We tried it but only once. It was indeed just like skiing in the daytime, except when you looked beyond the lighting rigs, but it was so much colder.

We only sold a few evening passes for it all season because, apart from the novelty factor and to say you had done it, why would you do a full day's skiing, come back into the warmth of your hotel and then want to venture out into much colder weather again? The locals appeared to be very pleased with it and there was always some mad ski-obsessed Swedes on it. I thought, from a marketing perspective when they were trying to encourage more Brits to the resort, it wasn't something I would have shouted about. It was already a common misconception amongst the Brits that it was always cold and dark here in winter, so why draw attention to the fact that you have an illuminated slope? I could envisage people at home watching a World Cup event on the TV confirming their belief "See... I told you... it's cold and dark there. We're not going skiing in Sweden and that's final."

Dropping off the guests at their respective hotels was the moment I could begin to relax again, parting with the "John will see you at the Welcome Meeting tomorrow evening" or, for the guests staying at my Hotel in Duved, "I'll see you in the morning with the lift passes" as I hopped off with my rucksack and scurried off to the office. There was always paperwork to do after a transfer and that often delayed our going to the bars by quite some time, rather annoyingly.

Stepping out into the cold early morning gloom of a ski resort at this time of year was never a joy, particularly if it followed on from a night out in the bars and clubs to the wee small hours, but it was part of the job and I had to keep reminding myself it was so much better than waiting for a bus to take me over Hammersmith Bridge on my way to squeeze on to a Piccadilly line tube. The back door to the Sporthotellet slammed shut because I forgot to hold it and I carefully descended the steps onto a short piste that ran between buildings and lead into the town square. I walked up the piste, hunched up against the cold – minus twenty degrees it said on the gauge outside my window. Why did I keep looking every morning? My chin was tucked firmly into my chest, squeezing warmth out of a fleece neck warmer. I cursed the lack of insulation in my left boot sole – it really was time to see what the ski shop had for sale – and tried to keep warm by mentally placing myself back under the duvet I had just left.

It was snowing again. The flake clusters were so thick the glow from the streetlights flickered as it was momentarily blocked out like an old black and white silent movie. As I trudged on up the piste and walked along the edge of a road for a few metres, it felt like I was the only one up and about. This was the industrial backside of the resort which few tourists saw but was my most direct route to lift company office. You had to keep a watch out on these early morning missions as sometimes a truck would pass noisily by, splashing wet snow to the side of the road and on me if I wasn't paying full attention. This morning, with the temperature so low, there was no splashing just the gentle sound of a truck's tyres scrunching down on fresh snowfall; the heavy duty snow chains rattling as it went by.

Across the road, I entered a yard where the piste bashers slumbered after their night's work, their caterpillar tracks clogged full with thick clumps of snow and their empty cabins now cold again after keeping their drivers warm and secure during their lonely and dangerous job.

The head of ski school's dark blue Saab was parked at the edge of the yard, close to the steps that lead up to the rather bland grey office building, hooked up by its umbilical cord to a battery conditioner post.

Pulling the door open, I stepped into the brightness and warmth of the Åre Lift Company's office and was welcomed by a trio of happy smiling chirpy girls – Jenny, Anna and Camilla. My spirits lifted in an instant.

It was time to try some Swedish again as they always encouraged me to say how many ski passes I needed in their language. It was useful numbering practice for me, combining the words, *vuxna* adults and *barn* children (just like the Scottish word, *bairn*). Many words are quite common to the north of England or Scotland for obvious reasons (the Vikings). The word for snow in Swedish is *snö* and in Yorkshire it is pronounced exactly the same as it is in Swedish. A church is a *kyrka* in Swedish, like *kirk* in Scotland, not to be confused as I once was with *kyckling* meaning chicken which made for an interesting if not confusing conversation. Whilst briefly on the subject of food, *gravlax* is an interesting one. *Lax* means salmon and *att begrava* means to bury which is where we get our word "grave" from. Old Swedish salty sea dogs used to catch their salmon, coat it in salt to cure it and bury it to preserve it.

Once I had collected the ski passes and stuffed them carefully into my rucksack, I had to hurry back down the piste and across the square to the Hotel Åregården to grab a quick breakfast. The basement staff eating area, which was annexed to the hotel kitchen, was already a hive of activity as the chefs prepared the breakfasts for their guests and some of the early bird resort staff was up and about. The machine that dispensed strong hot coffee was busy bubbling and gurgling away and people lined up to fill tall glasses with the hot brown liquid. Oddly, no one seemed to use coffee cups but instead the 0.4 litre beer glasses labelled with the *Spendrup's of Sweden* logo served the purpose. The Swedes don't use possessive apostrophes like we do but as the "of Sweden" part was written in English I was impressed, perhaps in a slightly nerdy way, to note they had used the correct grammar. As the saying goes; *Grammar is the difference between knowing your shit and knowing you're shit*. I would always search out a coffee cup as I was convinced if I poured the steaming coffee into my glass it would crack. Breakfast was usually a quick grab and go on these mornings but I made sure I had my body warming porridge and a slice of toast before heading up the narrow servants' stone steps to the ground floor and out into the cold air again to catch the first ski bus to Duved, hoping not to have to stand in the cold for too long.

Now and again, I would miss the bus, which meant I would also miss Toni Braxton's singing but have to blag the use of the Mean Machine from Hanson. They would very generously oblige, but I often had an anxious wait to find out where it was or who had the keys. It was so much easier and quicker to drive it there and back instead of waiting for the ski bus. I would often sit patiently in the ski shop only to see another ski bus go by, wondering if I shouldn't have just jumped on it.

One such morning, I was idly nosing around the shop, waiting for news of the van, when the owner, Örjan Hansson, turned up and offered to take me over to Duved. Örjan had a twin brother, Håkan, and the two of them competed for their country at the 1988 Winter Olympics at Calgary, so were a pair of local legends. They both took part in the inaugural *Puckelpist* or

Freesytyle Moguls discipline at the same Olympics, incidentally, as the Jamaican Bobsleigh team first hit the icy slopes.

The story went that Örjan was marginally better than his brother but, the day before the event, he came down with flu and could not compete. His brother took his place and won the gold medal. High up in the shop itself the medal was displayed, but I never got a close look at it. I could only imagine how Örjan felt every time he saw it, thinking "that could have been mine". Perhaps that is why it was placed so high up. His brother was one of the co-founders of the now very famous worldwide brand, Peak Performance, and busied himself with developing that business, but Örjan ran the ski shop business. We had a very distinguished team of shop assistants in our little ski hire shop, which included two former Swedish Olympic skiers and one former American Olympic team skier. It wouldn't be too long before I would find myself standing on my skis with them at the top of a mountain one night about midnight, feeling utterly outclassed, peering down the face of a black mogul run.

Örjan was a genial man, with mousey hair and friendly big blue eyes, not your typical Swedish look. He was quietly confident, in great shape and still moved like an athlete. All our lady guests appeared to like him a lot, some of them making what seemed like unnecessary return trips to the shop to get their boots refitted.

"Come on. Let's go, Andrew," and we went outside to the waiting van. He and his staff were very patient with all our guests' requirements and he was very generous to us reps, letting us try whatever skis, boots and snowboards we wanted *and*, what was music to my ears at that particular time, a 40% discount on all the stock. That meant I could finally buy some new boots. My left foot already began to feel warmer. We talked about the business and how he had set it up and he asked me about my business field in England, being astute enough to recognise that I was just doing this job for a season.

"I can see you have more about you than the normal ski leader." I was liking him more and more and wondered whether he was having a little dig at John, whom I had often seen being quite pompous with the staff in the shop.

"You and me, we're about the same age, right? We have experienced a bit of life and know a little about people, you think so?"

"Err... yes," I answered, not really sure where the conversation was going now.

He went on to tell me the hardest thing about managing his business was dealing with the younger people and their work ethics.

"Don't get me wrong, I have a great team. It's just, sometimes, I don't think they realise they are lucky to have a job working here in such a beautiful place... and with such a nice boss, of course." He beamed a big smile at me as he shifted up a gear and we headed out to the lake road. It was a perfect blue sky morning by now.

The fresh dazzling white snow sat precariously on all the tree branches and smothered the roofs of buildings and cars alike. I noticed the more remote farm buildings we passed only had snowmobile tracks leading to them from the road.

We were making good progress and he was planning where we would have our coffee break in Duved after I had seen to my guests when, all of a sudden, he slowed to a halt using engine breaking, going down through the gears gently but swiftly. I thought there must be a problem with the van because he cut the engine, but no.

"Look," and he stretched out his right arm across to my corner of the windscreen, his finger pointing to an empty clearing in the forest on our right. I was beginning to think he was having a bit of a mad moment and the business had got to him, or he was having visions of an Olympic gold medal that should have been his.

"Look, over there," he insisted, a hushed urgency in his voice as he continued to point to the corner of the glade. "Look, Andrew. You may never see this again in the next few months you are here." *Yep, he has really lost it,* I thought. *I am definitely going to see a small field of snow surrounded by fir trees again. I'm certain...* and then I spotted it.

"Oh, my God!... I see it now! Yes!" And there it stood, not more than fifty metres from where we had come to a rest; a very large male elk. He stood proud and very still, looking out towards the lake, his dark brown haunches still partially hidden by tree cover, the wide fan of his antlers blending perfectly with the dappled shadows of the tree branches that surrounded him. After a few moments, when I readjusted my focus, I could see his chest steadily expanding and contracting as he breathed in and out and then I saw the plumes of warm air swirl up from the nostrils in his dark bulbous nose. He moved his head slowly and looked right at us, his chest gently heaving still. *Had he just run from somewhere?* I wondered. There was no one but us here. No traffic. No noise. The snow seemed to muffle noise anyhow. We three beings were caught in a moment. We just sat there watching him watching us. Then he must have got bored or presumed we were no threat and with a shake of his big head he turned away and sauntered back into the cover of the trees.

"Wow," we both said in unison.

"I can't remember the last time I saw that so close up," Örjan said to reaffirm the uniqueness of the occasion.

"We were lucky then," I replied, not knowing quite what else to say. He nodded his head, pressed his lips tightly together and reached out to turn the ignition key on. "*Absolut,*" he said in his native Swedish.

4

FEBRUARI

I Do, I Do, I Do

February began with a burst of excitement for a number of reasons. The weather improved and we started having brighter, sunnier days, although it was still cold, averaging about minus fifteen during the day, colder at night of course. The resort itself opened up the top zone now that the strong winds were not bothering us so much. There were suddenly a lot more people in the resort, which gave it more of a buzz. There was also another kind of buzz around town that the king was coming to ski here. I know we live in a modern world where kings do modern things but I couldn't stop myself from imagining a portly gentleman in robes wearing a golden crown, a couple of aides by his side helping him onto the ski lift or carrying his skis. The song *Minnie the Moocher* from the film *The Blues Brothers*, refers to the King of Sweden, and would refuse to leave my head. Consequently, every time I went skiing now I kept an eye out for the unusual sight of a skiing king.

Instead, I was rewarded one early afternoon with another

wildlife experience and one you just don't get in the Alps, to my knowledge. I was sitting on a ski lift, enjoying the sunshine of a slightly milder late morning, heading up towards Mullfjället above Duved, when there was a bit of commotion in the two chairs in front of me. Some agitated pointing and raised voices drew my attention to a mass of grey-brown dots up ahead on the side of the empty piste. They were moving away from the line of the lifts at a slow steady pace, picking at bushes as they went.

"Reindeer!" showed one of our guests. "How wonderful," exclaimed another. It was to be a fairly regular sighting in this part of the ski area and one that I always hoped the guests would experience when they came on the ski escorting morning in Duved. Looking on the map afterwards, I noted that we were close to the Njarka Sami camp so presumed the reindeer were part of their herd. Following on so soon from my elk experience, I was beginning to wonder what other life forms I would encounter in this very alternative skiing environment. Northern Sweden is home to a whole host of animals including the brown bear, arctic fox, wolf, golden eagle and lynx and now the upper part of the resort had been opened up who knows what we might see.

Sweden has over 2,500 brown bears, some of them growing up to 350kg in weight. Fortunately, they would be hibernating at this time but, in recent years they had been spotted a long way south. I would see two bears this winter. The first one was well over 7ft tall and surprised the life out of me when I saw him. He was standing at full stretch, teeth bared, arms outstretched as he guarded the entrance hall to the waffle house at one of our most popular excursion locations – Tännforsen, Sweden's highest waterfall.

Naturally, at this time of year there was not much water falling. In fact, none. However, the spectacle of the frozen waterfall lit up by floodlights was really quite something. It was possible to visit it during the day but it was best viewed at night, and that meant it would be a cold experience. Everyone had to don full ski gear after their evening meals, some guests ignored that advice, of course. A trip to Tännforsen one night proved to be my coldest ever night time experience at a spine freezing minus thirty three degrees – the gauge at the front of the bus was accurate this time. After that I was able to convince everyone at my welcome meetings just how very cold it could get and nobody else took a chance in jeans and a jacket.

The waterfall was a short coach ride out of the resort and we collected the guests staying in Åre first, followed by the Duved ones. I really enjoyed this once a week excursion as it was a chance to have a relaxed chat to the guests and I loved seeing their reaction to the frozen waterfall. The coffee and Swedish waffles dripping in honey and cream we devoured afterwards only added to the evening. The man who ran the site, and I suppose owned the land the water flowed through, was a tremendous character called Bertil. He was old farming stock aged about sixty with ruddy cheeks and a splendidly ornate ginger moustache and beard combo. He spoke a little English, just enough to give his welcome speech and answer a few questions. The intonation of his voice was, I am absolutely convinced, the basis for the Swedish chef in *The Muppets* and I primed my guests to expect that. I could often see quite a few of them trying to stifle a snigger when he spoke, but they loved it and he was so welcoming, enthusiastic and warm. After his short speech, he would stand by one of the doors of his large wooden cabin and hand out a ski pole to each visitor and then point them through the back door.

Leaving the warmth of the restaurant, you entered a magical forest where fairies, trolls, hobbits and yes probably wolves lived. The pathway led you away from the collection of timber buildings and was lit up either side with spot lights that pointed up into the trees. Looking ahead, you could see the route marked out clearly and beyond the trees a strong white glow emanated from an area slightly below us. The path itself appeared to glow white against the dark trees bordering it from the reflected light of the spots and was pitted with fallen pine cones, which gave some grip underfoot. It wound its way gently downwards, doubling back on itself a couple of times to tease us and increase the sense of anticipation.

After five minutes' walking through the forest we gathered at a small square timber viewing area, high up on the riverbank, gazing at the snow formation before us. It was as if the waterfall had been frozen in an instant by the wave of a magic Disney wand. Funnels of water, now thick ice, appeared to be caught in a moment of time, the snow providing a soft winter dressing echoing the shapes. The spotlights shone at the waterfall from our side of the river and were angled up to the head and down to bottom of the fall, a drop of 38 metres. In summer, it would have been a raging torrent of frothy white water that charged noisily through this stretch of the river; 740,000 litres a second, according to Bertil. We were standing level with the middle of the fall and everything was still. The path continued along the river's edge, leading us down further to a large pool of frozen water under a snow blanket dotted with tracks of tiny footprints. Lining the far edge of the pool on the left side was a short line of small trees, but the landscape opened up beyond the pool as the land fell away, revealing an expansive plain before a mass of black trees merged with the night sky. Those trees seemed to get darker and darker the more I stared at them.

By some quirk of fate, we had stumbled onto the edge of Tolkien's Middle Earth and were gazing out at Mordor, Land of Shadow, with the great Anduin River frozen at our feet. I'm sure I had seen a sign to Gondor on the E14 earlier. As I stood there,

I convinced myself I could see eyes peering back out at me from the gloom of the forest. A shiver went down my spine and not because of the cold night air. Turning around to speak to one of the guests, I realised something terrible had happened. They had all buggered off to the waffle house without me. I scarpered, scrambling up the steep path as fast as I could, grateful for the shorter route back, not wanting to be leaving my guests on their own, you understand.

The second bear was a small round cut of one on a plate in front of me accompanied by a large spoonful of red currant jelly, half a tomato covered with cheese, a fresh herb, and some boiled potatoes. We were sat on dark wooden pews at a curious roadside restaurant in Morsil, on the E14, which I could more accurately describe as a truckers' café, some way out of the resort.

To say it had "rustic charm" would have been pushing it a bit. The owners had asked all the reps in the resort to pay them a visit one afternoon with a view to having our guests dine out on "local specialities". Bear steak was about the only dish on the menu most of us could face. The husband and wife team, unusually did not speak much English so had to convey the meaning of each dish listed on their fairly extensive menu by impersonating each animal's movements and the sound they made. I hadn't appreciated there were so many dinosaurs still roaming these northern parts. We had given up guessing what most of the dishes were and declined the man's kind offer to inspect the freezers in his outhouse. A couple of the reps opted for tomato soup and a bread roll. We couldn't even say in theory it was a nice idea, because it simply wasn't, but the ever-enthusiastic tourist office people in the village had suggested it and we were interested to explore all suggestions. I had no bad after effects from this roadside dining experience and, although a little tough, it tasted OK to me, but it was too far out of the village and frankly too odd to be considered as an excursion venue. Having *Googled* the name of the place in the course of research, I discovered it now describes itself as a *strippklubb* and has an amusing logo very similar to the golden M of a well-known hamburger chain. The M takes the shape of a pair of women's legs as she lies on her back beneath which is the phrase, in English, "I'm loving it". I guess the restaurant was still catering in "local specialities".

The lovely Ulla, from the tourist office, accosted me one grey Monday morning, as I crossed the town square cradling a coffee and a donut, bristling with enthusiasm.

She was a slightly built woman with long, prematurely greying hair and worked all hours, so passionate was she about the resort. In any other town, she would have been a librarian. She clearly wanted to impart something of great importance or significance to me.

"Well, good morning, Andrew," she called to me, smiling from beneath her beanie.

"*Moron*, Ulla," I replied in my developing Swedish (*Morgon* with a silent "g" meaning Morning). I was still not wholly comfortable addressing people as stupid first thing in the morning.

"We have some very important news and need your help."

"Oh…?"

"We have yust heard that a Wee IP journalist is coming from England to wisit Åre and write a report for the British newspapers and we need you to look after them whilst they are here," forgetting her Js and Vs in her excitement.

"OK… sounds fine," I said rather dismissively, wondering why a journalist had been given such VIP status, or Wee IP, as she put it.

"Can you make sure you are available please on the 21st and 22nd of February?"

"Err, yes. I'll put it in my diary. For the whole of both days? What do you want us to do with this journalist? Just answer questions or go skiing with them? What's the plan?"

"Well, maybe you meet them and talk to them about the resort and, yes, go skiing with them and take them for a meal?"

"Oh..OK. That seems quite a lot of time. I'll have to check the diary and see what's happening then."

She sensed my short-lived enthusiasm had started to wane and I took too large a bite out of my donut before it froze.

"She's called Mariella Frostrup – you have heard of her?"

"Maarieyya Ffrosffrupph!?" I exclaimed through a mouthful of donut?

"Yes, you know her?"

"Mmmmmm," was all I could muster, still trying to clear my mouth of donut. Her deep, sexy-husky voice resonating in my head.

"We can pay you..." she offered, trying to win me back. "You will have to take her out for a drink and show her the night clubs too."

"Hhmmm… mmmm," I was frantically biting through the sweet dough, nodding my head trying to convey my agreement but Ulla still thought I was trying to decide.

"We'll pay all the drinks and the food and give you some on top."

Finally, I cleared my mouth.

"Really no, Ulla, you don't need to do all that. You have been so kind and helpful to us."

"Yes, of course we will," she insisted. "It's important for her to have a good experience."

I paused a moment. "So let me get this straight. The tourist office is willing to pay me to meet Mariella Frostrup, wine and dine her, take her out to the night clubs and buy her drinks and go skiing with her?" I couldn't stop a smile appearing on my face. The boys back home wouldn't believe it.

"Yes. Would you please…? I would have asked John but… you know, I think it would be better if you do it."

"Yes, of course I will. And we don't have to tell John anything, do we?" I was discovering that John wasn't as highly regarded in the resort as he perceived himself to be.

"No. Thank you so much. You won't forget, will you?"

"No, Ulla, I won't. Don't worry. I'll put it in my diary as soon as I can."

"Thank you. Oh and BBC Radio Scotland are here later today for a few days and want to do an interview tomorrow at 3.30pm. Is that OK? Perhaps you and John could take them snowmobiling?"

"Sure. Of course we can." I felt like a minor celebrity myself now. I certainly never expected all this extra-curricular activity, but it was welcome and would be fun. I continued across the square, taking stock of the latest secret new arrivals list; BBC Radio Scotland… the King of Sweden himself but… *Mariella Frostrup.* How much better could this month get? Well, calling into the hotel office at the Åregården to check any incoming arrival lists, Camilla handed me a fax copy of a typed letter that had been sent to head office in the UK.

It had been written by one of our guests who had visited with a couple of friends in January and was addressed to "The Managing Director…" It was dated 24th January and had obviously been passed from pillar to post in the organisation so quite a few important people had seen it. It read:

Dear Sir,

I am writing to you to express our gratitude for a fantastic holiday that myself (sic) and two colleges (sic) have just come back from.

' *The three of us have just come back from Are in Sweden where your two representatives Andrew and John look after your guests. From the word go they have treated us more as friends than guests, something that we have not encountered from other tour operators, they managed to sort out all our entertainment from husky sledding to Ice Karting! Most days they gave us guided tours around the slopes and showed us the best places for après ski.*

Our evenings were full of entertainment visiting pubs and clubs until 3–4 o'clock in the morning and they were still ready to take us out at 9am the next morning.

We are all hoping to visit the resort again later in the season and look forward to seeing them again.

Perhaps you could pass on our thanks for a holiday that will be remembered for a long time.

Yours,

Tim M

"Yes!" I exclaimed, "Thank you, Tim M." To get a letter like that was fantastic and, although he had promised us he would send it, it was so nice of him to actually do it.

Tim mentioned ice karting, which if I recall correctly, he and his two friends bravely took part in during a rare day of rain. They were cold, soaked through to the skin and a little splattered in oil at the end of it, but had a good time. The karting track was on the edge of the village, close to the lake side. Pre-season, we had tested it out with limited success, from the operator's point of view, and it never really took off to become the activity it could have been, mainly because the karts were rubbish.

Trial number one had us hanging around the freezing course for half an hour whilst the guy got one of his kart engines to start and run for about twenty seconds before spluttering to a halt. We said we would come back the following week. Trial two saw me complete three laps and John four laps before both our engines conked out. We promised to give it another go a few days later. For trial three, we turned up to find only one kart could be started and we took turns in going around the track practising our four wheel drifts. It would have been a lot more fun if another kart could have started. Trial four was the most successful and he proudly got three of his six karts all running together for a quarter of an hour and then the snow started to fall so heavily we couldn't see where the track went so we called it a day. Tim and his friends were extremely fortunate with their timing in one way, because all their karts worked for a solid half an hour, but the weather was against them. After that, we had a few days' rain, which washed the track away, followed by a further period of lower temperatures and lots of snow. The tiny shed from which the chap ran his karting empire never re-opened and I heard later he had loaded up a sledge, strung up a team of dogs and headed across the frozen lake for the hills to sit out the winter in splendid isolation.

Riding Icelandic horses was another activity that never really took off. I think we had just two horse mad people try it and they spent two hours battling slowly through deep snowy fields but they loved it.

The next day we met with Andrew and Tom from BBC Radio Scotland for our recorded interview in the Diplomat Ski Lodge hotel, where our office was located. Off air, they were eager to experience the nightlife and, since it was a Tuesday, that meant it was Bygget night. Bygget was the resort's biggest *nattklubb* and was housed under the Åre Fjällby Hotel and Apartments complex, a little out of the main central area on the way to Duved. The name didn't come from its size but, instead, rather boringly it translates as "construction" and, in the cold light of day, the inside was just a big concrete box. I never found out how many people it could accommodate but when some of the popular DJs and Swedish bands with very un-Swedish names played there, like Kent and E-Type, it was rammed. It opened at 3pm each day for After-Ski and closed about 3am on Wednesday mornings. We arranged to meet the Radio Scotland boys at 11pm at the Hotel Åregården and they arranged for a taxi to the club and bought us drinks all night. It was mainly a much younger crowd here, but seeing as it was Bygget's big night of the week, it was full of all ages. The music was predictably much louder and not quite as tuneful as elsewhere so, after at about 12.30am, we were happy to call it a day. They asked about the other night clubs, so we offered to show the Country Club the following night, which would probably be more theirs and our scene. The next day they had taken part in a ski lesson in Duved, experienced some cross-country skiing, been on a snow scooter safari, and visited the frozen waterfall in the early evening, but were still keen to do the Country Club, all in the name of BBC research.

The BBC paid for our drinks again and they were happy to drink, chat and ogle the beautiful girls, feeling more comfortable with that now most of them were over twenty one years old.

They were both envious of our jobs here, seeing as how we could ski every day and drink every night surrounded by such beauty. We knew more of the girls in the Country Club who would come up and say hello to us, which would make our two guests even greener. By the end of their third day, which was rounded off with a session at the Sunwing After-Ski party and more drinks courtesy of the BBC, I felt they had had a good time and I had certainly recovered most of the cost of my annual TV licence fee in alcohol, so I was happy too. They were probably less than happy with their proposed 3.55am departure pick up for the transfer to the airport for their connecting flight to their next destination.

We had a similar experience with another couple of journalists. Or rather one journalist, Ian, and his photographer, Geoff; both of whom appeared to be on heat the moment they had landed in Sweden. They worked for *Fall Line* magazine which, due to the title, I had rather assumed to be about skiing and snowboarding but their editor had sent them on a mission to Sweden to find the ultimate Swedish blonde (and check out a bit of skiing whilst in Åre). They had been in town for a few days when we bumped into them and started talking. Unbelievably, they hadn't had much luck and their bright yellow Renault Twingo hire car, which had "Hire me for 199SEK a day", had surprisingly not managed to attract the girls. Nor did chatting up girls who worked in pizza parlours, asking to take their photos, really work either. The only Swedish blonde babes they had met close up were ones they had seen on the pay TV channels on their hotel television.

They had done their ski research but were failing miserably in their ultimate quest and now Geoff had fallen off a toboggan, his knee getting tangled up in some catch netting at the bottom of a run chipping a bone and damaging some ligaments. Geoff had even been seen chasing after a couple of girls in the town square, hobbling along on crutches, camera slung around his neck asking for a photo.

It was all rather desperate but, as they were based in Duved, they had not been to the Diplomat Bar or The Country Club night clubs. So, on the promise of a pizza, free beers all night and a favourable write up in *Fall Line* magazine, we offered to show them the sights. They weren't disappointed and Geoff's flashlight on his camera was feverishly working overtime. The girls we knew came up to us and asked us what was happening and seemed only too willing to take part, even strip off their shirts and pull on *Fall Line* tee shirts for the camera, rolling them up to expose their bare mid riffs. The *Fall Line* chaps couldn't believe their luck, or our luck, working here. I think Ian seriously contemplated giving up journalism to become a ski rep in Åre next season. The highlight of their evening was heralded with the arrival of Mariha, tottering along in high heels and tight black jeans, accompanied by Lena the Smirnoff promotions girl. Ian couldn't believe it when both of them came straight over to us to say hello and Geoff was scrabbling with his camera so much I think he almost dropped it, though it must have been tricky balancing on crutches in a dark night club with an expensive camera around your neck.

Ian could hardly speak with these two girls standing so nearby but I could tell what he wanted to ask them and so I explained where the guys were from and, of course, both girls were only too happy to peel off right there and pull on the *Fall Line* tees. Mariha explained to me, shouting in my ear, that all Swedish girls love the camera lens. That couldn't be said of Ian and Geoff's experience up until that night.

I Have a Dream

We were frequently invited on freebies so that we could sell the restaurant, excursion, ride, experience or whatever to our guests. One Thursday afternoon in early February, John and I had an appointment at 1pm to meet with a Sami man called Radar. Ulla introduced us to him at the tourist office saying his dream was to have lots of our guests pay lots of money to have lots of arctic fun with his reindeers. We chatted, mainly via her as an interpreter, for a while before we climbed into his ageing GMC 4x4 pick-up truck. The three of us sat on the front bench seat amongst lengths of ropes, axes, sheathed knives and a heady aroma of venison and vodka.

We headed off to an area called Björnen, a family orientated area on the south eastern extreme of the resort. The road wound its way past the holiday chalets and on into the forest. We were soon the only people on the road and conversation had run out. Radar continued driving away from civilisation and began chewing on something noisily. I gave a sidewise glance at John who just raised his eyebrows and shrugged his shoulders in response. We already had the feeling this proposed excursion wasn't going to work but were now intrigued to see what unfolded.

The gentle snow started to develop into a heavier fall and by the time we were in a full blizzard I had lost my bearings. We drove on through the snow storm and, from what I could see looking out of my side window, deeper and deeper into the forest.

I was no longer certain we were still on a proper road. I was developing a funny feeling that this was going to be a strange experience and kept thinking to myself... "It's two o'clock on a Thursday afternoon and I'm in the middle of Sweden in a

4x4 being driven through a blizzard deep into the forest with a strange little man and his collection of blades smelling of meat and alcohol. How bizarre?! I thought of my friends back in London returning to their desks after a pub lunch, sitting down at their computers and carrying on with a normal day. This was anything but normal.

After a while, Radar pulled up to the side of the road, or track or whatever we were travelling along, and hopped out. In an instant, the snow eased off a lot and we were sat there in the muffled silence that always follows a heavy snowfall.

"I guess we hop out as well?" I said to John, pushing down on the door release.

"Your guess is as good as mine." He shuffled along the seat to follow my lead.

Radar stood on the other side of the truck and, reaching behind his end of the seat, brought out a heavily jewelled belt that he wound around his woven tunic. Then he donned a colourful Sami hat, grabbed an old rucksack and a cluster of knives, attaching them to his belt. He beckoned us towards the trees. John and I looked at each other again, apprehensively thinking, "Now what?"

Radar charged off into the trees and pulled back some fir branches to reveal an old snowmobile, a very old one. How he knew exactly where to pull in on the track amazed me for these snow covered trees looked just like the snow covered trees a hundred metres further back and they were identical to all the other trees along this stretch of forest for the next two hundred or three hundred metres or more. Only the deep ruts of our tyre tracks gave any point of reference as they wavered unsteadily along the route we had followed.

He signalled for us to sit on the trailer on which he dumped his rucksack. The trailer was fitted with skis and attached to his snow scooter, with an old screwdriver jammed into the towing hitch and secured with garden string in a very Heath Robinson sort of way. He started his engine first time and we were off, heading deeper still into the forest, the blue smoke from his tired engine choking our lungs as we held onto the flimsy trailer. Ducking branches and leaning over to counterbalance the turning, we arrived at a clearing after three of four minutes. There were five wooden huts of varying sizes, their roofs heavy with snow, and to the left of the clearing was a small corral. Through the lighter snowflakes that now danced their way to the ground, I spotted movement and then, as my eyes became accustomed to the surroundings, I saw half a dozen reindeer. Radar led the way to the largest hut, which had been built in the shape of a tipi, and opened the hatch.

He lit a gas lamp and hung it from a beam that spanned the diameter of the hut before he started to get the central fire burning stronger again in order to make some coffee. We sat around the edge of the hut on reindeer skins and, as my eyes adjusted to the dark, I could make out bows and arrows and a pile of harnesses, more reindeer skins, and other oddly shaped tools and hunting knives. Here was a man who liked his knives… and we were alone in the woods with him.

Looking out of the little window in the side wall, I saw the blizzard had picked up again but the hut quickly warmed with the fire gaining strength, and soon it felt quite cosy inside. We began to make some progress with conversation and Radar started to smile more, which relaxed us. His English had suddenly improved. Clearly, he felt more relaxed and confident with us now he was in his home environment. As the storm properly got going outside, we ended up talking reindeer, his favourite subject after knives, for about an hour and drank several cups of very strong thick coffee.

At one point, he brought out a small white plastic bag

from which he released a bloodied slab of dark red meat. As he peeled the sides of the bag away from the meat the blood trickled back down to the bottom. He placed the meat on a wooden board and very carefully used his penknife to slice off pieces of raw flesh before offering the morsels up to us. It was very salty to the taste, had a distinctively strong smell, and needed to be washed down with a big gulp of coffee. My fingers would reek of it for days after, in spite of some rigorous washing of hands.

For the next hour, he delighted in telling us how to make tasty reindeer dishes such as reindeer tongue, reindeer stew, dried reindeer chews, and blood pancakes. The Sami even liked to add reindeer fat in their coffees instead of milk. We learned that there is an annual reindeer round up; they cannot be penned in and have to follow food supplies so the Sami have to move with them. Nowadays, they used snowmobiles to "steer" the reindeer and each herd is about two to three hundred beasts. I asked him how they fed themselves when the land was covered in snow. The answer was that their main food source was actually buried beneath the snow. It was the same lichen that we had been feeding them in the Sami camp. It did not contain much protein but lots of carbohydrate from which they could generate heat to help keep warm.

It was time for another game of Swedish charades as he took to the floor, bent low down, and started sniffing the ground. Then he used his foot to scrape the floor. At the Sami camp, they had described the reindeer's paddle shaped feet that work like shovels to dig down to the lichen. He described and mimed how each spring they check the state of the teeth of the reindeer because the lichen they eat is gritty and grinds down their teeth after time. The animals that show teeth that are too worn down are culled as they would starve through the summer. We were getting good at Swedish charades, although we could have got all this horribly wrong. What he might have been trying to tell us was that he hadn't been to the dentist for ages because he couldn't afford it and hadn't discovered any buried treasure and he would rather spend what little money he had on a new pair of boots, which had worn out because he had a problem with dragging his feet backwards.

Long after we had finished our meaty treats, he abruptly halted his description of life with the reindeer. He seemed to have forgotten something, like a dinner party host exclaiming, "Oh my word, I forgot the cheese and biscuits!" Only he asked us: "You like beetles?"

"Err…" again John and I glanced at each other apprehensively.

Before either of us could answer, he continued, "I like them a lot."

I was thinking, "OK… when in Rome…"

"You like?" He nudged John's knee with his hand still clasped around his bloodied knife.

"Um. Yes, sure, why not?" John replied.

Radar stood up, turned away from us and moved to the back of the hut and began to rummage around for something. John and I looked at each other, knowing exactly what the other was thinking but not daring to say anything. Radar made a deep frustrated-sounding grunt followed by an odd higher-pitched noise and I imagined him attempting to extricate a stubborn little object from some horrid little plastic container. The raw reindeer felt like it wasn't sitting that comfortably in my stomach but maybe it was the anticipation of beetle pudding to follow that was unsettling me. At that moment, there was a click and a shutting of a lid and then…

The words to *Love Me Do* bounced off the walls of the hut.

"Oh, thank God for that!" I exclaimed.

"Ah… The Beatles!" said John, turning to smile at Radar, the relief so apparent to see across his face.

"Yes, of course we like The Beatles," even though neither of us had ever confessed to liking them. "We're English. We all like The Beatles. Yes... Beatles." He was getting carried away with his enthusiasm.

"OK, John. He gets the message." I held up the palm of my hand to him to try to stop him jabbering on. Radar was pleased too and he began to dance awkwardly, as a man does with a dozen sharp hunting knives dangling around his waist. He then looked at John, who was still praising The Beatles, and must have wondered why such a big fan was, only two minutes ago, oblivious to their very existence.

I glanced out of the small window and noticed the snow storm was easing off again. Radar soon decided it was time to move out and, snuffing out the fire, he tidied up and then handed us each a lasso, harness, and a reindeer skin. We stepped outside and paused for a moment, appreciating the absolute quietness of our surroundings. It struck me there was actually something eerie about snow, eerie but at the same time beautiful; a claustrophobic smothering in one way and a comforting protective hug in another.

The thick snow seemed to muffle any sound but as we stirred so did the reindeer, one bell tinkled gently as the animal sensed our movement. The three of us walked slowly across the centre of the clearing through six inches of snow and over to some big wooden sledges which were stacked up against a tree. Placing the reindeer skins carefully on the flat boards with the harnesses on top, we ventured into the corral and, like a magnet to iron filings, the reindeer trotted to the other side of the enclosure.

Radar skilfully demonstrated how to lasso a reindeer and caught one straight away. What had up until now been a kind of *Northern Exposure* afternoon became more *Monty Python*. As the two ski reps charged around the corral trying to capture a reindeer each, the *Benny Hill* theme tune started to play in my head. As our attempts failed time and again, we began to giggle insanely like children playing in the snow for the first time. The reindeer were having none of it from these two amateurs and evaded capture. We fell over in the snow, getting entangled in our own lassos, and had to heave ourselves up quickly.

On my eighth or ninth attempt, the rope uncurled itself and flew through the air almost in slow motion to land in the rigging, entangling itself in the antlers of my quarry. The beast knew it was caught and didn't bother to fight or shake the rope off. It just stood there staring straight ahead, waiting for me to reel it in. We manhandled the animals out of the corral and into the main area of the camp with Radar's guidance and John attached his to a tree. There is a reindeer pecking order apparently and these two were not the best of friends. It took a massive effort to hold them off each other when we endeavoured to harness them up. John's beast managed to work itself free and head-butted mine in the hind quarters, breaking off a piece of its antler in the process. It left a weeping bloody wound that dripped and stained the pure white snow. It wouldn't have hurt him, Radar reassured us.

The angry *ren* (reindeer) was, thankfully, harnessed to Radar's sledge in front of us and, while John sat ready in that sledge holding the reins, I used all my strength to hold my one back to prevent it retaliating. Both animals were very excited and itching to get going. The sledges kept edging forward as we continued to settle the second reindeer into its harness. The tension mounted all the time as Radar made his final checks. John and Radar traded places and no sooner than they had taken up their positions than the reindeer were off. I had a split second in which to release my hold on the harness and leap onto the back of John's sledge, landing on a narrow running board as it whizzed past me. Luckily, I managed to time it just right, but my left ski glove had got wedged into the harness I had been holding and was flapping around madly in the wind.

Radar, being in the lead, was blissfully unaware of our predicament and was already some way ahead of us. Ours was trotting ungainly but eagerly to catch up to him. I held the reins tightly and attempted to steer a safe course through the trees, ducking the low branches and leaning right over to stop the big sledge tipping over, which it felt keen to do. I waved frantically on the turns to try to get Radar's attention so we could stop before my left hand froze solid and fell off in the bitter wind-chilled air. John was just giggling all the way as he held on for dear life, not daring to move his bodyweight in the turns.

We came to an abrupt stop and, mercifully, Radar looked back to check on us and realised what had happened. After retrieving the trapped glove, we were off again at a cracking pace, up over banks then thumping down the other side, where we would be thrown clear of the deck only to come crashing down a second after the sledge landed. We plunged down into ditches and were hauled up the other side, the sledges becoming airborne as we crested the ridges. Mostly, we squeezed through gaps in the trees barely wide enough for us to pass, all the time on the lookout for low branches that could have easily swept us clear off the deck. It was sheer exhilaration. but also utterly bonkers.

After half an hour or so, the snow began to fall so heavily again that I could hardly see beyond the bucking antlers in front of me. Heaving the sledges around the trees and trying to stay on board had required huge physical effort and I had been trying to catch my breath. In doing so, I was now catching a huge amount of white fluffy stuff in my mouth. Radar sensed it was time to go back to camp, peeled off right and soon we were back to his place again.

We unharnessed the animals and returned them, steaming and snorting, although no longer fighting, to the enclosure. We packed everything up quickly and headed out on the snowmobile trailer to find the 4x4 buried deep in snow. It took us a further five minutes to uncover it and find the door handles then we leapt in and Radar returned us to what now felt like planet earth after wherever we had just been.

In the village centre, normal ski resort life was still going on and the sun was shining. We thanked Radar for the experience and left him with the promise of a lot of customers but, in reality, we could see it would be asking for trouble with too many guests falling off, getting hit by branches or very foolishly getting their gloves stuck in the harness. As we headed back to the Sporthotellet, passing the supermarket, Broken Dreams bar, the pizza hatch, and the ski hire shop, I felt like Mr Benn walking along Festive Road after a magical adventure.

We were still buzzing with adrenaline and, of course, nobody out in the square here could possibly know what we had just been doing. We passed a stuffed elk in the window of a shop. I'm sure he was grinning at us as we walked back to our rooms.

Not having any work to do for the remainder of the day, I headed back to my room to get some more rest and bumped into Ulla, who asked if I was still OK for meeting Mariella – as if I would forget. No one else was about when I walked through the main hallway and up the steps, past the fireplace and underneath the swastika-emblazoned hanging candelabra. I turned left at the top of the stairs and opened the fire door to the corridor, closing it quietly behind me. I could see the whole length of the corridor and there was only one door open about half way down on the right.

All was still but I had a funny feeling. I felt my heart rate increase a little as my anxiety level rose. And then, through the open doorway, came Elsa the Rottweiler, her claws rhythmically scraping along the floor as she walked steadily towards me, her neck chain jingling. For a few metres, she was quiet but the moment she sensed my fear, she emitted a deep growl.

"Oh God, is this the end for me? Why isn't her owner in her

room? Why is no one else around?" I had passed her before a number of times but we had never had a one-to-one encounter.

Micke, her owner, did not work in the resort every week but he and everyone else had told me that, if I did happen to meet her on my own in the corridor, it was best not to show any fear! Trying not to show any fear when confronted with a strange Rottweiler alone in a corridor was never going to be easy. I had also been advised the best thing to do if I met her in the corridor was to growl at her. *Really?* It was counterintuitive but I had no better ideas and the rasping clickety click of her claws was getting louder as she moved closer.

"Raah," I said feebly and she paused to get a better look at me. Was she about to charge me down and savage me? "Raaaghh," I repeated, only much louder and stronger. I bravely began to walk towards her. "Raaaghh, Elsa," I growled as best I could under the circumstances – in a stronger but not, I prayed, a menacing way.

What if she didn't understand my English accent?! Do Swedish dogs growl differently? I quickly changed my "raaagh" to a "ggrrrr". I didn't want her mistaking me for a lion or something. She growled back at me in a frightful low pitch.

"GRRR, ELSA." I shook my head and probably my whole body as I got closer to her. Her tail wasn't wagging and she was about two metres from me now, staring at me with evil eyes and menacing teeth bared. I had to walk right by her and growled again. She turned her head to follow me. I didn't dare reach out to stroke her. Then I had a terrifying thought. Of all the days we have to meet one-on-one, it has to be this one. She must be able to smell reindeer! I walked by the open door to her room, glanced quickly in to see no one there and fumbled for the key to my room. *Where was Micke!!??*

Unlike most horror movies, I did manage to get the key in the door straight away and turn the lock to open it. I didn't turn to look at her again but opened and closed the door in a flash, breathing a big sigh of relief once safely inside the confines of my own room. I listened carefully for the sound of her feet padding away back down the corridor to wait for her next visitor. In a few hours' time, I would have to go back out along the corridor to meet up with the guys from the hotel. I prayed that she would be in her room or someone else would be about. I toyed with the idea of sliding out of the window to my room but, although the lower part did open upwards on a hinge, it was only about 25cms high and it would have been too embarrassing to have to call the fire brigade or piste patrol to help free me in the event I got stuck. And besides, there was also a good party in the offing.

I read for a while before dosing off a bit and then got ready to head out. I could hear more sounds of life in the corridor now and decided to brave the walk. Out of interest, I checked the temperature gauge again – minus twenty five degrees. I had noticed that below minus twenty felt really cold. For sure it was cold in the minus teens, but it was still a dry cold. At this temperature, the cold sort of whacked you about the face as soon as you stepped outside. I had developed a slight winter cold and a runny nose and noticed that, merely seconds after I stepped outside, if I made a little *Bewitched* sort of wriggle with my nose, I could feel a crunching as the "nose juice" froze. It was a wonder your eyes didn't freeze too, but I guess they were just a bit warmer.

Taking big breaths was almost painful, like swallowing razor blades, as the air felt like it was cutting the inside of your throat. You had to take gentle breaths. If you took one almighty intake of breath, as if to blow up a lilo, I imagine your insides would freeze and you would keel over and die.

I met up with Anna, Camilla, Annelie, Åsa, Stina, Carolina, Danny, Fredrik and Ronny (not even one Ulrika or Björn among them) for a few drinks in the hotel bar, where they worked, so the drinks flowed quite freely. After an hour or so, we drank up, wrapped ourselves up against the cold, and stepped out into the freezing night air, heading down the hill to a restaurant and bar called Tottebo. The venue was close to the Åregården Hotel, set back from the square at the other end of what was presumably a small park most of the year.

The building was a beautiful old timber structure, painted in a gloriously-rich, deep red. It was very similar to the shade of red with which some people decorate the statement wall in their dining room. Inside was all cream walls and light polished wood. On the ground floor was a classy, white table cloth restaurant and upstairs was an airy wine bar with a high ceiling. It was where the beautiful and sophisticated headed to for a night out but tonight it was closed to them after 10.30pm and reserved for the staff and their invited guests, of which I was now one.

More staff discounted beers were gratefully downed, the music got cranked a up a notch or two and people began dancing. It was good seeing so many people you knew all in one place for a change, rather than spread out across the resort in various offices, shops, hotels and restaurants. Sometimes it took a moment to recognise them without their faces being partly obscured by a familiar hat, hood, jacket collar or goggles, but I had got used to recognising eyes. There was a great sense of camaraderie, in that we were all working together to make the whole resort function, and I really felt part of a much larger team than just us two reps. Besides, although we had had a good afternoon's experience together, things were becoming a little strained and I was starting to spend more of my free time with the Ski Skandinavia reps, Mellissa, Daniel and Katrina/ Natasha. For now, though, there were enough people mingling and chatting and dancing with each other that I could socialise with whoever. It was a chance to take stock of the various people we were working with.

Gathered here was a complete cross section of the *ski*

seasoners. We had: long-haired grungy snow board dudes with scraggly beards and baggy clothing; scruffy lumberjack and tee shirted guys with faded jeans and big boots; freakishly tall guys with floppy hair and pointy sideburns that matched their pointy boots, who were wearing smart jeans and shirts. Then there was a collection of rakish, bushy, wild-haired chaps, nurturing newly-formed beards in white tee shirts under smart jackets and jeans. Among the crowd there were, as you might expect, more than your average number of beautiful blonde girls, many with their hair tied back in plaits. The striking blue irises exaggerated the whiteness of their eyes. But what had come as a surprise to many of our guests was the girls weren't all blondes. Another quirk had been keenly observed and noted down by one of our fellow reps, Simon (who had been posted to Geilo in Norway), that the women were far more attractive than the men, and he wasn't trying to be overly heterosexual.

He had popped over to visit us on a number of occasions when his weekly Arrivals Sheet had been faxed to him and he was void of guests; Geilo, being that much smaller a resort than Åre. He wrote in a fax sent to us from his base in Norway, wondering "...*why the said beauty gene does not extend to the vast majority of the male of the Nordic species? For it does seem to us experienced travellers that, if one surveys the French, Italian, Spanish and Portuguese youths, for example, it is quite apparent that many of both male and female gender are equally blessed with beauty genes. Why is it, therefore, that the beauty gene is only seemingly passed down the generations via the female...?*" What was also apparent was that Swedish girls knew how to deal with unwanted advances in a most genteel fashion and not in the traditional British way of "Piss off, I'm wiv me mates." "*Skall vi mingla?* (Shall we mingle?)" was usually the line one girl used to her friend when she came to the conclusion that our time was up and she didn't want to speak English anymore or, more to the point, didn't fancy us. That said, we British boys were certainly proving to be such a curiosity amongst the female Swedes in resort they felt we needed to be explored. For the first (and last) time ever in my life, I had been described as "exotic". The evening at Tottebo was turning out to be quite a drunken party, mainly due to the amount of free alcohol on offer, and I was hoping more explorations would be embarked on later.

After doing a fair bit of mingling myself, including talking to Ulla, who reminded me about Mariella's visit again and urged me not to forget, I got talking to Anders – aka Jesus, owing to his long brown wavy hair, dark beard and brown eyes and gentle manner – who was DJing for the night. He loved to talk English, and loved all the British bands and all the girls seemed to swoon about him. That similarity with Jesus soon stopped when it came to him and girls, but he certainly worked his miracles with a fair number of them, by all accounts. Strangely I think I heard him speak more English than I ever heard him speak Swedish but it turned out he had spent three years living in Notting Hill.

He took his headphones off to talk to me once more and asked: "You wanna choose some music?" He pointed to the stacks of CDs that filled the pine IKEA-style racks on the wall to the side of his mixing decks.

"Really?" If I heard him correctly above the noise of the room, I could have sworn he had just said I could select some tracks, so I squeezed in behind him and finger-searched the titles on the sides of the cases. Knowing his penchant for Brit music, I dug out some cases and, when I got his attention, pointed to the tracks. He nodded and gave the thumbs up at my suggestions, then took the CDs out and lined them up ready to play. He put the first one on (which followed his quite well, I thought) as he faded in and out – or "mixed", I should say. Another of my choices followed on and, again, the dance floor remained full and lively. The crowd liked it, responding with renewed enthusiasm on the dance floor. Then he showed me how to tee up the next track on his double-CD player, and fade in and out, before saying he was going into the cellar for a cigarette so it was all mine.

"What?!"

"Yeah, you'll be fine, my friend," he said with a big reassuring smile and a hefty pat on my shoulder, before ducking under the door frame and disappearing into the crowd. And there I was; DJ Snoop Doggy Pooper Scooper, with a hundred or so people on the dance floor as yet unaware that their whole evening could now fall apart under my control if I failed to keep them entertained. After a few tracks that got them all revved up, I slowed it down a bit, although not to the extent of playing *slowies* obviously.

It was so much fun controlling the pace of the gyrating bodies in front of me, and getting the tacit approval of the crowd. Some of the people I knew better came by the front of the desk and pointed at me in amazement and clapped in appreciation. Feeling confident and wanting to inject some humour, I even stuck on *Minnie The Moocher*, remembering it had the line about the King of Sweden, which got a big cheer.

After a few tracks, I realised Anders had been away for much longer than a cigarette break and, when I could, I stuck my head through the archway to see him chatting up a lovely girl all dressed in white. On closer inspection, I think she was actually chatting him up, the way she kept pulling her hand through her long hair in an exaggerated way. He was holding two bottles of beer and, when he spotted me, he excused himself briefly from her and brought one over to me.

"Are you OK for a bit longer?" he asked, handing me what had probably ten minutes ago been an ice cold bottle.

"Sure…" I said, not sounding very sure as I felt my good run of tracks could come crashing to an embarrassing halt any time soon, but how could you refuse the charming Jesus?

I slipped back to my decks in time to fade in the next track like the old pro I had suddenly become and started to have ludicrous thoughts about becoming a DJ full time back home, then touring the clubs of the world. I needed a good DJing name and was thinking of what could work when Anders politely reclaimed his equipment and effectively faded me out with a thumbs-up and a congratulatory, "Cheers, mate!"

I returned to the crowd to *mingla* and seek adulation from my new fans. That was remarkably short-lived. Amid revelations of who was currently sleeping with whom and the major news that McDonalds was set to open a branch in Östersund in April, I did glean some useful information that could turn out to be a bit of wheeze. Apparently, as part of a day's organised activities, everyone attending business conferences that ended up in the restaurant, Skogstugan, took part in snowmobiling as the last event of the day. After the snowmobiling, they all had dinner and got totally smashed, so they couldn't drive the snowmobiles back to the village. The snowmobile company that provided the machines never had enough staff to retrieve the machines so were happy to pay anyone who volunteered 100 kronor for driving them back down through the trees to their HQ on the lake shore. Everyone knew how to drive the machines so no checks were needed and, by this time, I had become quite proficient. All you had to do was register your name with them on the notice board in the kitchen of the Åregarden a day before the next conference, then turn up in the evening to be picked up in their minibus and taken up to the venue.

Music, alcohol and mingling continued apace until the early hours of the morning and it must have been about 3am before I retrieved my jacket, ski gloves, hat and scarf, and a small group of us headed outside for the short walk back to the Sporthotellet. I was in an ebullient mood as I strode out purposefully up the pathway leading home, less aware that my nostrils had frozen again, inhaling cold air laced with razor blades.

It had been snowing again during the night, so that wonderful soft crunching sound emanated from under boot steps. I spied a mound of snow about the size of a small football on the side of the path and, probably buoyed by the alcohol and the success of the evening, I broke into a run and gave it a mighty kick. It didn't move.

For a brief moment, nor did my foot or leg as it absorbed the impact and I tried to take in what had just happened. It was a frozen solid lump of ice and very foolishly I had attempted to wellie it up into the trees. The others just fell about laughing as I tried to suppress a shriek of pain and prayed I hadn't damaged my foot.

I began to hobble but was soon propped up on each side by Annelie and Åsa, who effectively carried me back to my room and drunkenly took off my boots and socks to inspect for damage. I didn't think it was necessary to be carried back like that, but I wasn't complaining being nursed by those two. Fortunately, apart from a little bruising, there was no lasting damage and I lived to ski another day. Not eating yellow snow was one thing, but kicking frozen snowballs was another, "no no".

Voulez–vous

One of the benefits of having the freedom to ski every day for a whole season was that you got to experience those perfect blue sky days that often followed a long night of falling snow. Of course, there were other days when you were duty bound to take guests out for a ski around the resort under heavy grey skies with poor visibility when you couldn't make out what was up or down, or see the ruts or lumps of rucked up snow on which you could easily catch a ski edge that would send you tumbling. Some days, the wind blew sharp pin pricks of ice into your face for the whole hour or so of the ski escorting session, the temperature never getting above minus twenty, but they were rare.

Some of our guests actually compared the conditions very favourably with the minus fifty degrees they had experienced in some North American ski resorts. I never needed to wear a face mask, although some guests came equipped with them. February produced more sunny days than the previous month and I was determined to make the most of them, happy to do more than my fair share of the ski escorting.

The resort was divided into three main areas; Åre village being the central zone with the mountain railway and the cable car station. Standing in the village square, looking up to the ski pistes, you could only see a small part of the skiable area.

To avoid any first morning of the holiday disappointment, I told the guests on the transfer to imagine a giant man sitting in a chair. Standing in the village square you were standing on his shoes. If you looked up you could follow the legs up to the knees but could see no further. It was only once you had reached the knees could you see the full extent of the resort. I had to use a man as the best example because there weren't a pair of smaller mountains three quarters of the way up from the "knee".

The free ski bus linked the central area to Björnen, over to the east, but it was possible to ski there and back. So many of the British guests were obsessed with the idea of doing every run in the resort and ticking them off just to say they had done that.

"Oh, we do that in all the resorts we go to," chirped Mrs B from Solihull.

"Well, it is your holiday, but it's not really worth skiing over there as it's a bit flat and mainly accommodates young families who want to ski with their toddlers in amongst the trees. If you really want to go there, I would take the ski bus one morning and do a few runs then come back to ski in the main area. It will take you about two hours to get there via ski lifts and ski runs," I suggested.

"Well, we thought we'd get up early and catch the first lift and head over and back. What time is the first lift?"

"Nine thirty."

"Oh. Isn't there an earlier one?"

"No, that's when they all start at this time of the year. You really would be better off taking the ski bus, which will get you there in twenty minutes, max. There's a nice little café there shaped like a copper cooking pot, nestled in the trees at the bottom of Sadelvägen, with a roaring fire where you can get a coffee." I pointed out the location on the piste map. "You can admire the view down the length of the frozen lake as it stretches eastwards."

"No, we like to do all the runs we can, thanks." *Yes, you said that*, I thought. "We're quite fast skiers, you know."

"Well, have a good day doing it then. See you later."

Later, much later, a conversation would be had revolving around the inordinate amount of time it took them to drag themselves over there and back. They barely had time to suck the froth off their cappuccinos before they had to jump into their skis again and make the return trip. They refused to take the ski bus back but did show me a piste map with green pencil ticks on all the lifts and runs they had completed with which they could bore their friends back home in leafy Solihull. I was puzzled why it had taken them over three and a half hours to get there until they came ski escorting the very next day when I understood their definition of "fast skier."

Duved was on the other side of the resort about eight kilometres from the village centre. The runs there were mainly blues and reds, with some interesting and mixed skiing above and below the tree line. It was a great area for the snowboard dudes as there were less skiers out there on the extremities; they were more likely to come across a reindeer than a skier. The entire resort was wonderfully uncrowded, even in the busiest weeks, and the skiing was generally of a very high standard.

Most Swedes start skiing at two or three years old and, consequently, they all seemed to ski like instructors. The instructors skied like gods but, more importantly, they knew how to teach. It was a rule of ski school that the instructors had to remove their sunglasses whilst teaching to maintain eye contact their students. Ski school for adults was seen as, well, just a bit weird, although they were happy to oblige us when we started booking adults in. The school groups were small, invariably being no more than four or five in each class, and all the instructors spoke perfect English of course.

I was on the *Bergbanan* (mountain railway) with my new friend, Åsa, as it chugged slowly up from the village square. She worked nights on the Åregarden Hotel reception and had just returned from a couple of weeks at her home down south, attending to some personal stuff. It was good to see her back and be able to go out skiing with her as she was usually sleeping during the day. We were both a little older than most of the resort workers and had become good friends as the season had progressed. We had the same sense of humour and I admired her feistiness when it came to dealing with some of the drunken idiots she encountered doing her job in the early hours of the morning. She didn't need to do the job and frequently wondered why she was still doing it, not being the most enthusiastic skier. She had striking green eyes below short black hair and wasn't the least bit interested in the latest ski brands. As we ascended the railway, she was recalling how she made good money doing some modelling a few years ago and the fact that she appeared on the album cover of a band.

It was a beautiful crystal clear morning, the smoke trailing up from Åsa's chain-smoking not really spoiling the moment and I was feeling very relaxed. I happened to look back down the railway line to the village and out to the lake and, to my amazement, I saw three vertical rainbows reaching up from the surface of the frozen lake to the skies. It was about minus twenty degrees in the bright sunshine.

The tiny particles of moisture in the air had crystallised and were caught in the sun's rays. Readjusting the focus of my eyes on the air immediately surrounding me, I could see myriad snow crystals floating lazily about us like dust diamonds as we ascended. It was sights like these that made this place so special and different to so many of the traditional alpine ski resorts.

Conversely, it was also different because of its snow record. From time to time we would get reports from other resorts via Dapper Bob. In the same week that Kitzbuhel had only 30% of its lifts open and skiers were being bussed out like packed sardines to ski on the nearest glacier, the top lift in Åre, the Tusenmeter lift, was temporarily closed in the early hours whilst the lift company first tried to find it and then dig it out of an enormous snow drift.

I saw more Telemarking here than anywhere else I have skied. It is the original skiing style and is said to improve balance, posture and agility to help you become a better downhill skier. "Free the Heel," is the Telemarker's mantra. It is cool to be a Telemarker and looks almost balletic when demonstrated by an experienced exponent. It looked like a recipe for disaster to me and I never really had the urge to give it a go. I reckoned there was a high chance of damaging my knees or ankles or both.

On the extremities of the resort, you would often spot cross country skiers, usually loaded down with a rucksack full of provisions for the day's outing accompanied or sometimes even towed by a couple of husky dogs. Again, a more traditional form of skiing, it looked tempting enough for me to consider swapping my carving skis for some thinner straight planks and to explore the wilderness following the red crosses attached to wooden poles that indicated the trails. The problem was I had not yet found anyone to give me any instruction and lead me out on a trail. A slice of traditional Christmas cake would soon be my ticket to a full afternoon of *längdåkning*.

Snowboarding had been welcomed in Scandinavia for many years before the resorts in the Alps had really accommodated it. A half pipe had been constructed near the village centre and *Snowboardland* had been specially developed for those who wanted to ride goofy or regular and practise those acrobatic jumps away from skiers. 'Skiers enter at their own risk,' said a sign by the entrance off the Farisvägen run. As there was so much space on the slopes, everybody seemed to respect the other mountain users. I never saw any dangerous manoeuvres.

One of our younger guests, a lad of about twelve years, managed to carry out a dangerous manoeuvre on himself somehow. The family was staying in my hotel in Duved and we had got a call to say that he had been in an accident and the rest of the family had taken all their skis and boots back to the ski hire shop as they couldn't face any more skiing. On hearing the news, I jumped on the next ski bus where Toni Braxton was still singing about her heart, to pay them a visit and see what I could do for them. John had told me the lad had cut his face on a ski edge and was in a bad way but I wasn't prepared for the sight that awaited me.

When I got to the hotel they were all sitting together in the lounge bar looking dejected. The father was the first to get up as I walked over to them and strode purposefully towards me. After exchanging greetings, he said in a hushed voice, "Try not to over react when you see his face as he and his mother are very upset about it. Well, we all are, naturally, but particularly his mother."

I nodded in acknowledgement and we went over to speak to the boy. When he looked up at me I did my best to hide my shock. His face had been slashed up and down by what looked like knife cuts but were, in fact, the razor sharp edges of the skis. The worst cuts had been heavily bandaged up. I didn't know what to say and wondered how his head had got so entangled with the skis.

"Hi, I thought I had better come over and see how you are all doing. Sorry to hear about your accident…" I was floundering. "Did someone crash into you?"

"No," he shook his head and looked at the floor again. His father explained that he fell over whilst trying to get off a chair lift and got tangled up with his and someone else's skis. It was no one's fault. I thought that was generous of them as they could so easily have reacted badly and pointed the finger of blame at someone else.

"OK, well… do you want me to check to see what the next flights are like and we can see if we can get you out of here and home as soon as possible?"

To my surprise, they said no they didn't want to leave on

such a bad note and wondered whether there were some places they could visit nearby that would give them something else to focus on.

What a lovely family, I thought. I was determined to help them out and make the rest of their stay as bearable as possible.

"There's the candle factory and the chocolate factory," I suggested, thinking of the cuff, "and you haven't seen the frozen waterfall yet, have you? The landscape there – it's like it's from a Tolkein book." I hoped he was the sort of age of boy who read Tolkein. As he lifted his head up to me I saw a flicker of interest and he tried to smile.

His mother piped up, "He loves Tolkein!"

"Excellent. I'm going to sort out a vehicle and for the rest of the week I am going to be your personal chauffeur. We are going to see a lot of the sights that many of the guests don't get to visit." Having made that grand claim, I only hoped I could get the Mean Machine whenever I wanted so I could deliver on my promise, but I was certain Örjan would oblige if he could. If not, I was hiring a car. For the remainder of their stay I did manage to ferry them around each day and help them make the most of their stay. One of the restaurant owners heard about what had happened and offered them a free lunch (at his restaurant, obviously – not at someone else's) and the girls at reception at their hotel got him a special box of Swedish chocolate. It was another kind and thoughtful act, although I didn't think he was going to be able to bite into something so hard for a while. When it came time for them to leave, our friendly taxi man, Stefan, offered to take them to the airport for free in his luxury minibus. The family were so grateful for all the help and kind offers and it was heart-warming to see that they finished their week on a reasonably positive note.

When the morning's ski escorting duties had been carried out, followed by a few hours' paperwork completed in the office, it was often necessary to catch up on some much needed sleep. During a normal week's ski holiday, you might have a few late nights and early mornings but you could always sleep in a bit if you wanted or just have an easy ski day. This is not possible when you are a rep. It was getting to the stage already where we were checking the arrivals lists to see if we could determine if the groups coming out were going to want to party every night and ski every day.

A list of a half a dozen names all having a different surname meant party week, so it was important to get some rest and have some quiet times when the schedules allowed. We had far more guests to deal with than our Ski Skandinavia colleagues, who were based in Duved and did their transfers from Trondheim in Norway. They were accommodated in a nice modern apartment in a quiet residential area and spent most of their free time sleeping or watching episodes of *Friends* on TV. They would call us up and say there were heading into Åre for a night out on a regular basis.

One afternoon, when the work was done, I visited the local branch of Sandy's sandwich bar and purchased one of their foot-long filled rolls, a can of Coke and a *Japp* bar, and retired to my room for a quiet lunch. Ulla had left a hand written message on my door about Mariella Frostrup, which began with the letters "*OBS!*"(meaning, "Please Note"). I had begun to see these letters everywhere about the town, in bars, restaurants, hotels, shops, ski lifts, and now on my own door. She was reminding me that it was only ten days until the visit and please could I keep the days free. I wondered whether Ulla thought Mariella was a much bigger star than she really was. I hadn't realised how tired I was and snoozed on my bed for the rest of the afternoon, waking when I heard the crashing and banging of doors along the corridor as people left the building to head over to the Åregården Hotel for our regular serving of salmon, mashed potato and krispbreads.

I walked across the square, still feeling a little groggy, but the sharpness of the cold night air quickly woke me fully. The temperature gauge outside my window had read minus twenty and I was thankful it was only five minute walk to the hotel. When I arrived in the basement, the hotel staff members were all buzzing around, carrying A4 sheets of red paper and excitedly chatting amongst each other.

"What's going on?" I asked Kai, a crazy Finnish snowboard dude who worked nights in reception at the hotel, who I had recently become pals with on account of my recent late evening meet ups with radio presenters and staff members.

"It's the mid-season staff party."

Mid-season already? I was staggered that we had reached that stage. It was going far too quickly. He showed me his invite and pointed to where his name had been hand written on a dotted line. Since his name was only three letters long I wondered why he held it for me for so long and I looked back up at him inquisitively. He still held it there smiling and urging me to look again.

"How's your Swedish coming along?" he asked.

I looked again and was disappointed that, although I thought my Swedish had progressed quite well, I couldn't understand anything.

"Hold it, I'll find yours." He rummaged around the table where all the uncollected invites still lay. I was surprised and touched to discover that my name was indeed on an invite and the management had taken the trouble to include us in their mid-season party, but concerned that I was totally clueless about what was required of me because it was clearly not a case of turn up at 8pm at a bar.

The typed invite read:

Nonu äror dodetot dodagogsos foföror

POPERORSOSONAIOLFOFESOSTOT

Sosomom kokomommomeror atottot bobloli

POPIRORATOTFOFESOSTOT

Vovi totroräfoffofasos sosomom popiroratoteror

Popå Cocounontotrory, ononsosdodagog 12/2

Koklolocockokanon 14.30

Vovidodarore inonsostotrorukoktotiononeror fofololjojeror...

O.BOB.SOS! Dodu,

Andrew

— — — — — — — — — — — — — —

Totilollolhohöror lolagog _ _ _7 _ _

Koklolädodsoselol: Popiroratot + vovarormomtot

Vovälol bobemomötottot!!!

You can see why I was somewhat bewildered by the coded invitation, but Kai informed me that essentially it was written in the way Swedish pirates talk. Oh, of course! Why hadn't I guessed that?

Unlike our pirates (who I thought were the real pirates) who say normal piratey things like "Shiverrr me timbers, Jim, me laad", "Hang 'im fram the yaardaarm" and "Ahoy me heaaarrtiees" Swedish pirates sound like idiotic *Bill & Ben the*

Flower Pot Men. No wait, Bill and Ben *were* idiots. Anyhow they just go "popalop a popirottot" a lot.

Reading between the lines, or rather between all the pirate nonsense, I could start to work out that it was the *Personalfest* (Staff Party) and this year's theme was pirates (so we wouldn't look at all out of place in ski resort, then) and we should assemble somewhere at 2.30pm on Wednesday 12th February. I had been allocated to Team Seven. Finally, it instructed us to wear pirate / warm clothing, I think.

It didn't take long to get a place accepted on the snowmobile recovery mission and I wondered why. It seemed like such an easy way to earn 100 SEK. *Why wouldn't you boost your pay by about a tenner for an hour's skidoo driving?* I didn't recognise any of the other volunteers that were hanging around the main entrance to the hotel one early evening. We didn't have to wait long for Mats to arrive in his minibus to collect us and drive us up the windy, snow-covered road to a restaurant I hadn't seen before, hidden away in the trees. It only took us fifteen minutes to get there and I was thinking this is going to be "money for old rope".

The party appeared to be in full swing already, judging by the cheering and laughing coming from within the timber building. In the darkness, we trudged around the back like a team of burglars to where the herd of snowmobiles were gathered together, following Mats and his colleague.

He straddled the nearest one and asked everyone if we were familiar with the controls, giving me the translation almost simultaneously. Yes, we were happy.

"OK. Let's go. Follow me and keep about three metres from everyone." He continued to speak in English as it was easier, rather than saying everything twice. "Jonas will be at the back in case anyone has a problem," he added, reassuringly.

Starting up all the machines in one go made a tremendous noise that bounced off the panelled, wooden back wall of the restaurant and across the stretch of snow out to the black forest. Mats gunned his snowmobile and headed off, still standing up, occasionally looking back at us. When we were almost in a line, he sat down and his machine reared up like a horse, charging off into the darkness, its headlight beam dancing wildly about ahead of him, up to the night sky then down at the thick snow cover. We accelerated to catch up with him as we weren't going back into the village via the road we had come up on and none of us wanted to get left behind. It was like the reindeers all over again; a mad dash through the snow and trees, only much faster and at night time and we were hanging on like cowboys in a rodeo. As we urged our machines faster to catch up with him, I think we all managed to get airborne when our route suddenly dropped a few feet without warning shortly after we left the restaurant.

Mats was jumping his machine around like a banshee and it wasn't too long before we had a machine go over on its side in a deep snow drift. Fortunately, Jonas was on hand to help right it. We all got thrown about quite a bit and it felt like we were in a race to get down through the trees as quickly as possible without a care for the machines. Another one overturned his snowmobile up ahead and this time Mats looked back to see it and hauled his machine round to come to the rescue. The guy who was thrown clear was a little winded but signalled he was OK to go on.

We didn't wait for him to get fully sorted out as Mats had spun round and was off again across what looked like an old unused ski piste before turning right and following its far edge downhill at full chat. It was every one for him/herself as no

184

one wanted to be left behind out here in the darkness. There was yet another one down who didn't see the deep ditch on the other side of the piste. They had overtaken a slower rider on the outside of the turn and hadn't had time to turn but managed to get themselves sorted out.

We looked like a wild west style posse chasing outlaws as we re-grouped on the move briefly before veering off to the right to line up with a narrow avenue cut out of the trees. This opening forced us to ride nose to tail, the snow billowing in large clouds from the machine in front as we peered through the grey mist for the rear lights and outline of the snow scooter in front. Our only real guide was the broken branches and thousands of pine cones that lay littered to the side of this rough, bumpy white pathway through the dark forest.

Ahead of us, in the distance, I could just make out the faint glow of lights from the village but we still had a fair way to go. There was no let up in pace as we launched ourselves out onto a meadow, but we soon slowed to negotiate a sharp left turn along the top of a high bank of snow. Finally, it was my turn for a mishap and, as I rounded the bank a little too tightly, the rear left caterpillar track slipped, the engine roared in a higher pitch and my machine started to lean uncomfortably to the left. It slipped down into some very deep drifted snow and got bogged down, still at a jaunty angle. I had come to a precarious halt and was desperately trying to keep all my weight to the right side to stop it toppling over. If it went now, I would go too and it would roll over me. What up until now had been a sort of rollercoaster snow ride of excitement had suddenly become a precarious situation and I began to see why they struggled to get volunteers each week. *Was it really worth the risk just for a tenner, bearing in mind how many near misses we had had?* I stood still on the scooter as it balanced precariously, an image from the last scene of *The Italian Job* coming into my head, wondering whether or not to leap off to safety. Jonas quickly came up behind me and encouraged me to slowly unhook myself from the kill switch lead around my wrist, switch the engine off and jump clear.

Thankful that the deep snow was piled up like freshly picked cotton, I landed very softly. The snowmobile slowly rolled down and onto its side and then eased over some more so its belly was facing me. Jonas then positioned his machine ahead of mine, attached a tow rope and dragged it out to a flat area, righted it and brushed off the excess snow. He started it up for me and beckoned me over to jump on and no sooner was I aboard than we were on our way again as if nothing untoward had just happened. I guess it was a regular occurrence but I could have been squashed by the snow scooter or buried or both.

The remainder of our little jaunt passed by without further mishap and we duly collected our money. We had only brought down about a third of the snow scooters so I was guessing that Mats and Jonas would have to rope in more unsuspecting volunteers for another raid but they said the restaurant kept ten scooters there permanently so they only needed to do one more trip. Incredibly, a couple of our group were keen to do it again. There were easier ways of earning 100SEK, like filling a minibus full of guests and creaming off the profit or persuading some guests they should upgrade from normal skis to VIP skis and that would make them ski and feel so much better. Many of them did upgrade. They believed they skied better. Our wallets felt much better.

Much later that very same evening, I was having a beer in the Diplomat Bar with some guests, though not spending my hard earned 100 kronor, as they were insistent on buying the poor rep some beers. The guests had had their fill of the Sunwing and weren't inclined to settle for the soporific Åregården Hotel bar, with its tartan trimmings and old skiing photos. It was a normal evening in the busy bar. Curtis Mayfield's *Move on Up* was filling the room, creating a good vibe, and people were relaxing and talking about their day's activities on the slopes. The huge stuffed moose head from the wall above the bar was watching over everyone as usual and the recently replaced spotlights were shining brightly on the old wooden skis that were fixed to the walls.

We hadn't yet moved from the bar and I was handed some more notes with which to buy the next round. It was easier for me to get the attention of the main barman at this busy time than them as he knew me. I turned around on the spot and politely, but forcefully holding my ground, waved the notes to get the attention of Andreas. He was built like a Norse god but was clean shaven with very blonde hair, green eyes and a friendly face. So, not like a Norse god really. He was very tall, though, and I wouldn't want to get on the wrong side of him. I felt a little awkward beckoning him over ahead of everyone else, but staff looked after staff here. Naturally, we were more important than guests. He nodded to me whilst serving someone further along and, after a while, came straight to me with his big smile even apologising for the wait.

"*Tjena*, Andrew!" which was the chummy greeting afforded to people when they were accepted as being friends, a bit like '*Wotcha, mate*'. "Sorry, but I was serving some important guests." He raised his eyebrows and nodded back to where he had been standing. "It's OK, no problem."

"What can I get you?"

"Four beers and a white wine please."

"Coming right up. Did you hear about the guests?" he asked as he reached for some glasses to fill.

"Which guests?"

"Our Vips."

"What?" It was a bit hard to hear above the music and hustle and bustle of the bar.

"Our Vips... V –I –Ps." He spelt it out. I still wasn't getting it and he nodded towards his previous customers whilst placing a wine glass in front of me.

"*Very* VIP…" He emphasised the word "very".

I looked down the bar to where Andreas had nodded and could see an ordinary-looking middle-aged man with short grey hair and wire-rimmed glasses standing between two sturdy looking chaps.

"Them?" I questioned when he came back.

"Yep," he replied, placing four beers on the bar top for me.

I gave him a quizzical look to say, 'I have no idea who you are talking about.'

When he gave me my change, he grabbed me by both wrists. His 6ft 6 frame bent down towards me and almost pulled me over the bar as he brought my ear closer to his mouth.

"It's the King of Sweden!"

What? I thought he said, 'the King of Sweden'.

"The King of Sweden!"

"Bloody hell!" I thought and turned to look down the bar, still being held firmly by Andreas.

He let me down gently and I turned around. I motioned to my guests to move in closer and handed out the drinks to them, waiting a moment before announcing:

"You know how your reps always take you to the best bars?"

"Yes" they replied or nodded.

"That's why we buy you the beers," one of them said, cheerily raising his full glass to me in salute.

"Well, you won't believe me… and please don't all look round at once… but about five metres down there," and I nodded my head in the direction "…is the King of Sweden!" They all turned their heads in unison, of course, like a bunch of meerkats.

"Don't make it so obvious!" I pleaded.

"Which one?" they asked, eagerly. It really wasn't obvious without his robes and crown.

"Guy in black polo neck, short silvery-grey hair, wire-framed glasses, with two other guys either side of him."

They all stared again, but I couldn't blame them. I'm sure I would have done the same. In fact, I did only a few moments before whilst being held across the bar by the bar man, which was even more obvious.

"No way… really? Wow!… He looks just like a normal person," they gushed.

And he did. He was just standing there like anyone else, sipping from his glass of lager, minding his own business… with his *minders*.

Oh, what I would have given to have been the DJ that night, for I would have got the crowd going with a little bit of the Blues Brothers' *Everybody Needs Somebody* and then slowed them down with *Minnie The Moocher*. It would have been great to have seen what old Carl XVI Gustaf would have done. Probably nothing, of course, other than give a wry smile, but I love to imagine that maybe, just maybe and just for a laugh, when the song mentions him he would have put his beer down on the bar, spun round and strutted onto the dance floor. He would then have grabbed a microphone and led all the "Hi-Dee" bits with the crowd responding with their "Ho-Dees". I know if I was the King of Sweden that's what I would have done.

The very next morning, I was on ski escort duty, standing in a cable car with half a dozen of our guests heading up to slopes on a beautifully sunny morning. The bright sunlight was streaming in through the glass and refreshingly cool minty air poured in through the open vents, speeding up the recovery of my hangover. Radio Rix was broadcasting Toni Braxton again through the speakers mounted in all four corners but, after she had finished crooning about her heart, there was a brief verbal interlude and a couple of local adverts for a pizza *restaurang* and the unfortunately named Zitt ski clothing company. I had been asked by the owner what I thought the chances of the brand being marketed in the UK. The product was good but I had big reservations about the name. As they weren't prepared to contemplate a change, the discussion stopped rather abruptly. They thanked me for my views, not believing that British people wouldn't be happy to ski with a pustular spot as the logo.

The next track began with a series of gentle guitar chords and then, all of a sudden, about a dozen girls at the front of the cable car broke into beautiful song, performing pitch perfect vocals to No Doubt's *Don't Speak*. Like the Welsh, the Swedes are renowned for their singing and this must have been a choir ski trip; just an ordinary bunch of girls would not have been capable of such harmonies. It created a wonderful atmosphere in the cable car and received a big round of applause when they finished.

It put the ski escorting group in a good mood and we had a fine morning's skiing in perfect conditions, covering a lot of ground as they could all keep up well. Feeling buoyant, I suggested we headed up high to ski down to a collection of coffee and waffle tipi style tents that had been erected. Everyone was up for it and it proved to be a unique experience for them, sitting in the sun on reindeer skins draped over benches carved out of the snow.

The coffee, served in polystyrene cups needed to be drunk quickly, even in the sun, for it cooled quickly, but free refills were on offer and the sweet tasting buns were a welcome accompaniment. The group was a great bunch of people from all walks of life and that meant for an interesting and rewarding morning, talking and getting to know them. It made the job a real joy and not like working at all.

To finish off, we headed over to the slalom course that had just been set up on the Tottbacken run. It had been laid out to the side of the main piste of a red run and effectively cut off a corner so it rejoined the main piste further down the slope. It was unmanned and roped off at the top before it entered the trees and, by sticking a five kronor (about 50p) coin in a slot at the start, you could time yourself on the short hundred metre course. After lining yourself up to reach for the slot, like entering a multi-storey car park ticket machine, you edged down to the little wooden starting hut, no bigger than a portaloo, careful not to accidently let yourself go and cross the timing line before you were really ready. With the palms of your hands on the top of your ski poles, you eased yourself into position inside the hut, pressed a red button and listened to the beep, beep, beep, beeeeep, and then launched yourself onto the course, your boots kicking away a needle-like wand that started the timing counter. The course was often quite rutted, with the number of skiers trying it throughout the day, so it was best tackled in the morning. It was essentially a sweeping curve but it was laid out properly, with alternate blue and red gates, and gave you bit of a buzz as your adrenaline started pumping.

The aim of all the groups was, of course, to beat the rep's time and so whenever I skied past it on a free ski day, I made sure I had a sneaky practice. I was only beaten once – by a ten year old girl who must have been some regional champion back home. Her parents were bursting with pride as her time flashed up at the bottom of the run showing 0.8 seconds faster than mine. Everyone thought it highly amusing. I handled the defeat graciously, even when she offered me a consoling, "Don't worry – I'm sure you will get better," knowing full well that I wouldn't. That made me feel really great.

What also made me feel great was seeing the mid-season sale sign in the window of Hanssons ski shop. It was finally time to upgrade from the Millets specials to a brand new pair of Rockports. As I had been paid some commission recently, and we got a "staff" discount of 40% from the already reduced 20%, I decided to buy some new ski boots too. Amazingly, after a full fitting session, I was offered the chance to ski in them for an afternoon, which is usually impossible. I was splashing out a lot of cash but I figured both pairs of boots should last for many years to come.

The mid-season pirate party came and went in a blur caused not by a snow storm but by alcohol. I vaguely remember us all assembling in our teams, sporting eye patches, stripy tops, bandanas pulled over our heads and, in the case of John and me, black boot polish applied to our faces as beards. Some of the staff had really gone to town on their costumes fashioning swords and hand hooks from bits of wood. You could tell who worked in the kitchens from the amount of silver foil they had used in their costume.

Each team was given a wicker basket that had to be filled with various items that could be found around the resort or bought in a shop, such as chocolate biscuits, bottles of wine, flags, salt and pepper pots – everything a jolly pirate needed on board ship. We had to call in at certain 'sea ports' (bars) for a drink before proceeding to the next destination. I recall our team coming out of one 'sea port' half way down a slope and being harangued by a lift company worker for stealing a blue marker pole. As we ran off, our boots proved to be hopeless for a quick getaway in the deep snow at the side of the piste. It wasn't easy to hide a seven foot plastic pole either.

The final 'port' was a wonderful restaurant in a large old log cabin on the edge of a slope, which had been hired out exclusively for us pirates. The ancient timber beams that made up the walls and the huge timber uprights gave the impression we were truly on board a ship. All the restaurant staff had got into the spirit of things and had dressed up as well; one barmaid even had a parrot on her shoulder. In spite of the food and copious amounts of wine and beer consumed, I was disappointed not to hear one pirate utter any "popalopalop" words. No one was made to walk the plank either, although when the music started later on, a couple of girls decided to strip down to their bras and dance on the tables in true *Swedish* pirate fashion.

At midnight, we tumbled out into the darkness like a ragged bunch of sea going ne'er-do-wells being kicked out of a dockside pub. The biting cold air had quite a sobering effect on some of us who suddenly remembered we had to get back to the village somehow. It took a moment to realise that the large snowplough about twenty feet from us, with its lights on and engine running, had an open flat-bed trailer hooked up behind it.

The mob surged forward like it was trying to reach the open door of a tube train in rush hour and half of us fell about in the snow, tripped up by others, their swords, ourselves, or our long beards and a slalom pole that someone still carried. I was in a group that missed the trailer and returned defeated to the shelter of the porch of the restaurant to wait the return of the snowplough.

John spotted a lone snowmobile tucked up around the side of the building and we sneaked off to check if the keys were still in the ignition. Our luck was in and he started it up and began to move off before being flagged down by Annelie and Mariha waving beer bottles at us. Since they also lived in the Sporthotellet, we slowed to collect them and then all four of us, very tightly packed in, lurched off in the direction the snowplough had headed. I am not sure if John had a plan as to where exactly we were going but it was an inspired move and he drove off in a very determined way. By that stage, I didn't really care, just pleased not to be stood out in the cold any longer than I had to. Being sandwiched as boy, girl, boy, girl, I was quite contented to sit tight in my drunkenness and go with the flow.

We hooned around a corner and nearly collided with the snowplough that was coming back up the road with its empty trailer but, after another two hundred metres or so, we came to a stop when we reached the main road.

That quick blast in the freezing air must have sobered us up some more. It would have been madness to carry on into the village, four up, and besides, we figured if we left the snowmobile here the owner, who presumably worked in the restaurant, would be able to find it there in the morning. On the other side of the road, a pathway wound its way down through a collection of small houses to another road that would take us back to our side of the village, so we stumbled along it and were back in the warmth of our rooms in about fifteen minutes.

All mid-season parties were underway now, with the different hotels and associated organisations that contributed to the resort running smoothly. It was like the run up to Christmas back home, where you only just recovered from one party / hangover before another one kicked off. But here Christmas was only the beginning of the marathon. It was gratifying to receive a fax message from our leader, Dapper Bob, who had not forgotten us up here in the northern extremes of our employer's empire. He sent us a message of thanks and encouragement that, for some reason, when I read it all I could hear in my head was the voice of Her Majesty as she gave her Christmas message:

Now that we have more or less reached the halfway stage of the season, I would like to take this opportunity to say a big thank you for your hard work to date. The Scandinavian programme is running like a well-oiled Swiss watch and all credit is due to you for your input and dedication to the job. Our relations with the hoteliers and suppliers are very good and credit in no small measure is due to you for this. Our percentage of QC complaints is probably the lowest in the entire programme. This not only bears testimony to the quality of the product but also to your skills as mediators, diplomats, agony aunts, marriage guidance counsellors and the like.

Then he proceeded to ask us to think about how things could be improved for the following season and if we had any suggestions. It was good to know that our company was willing to listen to the ones with the experience on the ground and happy to listen to any ideas we had. We would do it for Bob, as he knew how to get the best out of us. He was a good man-manager and I liked and respected him. The same could not be said of John who, to be fair, had no experience of man-management. I had one suggestion to make to Bob for the training week that all the reps that were to become Senior Reps in charge of other reps should go on a man-management course.

Things were getting more strained as he lectured me about stuff, often in a very patronising way. I don't think he meant to be like that, and he probably wasn't aware of how he came across, but it was becoming very irritating. It culminated when, one afternoon, I was walking through the village centre, not on duty I hasten to add, wearing my plain dark blue ski jacket. I heard a shrill whistle and turned my head to see John looking at me with his thumb and forefinger shoved into his mouth. His other fingers were signalling for me to walk over to him. It was still below freezing but I could feel my blood beginning to boil.

I looked around to double-check he wasn't whistling at anyone else. He wasn't. I took a deep breath and strode purposefully over to where he stood. He looked cross.

"Andrew!" he said abruptly and before he continued I interrupted him with

"I'm not a bloody sheep dog!"

"Andrew. Why are you wearing that?" He stared at my jacket.

"Erm... It's cold?" I felt like a naughty school boy being questioned by a teacher. "Yes, but why aren't you wearing your company jacket? You are still representing the company twenty four hours a day."

I looked at him incredulously. "I'm not working at the moment. And when I meet the guests later on tonight I shall be wearing the company kit."

"Well, you should be wearing it all the time," and with that he spun around and waltzed off.

I shook my head and under my breath uttered some expletives. What I didn't want was for him to be bad mouthing me to the management and for me to be sent home. There was far too much fun still to be had. I suppose he was right. I knew he was right, sort of. I was reverting to childhood. However, what incensed me the very next day at about the same place at the same time was John mincing his way across the square wearing tan coloured trousers and his cowboy hat. Under his armpit was wedged his brown leather satchel, not his company rucksack. I couldn't whistle like he could or I would have given him the same treatment, and he was too far away for me to say anything without shouting. And besides, I was speechless. I hopped on the next bus to Duved, swore at Toni Braxton, and joined my Ski Skandinavia chums for a pizza and beers. Whilst watching *Friends*, we planned how I would bring up the subject of dress code again. A phone call from our office to Dapper Bob in Austria enabled me to express my concerns about dress code standards and management issues.

I had the fortune of a slight lie in on my birthday, as John had offered to do the early transfer. His attitude had changed after a bit of an ear bashing from Bob. In my waking moments, I had heard the thump, thump, thump of rotor blades approaching and came to with the sudden realisation, much to my relief, I wasn't actually in Vietnam.

I lifted myself up out of the duvet enough to reach a corner of the curtain, pulling it back to reveal a triangle of window. A helicopter was descending out of the grey sky and as it landed it whipped up a great cloud of snow. Two men rushed out to it, hunched over. They had a quick word with the pilot before grabbing several bags from the rear passenger area. *How nice of everyone at home to remember*, I thought, wistfully. To my surprise, when I opened my door there were a few cards and a couple of presents piled up in the corridor, even a big bar of Swedish *Maribou* chocolate from John. That had made me feel a little uncomfortable. *We just needed to clear the air*, I thought, *maybe now we could just move on from our moment?* It's never easy working with just one other person, in spite of all the other people around.

I had saved a piece of my mother's Christmas cake for this day and decided to have it now whilst I opened my cards. Some were from England and John must have been gathering them up for me. John had got about twenty people to sign another card, which was kind of him. Even the hotel manager had signed it, I saw. The card depicted three frogs getting smashed on beer and read: "*Det är din födelsedag och skummet yr…*" (It is your birthday and foam dizzy…). Then inside there was a picture of one frog with his head over a toilet bowl and the words: "*Men ta't lugnt så du inte…*" (but helping ourselves, calmly said you cannot…). It loses something in translation.

The day continued with ski escorting at 10.30am, and coffees and cake bought for me by some guests; a coffee and another cake with Jenny from ski school at midday; lunch at the Hotel Åregården, where my name had been added to the weekly newssheet in the birthday announcements, along with a Micke, Martin, Ronny, Åsa, Camilla and a Bengt. They all had their jobs after their names, mine had "Our Englishman", which was touching.

I had snowmobile duties at 3pm so had to make the first pick up at 2.45pm. The guests were staying at the Hotel Åregården, which was the most expensive hotel in resort right on the village square. We had one very posh family staying this week; Mr & Mrs J of Godalming and their offspring. They were all charming but hopelessly disorganised and were late for almost everything. I was sat on the front passenger seat of Stefan's luxury taxi minibus – the one with blacked out windows for extra privacy – thinking about the bigger than normal profit we were going to make on this taxi ride, wondering where Mr J had got to. The rest of his family were, at long last, assembled and sat in the back of the minibus, helping themselves to the luxury water bottles and luxury 'complimentary' fruit.

Mrs J was starting to flap about the tardiness of her husband. "Oh, I just don't know *where* he could have got to? He is a silly man." Time was ticking on and, although we didn't have far to go to Mats' *Skotersafari* base, there would be others waiting when we got there. The engine hummed gently and Stefan busied himself with his newspaper crossword, pausing every so often to watch a pretty girl walk by, which was very often. I don't think he completed any clues.

"Stefan, you must come by the office soon as we need to pay you. It's been weeks since we did," I said.

"It's OK. I trust you guys," he replied and then read another clue.

"Yes, but we have a lot of kronors for you and we need to balance our books." He had such a laidback attitude to the financial side of his business, although he was a hundred percent reliable as a driver.

There was a sudden movement from behind as Mrs J lurched for the sliding door handle and leaped out and began calling out to her husband.

"Oh, do hurry, darling! Come on, we've all been waiting an absolute age!"

I looked into the huge door mirror just outside my side window and saw Mr J heading across the square with a plastic bag full of something he had just bought, waving at his wife every three or four paces. He was literally trotting across the snow in such a dainty way, almost hopping from foot to foot, that it reminded me of the wild reindeer I had seen at the side of the pistes. It was at that point I posed to myself an important question: 'Do reindeer run like posh people or do posh people run like reindeer?' There was a remarkable similarity. I have since noticed the very same trot amongst certain types of holidaymakers in both Salcombe and Rock.

We were ten minutes late but their gushing apologies to everyone already there prevented any grumpiness and I sensed the rest of the group were all a little amused having their very own Margo Leadbetter join them.

Later in the day, I had a 5pm pick up to attend for a trip out to the frozen waterfall. Although, after I had done the collection in Duved, checked off all the numbers and given them a brief chat in the stationary bus, I had to grab a bus back to the village to get changed for the evening's entertainment: The Hansons' ski hire shop mid-season party.

We had been instructed to assemble at the bottom of the Olympia Lift at 6.30pm in full ski gear; skis and boots too. Considering that out of the handful of staff that worked in the ski hire shop three of them were ex-Olympic skiers and the others merely skied like gods, it was a little daunting. Still – nothing that a few beers wouldn't put right. We all rode the lift up to the Café Olympia, which had been hired out by Örjan for our exclusive use.

Örjan had arrived earlier to greet us all with a beer or wine as we entered the big room. Several tables had been pushed together in the centre of the restaurant, covered with red and white gingham tablecloths, and wooden chairs placed around all four sides of what had become one large table. It was odd to be up there at night time with no one else around, just a few waiting staff. During the day, it was bustling with life and the stomping of heavy ski boots across the floor. The drink flowed and there was a very convivial atmosphere. Bearing in mind it was their staff party, I was very touched that we had been invited along as other reps from Denmark or Norway must provide them with far more business and hadn't been invited.

After just a short while, there seemed to be a lot of drink already consumed and the conversation level had got noticeably louder as everyone began to let their hair down. We were served a fine dinner of meaty soup with warm crusty bread then a chilli con carne and rice with huge bowls of salad. It was simple food but very tasty and a good base to soak up some of the alcohol.

Before dessert was brought out, Örjan got up to say a few words of thanks to his team. As he was wrapping up, he announced that, "…not only is this day a special occasion for the team, it is also Andrew's birthday! And in Sweden, on such a special occasion, we need to drink champagne!"

That got a cheer and a round of *Happy Birthday*, some singing in English, some in Swedish. The restaurant staff produced champagne flutes for all fifteen of us and several bottles of champagne, which was downed amidst clinking of glasses being toasted and birthday kisses for the birthday boy, who by this time was feeling quite merry.

By about 11.30pm, the staff had finished discreetly stacking up chairs and tidying up around us and the lights above the bar area were switched off. They loitered around the kitchen doorway, politely waiting. We took that as a sign to bring the party to an end and gathered up our jackets, gloves and hats. I had totally forgotten that we were half way up a mountain and it dawned on me with some horror that we were going to have to ski down.

As soon as I passed through the entrance door, the sharp freezing night air assisted in shaking me to my senses. Only then did I realise how much we all must have drunk. Disconcertingly, no one else appeared to be the least bit wobbly on their feet. Only moments before they were all holding onto each other, laughing and singing and generally back slapping each other massively.

Hmmmmnnnnn... I thought to myself as I struggled to find my skis, let alone attach my boots to my bindings. It took several attempts to click the heels in without a boot slipping off the edge of the ski. *And now I am going to have to ski down with this lot in the dark.* I figured if I were to die that night then it would at least be a nice round number of completed years. And, with that cheery thought, I shoved off with my poles and followed three of them along for about twenty metres, stopping just short of what was the start of a black mogul field.

Where were all the others? I wondered. The three of them were pumping themselves up for the attack on the run and seemed surprised that I had followed them. I had presumed all the others had gone ahead of them. I happened to glance up at the night sky, as it was a full moon and all the tops of the mountains were beautifully picked out by the moon light. I scanned around whilst they continued to rev themselves up and suddenly noticed the rest of the group all lined up in the middle of a freshly bashed piste a little lower down.

They had gathered in a line for a photo shoot and some of them were waving poles or gloved hands in my direction. I had come perilously close to chucking myself over the edge and into the abyss and the horror of what I was about to do immediately snapped me to my senses. I performed a neat hundred and eighty degrees jump turn and high tailed it out of there down to where the others were waiting, swishing my skis roughly through some low lying bushes as I crossed a couple of banks in my haste to reach the safety and sanity of the main group on the groomed piste.

"We wondered why you were up there… They are the crazy ones," they chirped when I was safely among them.

We only had two former Olympic skiers in our midst – Örjan and Ellen, who was in the US ski team (not to mention being a two-time freestyle World Champion) – plus a few national squad skiers. After a few poses for photos in a line under the moonlight, and us trying to stay balanced on the edges of our skis without falling over and causing a domino collapse (or was it just me?), Örjan moved out in front of the line as if he was about to address his troops.

He raised his ski poles above his head, clicked them together two times, let out a whoop and then hopped through ninety degrees to face down the slope and begin his purposeful attack of the manicured Manchester or *mahnshayssterr* slope, as they pronounced it in Swedish. It was the corduroy effect: the piste bashers had left the snow like corduroy and, as we all know, or at least all the Swedes told me, Manchester is famous for its corduroys. It's sometimes surprising how much you learn about your own country from foreigners.

Most of us who have done quite a bit of skiing like to think we are pretty competent and this slope was a nice wide red with sweeping turns. On a regular day with good visibility most reasonable skiers would probably look to complete it, top to bottom, in fifteen or sixteen turns given a clear run with no slower skiers getting in the way and with a longish straight 'schussy' bit half way down. Örjan headed off at quite a pace, steady as a rock and perfectly balanced, carving big arcs across the corduroy snow. He looked like he was on rails and reached the bottom in just four turns. He was in a different league and I am sure he had been drinking just as much as anyone else. It was quite something to witness, even though it was just a red slope, but I'm sure he would have done the same on a black.

Then the rest of us headed down; I felt so elated skiing in this group, at night time, with the run to ourselves, on my birthday evening. Every now and then I looked down at my skis to see the moonlight reflected back up at me as they turned in unison from edge to edge as I carved my way down. What a unique and memorable birthday it had been.

The next morning, there was a photocopied timetable of Mariella's visit neatly folded inside a crisp white envelope stapled to my door with a note from Ulla reminding me of her imminent arrival and urging me not to forget. I read that she had been lined up to ski with an instructor for three days between 10am and 12pm, and a snowboard lesson had been booked in for a Joseph, whoever he was. She was certainly being given the full tour, with a snow scooter safari, dog sled ride and tobogganing, plus a couple of dinners scheduled in.

John and I had both now been allocated a first meeting slot at the Sunwing Hotel before her evening meal and then another 'date' the following night at another bar. We duly met up with her for a drink and a chat and she was very charming, and lovely and the wonderful gravelly voice was as captivating as expected. All the attention was on her, as there were a couple of people from the tourist office also present.

Her other half, had been somewhat sidelined and seemed at odds with the situation. When asked about skiing, he said he didn't really like it and preferred scuba diving, which was a bit of conversation stopper. He proceeded to tell me he and Mariella go diving in Cornwall and then pretentiously named dropped how they stayed at Andrew Ridgeley's house.

"Who?" I asked mischievously.

"Andrew Ridgeley... from Wham!?"

"No. Don't know him," I lied. He looked at me incredulously and I returned my attention to the ski chat as we had quickly run out of things to say. For all of Ulla's enthusiasm and efforts, we only met up with Mariella twice and sadly she didn't need escorting round the clubs or the slopes.

I was amazed that birthday cards and little presents continued to appear at my door, which was very kind and thoughtful of everyone. One of the girls in the Sporthotellet, Lena, had her young cousin, Anna, stay for a week while she tried to find a job in the resort. They drew me a fabulously useful card with a whole host of new Swedish words for me to learn. Lena told me one evening at a bar that her cousin was known as 'Friendly Anna' and she thought she had a crush on me, which was all very high school-ish. It got more contrived. Lena was working on night duty on Saturday so Friendly Anna would be all alone in her room. Could I take her out for a drink? What would we have in common to talk about? She was more than ten years younger than me!

"Oh, don't be so British! Just go for a drink with her". The Swedes can be coy about some things but very direct about other stuff. Friendly Anna proved to be very direct and gave me a very personalised belated birthday present.

5

MARS

Does Your Mother Know?

February had been a manic month, one way or another, and we had expected March to calm down a little. It felt like we had crested the mid-season hill and we could now almost cruise downhill to the end of the season. For us, though, the season would continue well into April for there were still more Arrival Sheet faxes coming through with yet more guests.

At the beginning of the month, we had a good intake of arrivals, some sixty people spread evenly between the main village accommodation and my hotel in Duved. The numbers were nothing like some of the major resorts in the Alps but they were enough for us to be kept busy with and, now we were into the more expensive months in which to travel, we had more guests that could afford all the excursions. John and I had settled down into a better working relationship after our mid-season wobble. He had certainly backed off a lot after Dapper Bob had given him a talking to. We both had plenty of takers for ski escorting as well as bar and nightclub escorting duties too.

Ski escorting became much more enjoyable now that I had developed a detailed knowledge of the entire resort. My skiing had improved enormously so that I could tackle almost anything, certainly anything that even the most ambitious guest would want to do. It amazed me how, every now and then, we would have a guest come on ski escorting who would be sizing you up and then after only a couple of runs would want to race you down to the next lift. What is the point in trying to race the rep to the next lift? He or she is usually a better, fitter skier, is supposed to be *leading* the group, watching out for the slowest skier of the pack. We were there to guide people around the resort so they could get a better idea of where to ski and which restaurants to go to.

There would also be the ones who would be all talk about how brilliantly they could ski and tell you all the places they had skied across the entire globe. Again, what's the point in telling your rep how well you can ski? Yes, they might be better skiers than the rep but so what? I had one chap who was just itching to get going on a really fast run and was very impatient with the group which, incidentally, included his wife. Time and again, when he had done his little speedy spurt he had to wait for the rest of us at the side of a run, then was champing at the bit as soon as we caught up with him. On that particular day, we were only doing blues and reds but he kept asking if we could do a black.

"No. Sorry, but as I've said, if you want to do reds and blacks that's Thursday's ski escorting," I told him.

"But we're booked to do the husky dogs on Thursday morning and my wife won't do a black with me."

"Can you not do it on your own?" I suggested.

"As you're here now, you can show me the best blacks."

"Sorry, but not when this group has booked to do blues and reds."

"What time are we finishing?"

"About midday."

"Can't you show me then?" he asked, as if he was testing me.

I had quite bit of work to do back in the office but he had begun to annoy me and I remembered they had just opened the top of the World Cup run. Most of it was an icy red but the top fifty metres or so was a black, dark black, almost Vanta black.

"OK. I know a place we can go," I said, nearly letting out a villainous cackle.

"I was beginning to think you didn't want to do a black."

What an arse, I thought. His final comment was like a red rag to a bull.

When the ski escorting had finished and I exchanged pleasantries with the rest of the group, I turned to Mr M of Brighton trying not to be too curt with him: "Ready? Let's go. We need to be quick as I need to be back in my office in half an hour. I've a lot of work to do." And with that I heaved away on my ski poles and quickly pulled away from him, skate skiing across the flat stretch of snow to the chairlift, pushing forcefully down on my skis with each leg in turn.

The lift attendant recognised me when I got closer and with a brief nod I jumped in front of the short queue and swished into position waiting on the rubber mat. With my ski poles gathered in the left hand, the right hand was held lower down with my open palm facing the approaching edge of the lift seat, ready to brace myself against its impact, before it swept me off my feet and carried me up over the treetops and onwards and upwards to my destination. I was eager to get this over with and didn't feel like engaging in idle chit chat whilst sat on the lift.

I virtually leapt off the lift at the other end, so eager was I to get going. Mr M followed along a few chairs back and, as soon as his skis had touched the snow, I turned around and headed down to the ridge just above the start of the black, edging my ski tips just over the lip. From here, I could make eye contact with the skiers who were taking a break, sat out on the terrace of the nearby restaurant. More importantly, I thought they could easily see us and, once we were in position here, it was obvious what we were about to do and there would be no turning back.

"You're in a hurry," he said when he finally caught up.

"Hm-mm. Well here's your black," I replied enthusiastically. I switched my gaze from looking at him to the steep icy bowl below us and back to him again. He was peering over the edge, his ruddy complexion fast draining of all colour.

"It's steep, isn't it?"

"Yes, it's a black."

"All the way down?" *Was he now searching for an excuse not to do it?*

"No, it goes into a red," I said reassuringly. "It's the World Cup run," I added, nonchalantly.

His face went rigid and he ran his tongue nervously around his lips.

"Are you still up for it?" I challenged him in a polite way, sensing his wavering bravado.

"Yeah, yeah, of course."

"OK, then. After you. I'll watch out for you."

"Are you not doing it as well?" He asked with a hint of panic.

"I'm still on ski escorting duty. I've got to make sure everyone gets down, so I'll be tail end Charlie and.." I almost said *when* "if you fall, I can pick you up."

"Oh, right. Good. Well. Best get on with it then."

"OK."

He still paused and started twitching a little, like a golfer with the yips before an important putt. He couldn't bring himself to go over the edge.

"Your best bet is to go over there to the left, then cut back quickly before the end of the sunny bit. Then you need to swing over that way to the right and loop left around that tree, although it will be hard to turn in the shade as it's still sheet ice."

"What are those hoses for?" he asked, looking disconcertedly at the whole scene before him and finding another reason to put off the moment.

"It's the World Cup run. They spray the surface with water to make it icier"

"Oh."

"I don't think they will have turned them on yet." I had no idea if they had or hadn't, but I just wanted him to get on with it.

I glanced round at the people sat out on the terrace who were eagerly watching us and cruelly said, "C'mon. They're waiting for us." I pointed towards them with one of my ski poles and, with that, he took a deep breath and pushed off with both poles. He immediately went into a sort of tuck position and went off to the right instead of left. Adopting a lopsided snow plough, with the downhill ski taking all his weight, he scuttled remarkably quickly across the icy piste in a crab like fashion and disappeared behind the tree at full speed.

I swooped down to the left before arcing right and then left behind the tree at a much more controlled speed, the turns slowing my speed, but I was still travelling fast after such a short distance. When I rounded the tree, I saw that he was way ahead, still in the tuck position with his poles flaying wildly about on each side like he was trying to wind the car windows down.

He had gone straight down without turning but was now headed towards a big sweeping right hand bend. His left leg must have been under a huge amount of strain as he desperately pressed down on his ski to try to make the right turn, but he ran out of room and ploughed into a steep snow bank before spinning around a few times, sliding further down the mountain and coming to rest in a crumpled heap on his back.

When I reached him I asked if he was alright.

"Yeah," he gasped breathlessly, probably winded.

"I think I must have caught an edge."

No comment was needed. He refused any help up to his feet and we skied on in a knowing silence. He knew he had bitten off more than he could chew. I knew he had been a prat and bitten off more than he could chew. I was also very relieved that I had not taken a tumble but I had just done a Technique Improvement session with an instructor on this very slope only a few days ago.

He wasn't the only one to make a fool of himself on the slopes. There was a Mr and Mrs D from Maidstone who were talking up their skiing in the welcome meeting and saying how they had skied most of the Alps. They were actually quite a sweet couple and, rather oddly, had matching all-in-one ski suits and bobble hats. He worked for the local council in the highways department and collected beer mats as his main hobby, he told me, and she spent her time baking cakes. They always holidayed in Bournemouth at the same B&B and spent their money on a ski trip once a year. On the morning of their first ski escorting day, they hustled their way forward so they could sit next to me on the first chairlift ride up, and were still banging on about where they had been skiing when it was time to lift the safety bar and get ready to ski off the seat.

I am not quite sure how it happened but Mr D fell flat on his face the moment his skis made contact with the ground, swiftly followed by Mrs D who executed a sharp ninety degrees right turn, skiing straight into the lift hut, hitting it with a solid sounding thud. She then got in a flap because she couldn't extricate herself from her situation. She was still stood in her skis facing down a two metre slope towards the hut, her ski tips wedged into the side wall. Everyone who had seen it happen and those still coming off the chairlift could see her right angled ski tracks and started to laugh. When the lift staff had picked themselves off the snow and tried to help her out of her predicament, they were still giggling. Mr D just stood to one side busying himself with brushing the snow of his bobble hat as if nothing had happened.

Oh, the Brits abroad! I lost count of the number of times some skiers would have one trouser leg covering a ski boot and the other leg hitched half way up resting on top of the boot. They would ski along quite oblivious to their faux pas, like a car driver with the end of a coat stuck in the door.

Some guests would want to snowplough all the way, which was unfair on the rest of the group. We had been told that we had the authority to tell them, in the nicest possible way, that it was probably best for everyone that they left the group. That was sometimes a difficult discussion, but most of the time it was accepted.

One individual insisted that he had "*paid good money*" to come on a skiing holiday and he was "*bloody well going to do the ski escorting*". Well, the big news for him was: "...other people had also *paid good money* for their holiday and having someone who persisted in snowploughing down every slope wasn't going to help them get the most out of their ski escorting day, was it?" The suggestion that he might like to consider some ski lesson was met with a stony stare. At times, I could so easily have slipped into a full Basil Fawlty rant.

People did do some bizarre things, such as come out skiing without any gloves when it was clearly very cold just walking along the street. Another guest kept calling the currency Swedish pounds, for some reason, which I think he thought was very funny. It wasn't funny the first time we heard it and certainly wasn't the tenth time. The same individual sat on the lift mumbling "hurdy, gurdy, gurdy" whenever he heard anyone speak Swedish. One man who had been skiing OK with us for about an hour, skied up to me at a restaurant stop and said he had to stop immediately because his feet were absolutely killing him.

I looked down at his boots to see what the problem might be and to my amazement saw that the buckles were facing inwards. He had foolishly managed to put his boots on the wrong feet!

I was momentarily lost for words. We helped him out of his boots and left the poor chap to massage some life back into his misshapen feet for half an hour before collecting him for the final run back into the village. He was still hobbling along later in the evening when I called into his hotel to take bookings for some excursions.

I became aware of Ronan Keating singing *Words* about half way through the song and the sound continued to drag me out of a very deep sleep. I lay there motionless, wondering where I was for a moment or two, with my eyes still closed. I wanted to wake up back in London and have a normal day. I wanted to walk down to the local Waitrose, do some shopping, meet up with some friends for lunch in one of the riverside pubs. Something nagged at me and told me that wasn't going to happen. *Where was I?* The Swedish Band, E Type's song, *Calling Your Name*, which Radio Rix played next, confirmed I was still here. Today I didn't want to put on salopettes and spend the day with my eyes squinting at the glare from the snow on the pavements, the roads, the trees, the cars, the roof tops and hedges. Strangely, I wanted to smell the traffic. I needed to see some green grass on the ground and smell the first hint of Spring.

I crawled out of bed and, crouched over, I hobbled to the window, as if that would stop the rest of my body waking up. Peeling back a tiny corner of the bottom of the curtain, I looked out on the familiar scene I had now seen for many months.

The same few buildings stood there, impervious to anything the weather threw at them. The gentle slope of the land that dropped down to the frozen lake merged into a large expanse of flat whiteness. On the far side the wooded hills looked back at me, motionless and emotionless, shrouded in a low misty cloud, turning their leaves dark grey from their natural green. I was too far away to see any actual movement of leaves or branches.

It wasn't that I was homesick – I was having a great time and enjoying the experience. I was probably just tired and weary of the same routine. I needed to pull myself together. It wasn't like I was going to work in a factory every day, doing the same thing day in day out. I was being paid to go skiing, for God's sake and, apart from the work entries in my day to day diary, noting arrivals or locations I had to be at a certain time for guests, there were also notes like *"snowboarding with Kai"* and the whole afternoon had been struck out. I also had plenty of *"coffee with Jenny, skiing with Annelie, drinks with Anna"*, and even a couple of highlighted *"fika med Madeleine"*'s, so there were lots of opportunities for fun and pleasure. I checked the temperature gauge which now read minus ten degrees; positively balmy. Jamiroquai were now playing *Virtual Insanity* on my clock radio, which perked me up, and I got myself ready for another day in paradise. It was just a momentary glitch in the fun, fun, fun I was having and I convinced myself that many reps and other ski workers must have the same feeling now and again at some stage during their seasons. It stuck with me for most of the morning, though, but by the time I had got geared up for the transfer later the day, I was almost back to normal.

As our transfer coach threaded its way through the streets of Östersund on the way to the airport, I came to the realisation that I had never spent so much time just in one place. Normal lives were being led down here in the town centre whilst all us ski resort workers were living and working in a sort of

Disneyland existence, helping the visitors escape from their normal lives. I had no idea what was going on in the news back home, actually I didn't care, and that felt good. I made a mental note to check when the trip to McDonalds was happening as it now seemed like an important thing to do, for mental health reasons, bizarrely.

I think I appreciated why so many others were looking forward to it. They too were keen to have a reason to get out of the village and do something normal. See – I was having a normal reaction after all. I was normal. In my head, I celebrated normality.

By the time I had jumped down from the coach and taken up my usual position in the arrivals hall, I had flicked the switch back to cheerful ski rep. The new arrivals were the usual mix of shapes, sizes and personalities, with the exception of three people. Two of them were a couple and they were both wearing bright pink and blue ski jackets. Both had matching earrings and fake tans. Both sported the George Michael three day growth look, trimmed to perfection. Both were as lively and outrageous as each other and were entertainment for the whole coach. They looked like they had come on a massive shopping trip with all the extra bags they had somehow managed to bring through customs. I heard one of them say to a woman in the next seat, "Honey, we're so gay we can't even ski straight," which brought a chuckle to their immediate neighbours.

"I can see you two are going to be handful," I commented with a smile to the one in the aisle seat and immediately wished I hadn't.

"Ooh, honey," he said to his friend. "I think our rep has taken a shine to me already!"

I moved on further up the coach to check numbers and deal with any immediate concerns and questions. I could still hear them chattering away all the way at the back of the coach and, as I returned to the front, counting up the occupied seats, Neil, in the aisle seat called out to me, "Let me know when you get to sixty nine!"

Chris, his partner, was now shaking his head. It was all good banter but already I thought it might wear a little thin if he was going to keep it up all week on every excursion.

Right at the front of the coach sat a Mr & Mrs P from Essex and their daughter Laura. When we had scanned through the arrivals list, we had presumed Miss L was aged about five or so. Correction: add twenty years, squeeze on some tight denim jeans, pull on a pair of pair of thigh length black leather boots, a lovely smile and thick wavy black hair and almond eyes and… "Hellooo," I gushed, all too Leslie Philips like.

Maybe it was a reaction to the antics of Neil and Chris, but I forgot all about her parents sat on the other side of the aisle for some time as I fumbled around with the arrivals list and checking to see what she had pre-ordered, somewhat unnecessarily.

"So, I see you have ordered boobs and skis..?" Damn Neil and his innuendos. I don't think she heard my blunder and I rustled the papers some more. She smiled sweetly.

"Yes and I want to do everything."

"What?" It was turning into a Two Ronnies sketch.

"I really want to do every excursion. Although I am not sure my *parents*…" she pointed to them across the aisle "…will do." I snapped out of it, realising I had completely ignored her parents who were sitting patiently waiting for me to include them in the conversation, as well as the passenger count up. I had no idea where I had got to with that and abandoned it, seeing as there were no other tourists wandering around the car park looking lost. Turning the charm on for Mr & Mrs P, I made a point of ticking them off the list and wished them a good holiday.

I chucked my file down onto my seat next to my rucksack and reached for the microphone that was lying flat on the shelf below the huge front windscreen. It was time to get a grip and do my job properly. The ABBA CD was inserted and we were on our way to Disneyland on snow. I was feeling perky again. Neil and Chris, of course, loved all the ABBA songs and sang along in their seats, making all sorts of hand movements.

I happened to be in their proximity on the coach selling excursions and doing money exchanges when *Gimme! Gimme! Gimme! (A Man after Midnight)* started playing. They couldn't stop themselves jumping out of their seats and dancing in the aisles and I had a job getting them back down again. Fortunately, all the guests close by found them very amusing. Certainly it made the transfer time seem very short.

Apart from that first evening, I must have spent more time that week with Laura than her own parents. She came to the welcome speech with her parents and booked herself onto every trip and event she could do. She told me she was having a drink in the bar, if I cared to join her when I had finished. She told me her parents weren't skiers so she would be coming on both ski escorting days and asked if I would be able to take her skiing on any other days, if I wasn't working. She offered to pay, which I declined, settling for payment in beers which suited her.

"So that means I am going to be seeing you in the evenings as well, if I am paying you in beer?" she said in a flirty manner.

"Yes, I suppose it does." And so the week progressed with a rendez-vous with Laura every evening in the Åregården Hotel bar and a couple of drinks before heading out to a different club every night and her sneaking back to her hotel room in the early hours of the morning so she could join her parents for breakfast.

By the third night, Ronny, the security guy stopped me as I entered the hotel lobby: "She's here again. Your beers are on the bar already". Word quickly spread amongst the hotel staff about my 'special guest'. Some kind soul even left a six pack of Red Bull outside my door for me. I think it was Kai, my Finnish snowboard dude pal, who, working nights on reception, I had really got to know well that week sitting in the lobby bar with Laura. She was good company, of course, but I couldn't help thinking it was a little ironic; all these Swedish girls and I'm spending time with an Essex girl.

I didn't see much of her parents at all but, on the return transfer, her mother even tipped me for looking after her daughter.

She and her parents did, however, come on the trip to the frozen waterfall at Tännforsen. So did Neil and Chris, who were both unusually quiet on the outgoing coach journey. That all changed when they clapped eyes on the stuffed bear in the entrance way. During one of the ski escorting mornings in the week, I had chatted to them both and learned that they shared an apartment in Soho. They were avid collectors of all things unusual but had no real theme to their collection. Anything goes, they said, as long as it's quirky or outrageous.

Neil was the first to spot the bear and grabbed Neil by the arm stopping him in his tracks.

"Oh... My God!" he exclaimed. Neil looked up and his eyes widened like a small child in a sweet shop seeing an extra large Toblerone for the first time.

"OMG... indeeeed!" he replied. I am sure the bear would have said the same in response if he could have read their minds. They were captivated. I was certain the bear's hitherto wild-eyed look changed in that instance to one of mild fear and apprehension.

"Andrew – we love him!" confirmed Chris.

I hoped they weren't thinking what I thought they were thinking.

"He would be fabulous in our hallway." They were.

"I'm sure he would but he's not for sale."

"Everything's negotiable, honey." *Not if you keep calling me honey,* I thought.

"Will you ask the owner if he would sell?"

"This bear has been here for years and, as far as I know, Bertil's grandfather shot it himself."

"Maybe, but you must ask for us. Pleeeease," begged Neil.

"OK, I'll have a quiet word with Bertil when we've done the walk to the waterfall and we're back here having the waffles," I promised.

Neil rubbed one of the bear's thighs before saying, "See you later, big boy."

They gave the waterfall a cursory inspection before hurrying back up through the trees to be reunited with their new best friend. When all the other guests had assembled and were tucking into their waffles, I sidled over to Bertil wondering how I was going to make myself understood with the man whose English vocabulary was limited to talk of waterfalls and waffles.

"*Hej*, Bertil," I began. "The bear... err the err... *björnen*," and I pointed in its general direction.

"Arh," he replied in that abrupt, slightly irksome, birdlike squawk some Swedes use to say "yes" in acknowledgment of something.

So far so good, I thought. *At least we're on the same subject.*

"Is it yours?" I asked, pointing to Bertil's stomach.

He glanced down at his stomach and then back up at me with a quizzical look.

"Did you shoot it?" I asked, making a pulling the trigger motion with my right hand whilst holding the stock of a rifle with my left.

"Arh," he squawked again. "*Min far sköt det i sextiosju.*"

I caught the father bit and sixty something and deduced that his father had shot it in nineteen sixty something, possibly sixty seven."

Buoyed up by my understanding him so far, I ventured more

questioning in Swedish, thinking if I threw a few words together he would get the gist of what I was trying to ask.

"*Mina gäster vill köpa det,*" – meaning *my guests want to buy it.*

In Swedish, he responded with something along the lines of "no, you have already paid", adding the words "*varje månad* (each month)". He must have been thinking I was offering to pay for all the waffles and the tour when we paid him each month according to how many people we had booked in with him.

Again he looked at me with a puzzled expression and I started to think I should just tell them the answer was no.

"*Nej, björnen* (no, the bear)," I repeated. He looked at his stomach again.

Neil and Chris now came over to me. *One more try,* I thought. Again, in my basic Swedish: "Two guests; him and him, want to buy the bear."

Bertil regarded their smiling, expectant faces then looked back at me.

"Naaaay (a long "Noooo...")." He shook his headed emphatically and then proceeded to tell us the history of the bear, I think.

Chris suggested I offer him some money.

"How much?"

"Ten thousand kronor?" That was about one thousand pounds.

"I'll try but think he's pretty adamant about it."

When Bertil had finished waxing lyrical about his stuffed bear, I suggested the offer to him. He paused for a brief second and then said again, "Naaaay" and turned away.

At the risk of antagonising him and damaging a good business relationship we had with him, I said to the guys: "I think we should back off and leave him be."

"We'd offer more," said Neil.

"OK. Well, leave it with me and I will speak to him another time…"

On the day before they were due to leave the resort, they asked if I had seen Bertil to talk about the bear. I hadn't and they looked as crestfallen, as if I was telling a pair of children that Father Christmas wasn't coming this year.

"You must try him again for us. We must have him back home – he's so divine".

"Oh, he's adorable!" chirped Neil, clapping his hands in front of his chest. Divine or adorable are not the two words I would have used to describe the bear and, like a lot of things that look good on your holiday, they look very different back home.

"I'll try again," I said, a bit half heartedly.

"Oh, you must. For us…!"

"OK," I replied, trying to sound a bit more positive and hoping that they would forget about it once they had settled in back home in Soho.

Fat chance of that. On the day they arrived home, they had faxed a note through saying what a wonderful time they had had, which was nice of them, and asked how "negotiations were going with the bear?"

In spite of the bear's apparent consternation, I believe I might have had more success negotiating directly *with the bear*. The fact was that I hadn't seen Bertil since and therefore had not any chance to speak to him. I didn't respond to the fax but was sat in the office one Monday morning nursing a hangover from the previous night out.

Sundays were the big nights in the village, as far as all the staff were concerned, and from our office it was only a short walk through the hotel building, along the corridor, up one staircase, across the walkway, past the 'sad single supplement' rooms, and down a secret narrow staircase, which lead to the entrance to the nightclub.

You could begin to hear the thump, thump, thump of the music as you crossed the walkway and we were constantly surprised that none of the sad single supplement roomers ever complained. It actually led to a point that intersected the main public queue to the nightclub entrance, but usually there was a friendly bouncer on the door who could let us in when he so chose.

All the nightclub bouncers had official licences to 'bounce' and wore, on their jackets or the chest of their shirts, a rather impressive *Ordnings Vakt* metal badge, gold in colour on a black leather fob with the three Swedish crowns symbol, essentially like a police badge. Unlike a lot of UK bouncers, aka 'aggressive thugs sporting for a fight', these guys were first and foremost diplomats, but you wouldn't want to cross them as they knew how to handle themselves. I had seen them on the doors of nightclubs in Stockholm, some even sporting white flower buds next to the badges, which seemed to emphasise they were there to keep the peace but also to lay down the law. They did actually have powers of arrest.

Surrounded by a bottle of water, a Coke and a mug of coffee, I was slowly beginning to function again when the office telephone rang. It was Neil.

"Hiiiiiiiiiyyyaa!" he wailed. I knew exactly who it was after the first part of that "Hi".

"It's your favourite gay! How are yooooou?"

I just about got the chance to say "hungover" but he was off again.

"We've decided to make it worth your while buying the bear for us"

"Oh yes?"

"How does five hundred quid sound to you?"

"Sounds good but…"

"We would want you to negotiate the deal and arrange to get him back here."

It hadn't occurred to me that if I was able to agree the price we would then need to remove the bear and transport him to the airport.

"How are we going to do that?"

"Easy, honey. We've spoken to people who know." *What sort of people do they associate with that know how to import stuffed bears into the country,* I wondered? I didn't dare ask.

"Alright, I'll see what I can do. How much do you want to pay for it? What's your maximum?"

He proceeded to explain that all I had to do was agree the price and get the thing to the airport. He had made some calls and had already put the wheels in motion for the authorities at Östersund airport to expect a large stuffed bear to arrive. We just had to secure the deal, get it wrapped, tagged with their London address and transport it to the airport. I began to wonder how we might fit it onto one of the transfers. Or, failing that, The Mean Machine or one of Stefan's Taxis. Maybe Father Christmas might lend me his sleigh? I was going to need some help.

Fernando

I had discovered that March was the best month in which to see the Northern Lights, or *norrsken* as they called it. More often they called it: the Northern Lights, being so keen to use the English language. It was a great snippet of *intel* to impart to the guests on the arrival transfer. It got them all excited and immediately they started looking out of the coach windows. Some of them even strained their eyes skyward during a day time transfer in hope of seeing something.

The transfers were usually co-ordinated, so that we took one coach load back to the airport and returned with a new set of guests. We were now busy enough to have transfers on Sundays and Thursdays, although there was the odd occasion where we could end up stranded at the airport if there wasn't anyone coming in on that day. The coach driver would not want to turn around and drive an empty coach back into the resort, certainly not without a lengthy *fika* with his friends. This meant that we would either have to wait around for ages or hope that one of the town's taxis was doing a private transfer with no return journey pick up. We never knew for sure on the way out of the resort what the situation was going to be on the turn around and, although the drivers knew they weren't doing a pick up for our company, they never asked if we had arranged to get back.

One particular Thursday morning, I had said goodbye to another set of happy tourists and returned to the coach only to find that it was parked up and locked in line with some others on the edge of the car park. There was no sign of the driver. Usually, if they had gone in to the terminal building, they would leave it unlocked. I walked back into the terminal building and found my driver, Jesper, with his chums, all wearing leather jackets or faded ski jackets, in a heated discussion about some ice hockey

223

game. The table they were gathered around was strewn with newspapers, paper cups full of dark coffee, chocolate bars and wrappers, and plates of bread and *bräckkorv* (smoked pork sausage). It looked like they were all set for the morning.

I got his attention and asked him politely what time we were going back, pointing back over my shoulder towards the coach.

"*Klockan... halv tre,*" he replied in a friendly way, looking at his wristwatch, by which he meant, two thirty, even though literally he said half three. It was that quirky Swedish thing.

"Oh," I said and he returned to his pork sausages and thinly sliced, dense dark bread. It wasn't his fault as he was merely carrying out instructions to drive to the airport. It was nine in the morning and I could do with getting out of here and back to the resort. It must have been a big game because as I walked from the table some more drivers pulled up chairs to join them. I walked back outside to look around for inspiration.

Apart from a few bright yellow Audi estates that were waiting for the lucrative private transfers, there were no other coaches with their engines running.

"Mmmmmmmmm," was all I could muster; I was stuck. I walked back into the building again with a view to asking Jesper if he knew whether another coach might be coming from Åre any time soon – one that I could hop on for the return journey – but he was deeply engrossed in the hockey debate. I couldn't think of enough Swedish words to make any meaningful sentence, and his English wasn't good enough either.

I stopped midway across the concourse and, after a couple of seconds, someone grabbed hold of my right shoulder from behind and wrapped a black leather clad left arm around my head so the crook of their elbow covered my eyes.

"Guess who?" they asked playfully.

"I'm hoping that's Stefan?!"

"No... it's your prime minister!"

Thank God it was actually Stefan and not John Major. I didn't doubt for one second that it really was, by the way. He released his grip and spun me around.

"Stefan!" I almost hugged him. "Am I pleased to see you!"

"So, are you not always pleased to see me?"

"Of course, but especially today, this morning, because I could really use a lift back if you are going back now? Or... in the next hour?"

"Well, you're in luck, my friend. I have a VIP pick up but, for sure, I think you can join them."

"If they won't mind, that would be great, and I have a strange request to ask you about a *special* transfer I need to arrange from Tännforsen to the airport. One way."

"OK, we can talk about it. You're not stealing our waterfall, are you?"

"No, but it might be almost as tricky as that."

"OK, Stefan can come to the rescue again, I'm sure. Now, go sit in the taxi and I bring you the VIPs," and with that he gave me the keys to his best VIP minibus. With some relief, I headed out of the building once more and let myself into his black VW, which was parked just outside.

I made myself comfortable in the main seating area and it wasn't long before the side door slid open to reveal Stefan's toothy smile and a gang of lads standing behind him, surrounded by guitar cases and travel bags. As Stefan struggled with loading a drum kit into the back, one by one they stepped up into the minibus, each one introducing themselves, some shaking hands until the last guy stepped in.

"*Hej*... Bo"

As I had said "*Hej*" to each and every one, but only "*Hej*, Andrew" to Bo, they had assumed I was Swedish until I gave my name.

"Oh, are you English?" asked Bo.

"Yes. I'm working in Åre for the season as a *resor ledare* (travel rep)."

"Cool."

"I presume you are this week's band? Where are you playing?"

"At Bygget."

"What's the name of your band?"

"E-Type – that's me. And these guys are my band" and he proceeded to introduce them all properly, saying what instruments they played, finishing up with the drummer. "We're all looking to do some good skiing, apart from him who's not allowed to in case he breaks his arm!"

"Are you quite well known then in Sweden?"

"Yeah, we've had quite a few big hits and one called *Vänner*, which was the theme song to a Swedish TV show. Another one was *Calling Your Name* and we have a new one out now called *Back in the Loop*."

"Oh – yeah, I hear that all the time on Radio Rix. You are big!"

"Well, in Sweden, maybe yes but not big-big like your British bands, but maybe one day," he said modestly.

We continued to have a chat about favourite bands and why a Brit was a ski rep in Sweden and how they knew my ski company from skiing in Austria for years. Then the conversation flowed like we had known each other for years. This band was very big in Sweden at the time and I couldn't wait to ask some of the guys back in resort to guess who I had travelled back from the airport with. We all got dropped off at the Åregården Hotel and I helped Stefan unload their drum kit and carry it into reception.

The reception girls, Stina and Helena, were clearly very excited to welcome them to the hotel and very surprised to see me come in with them. They were eager to learn how I had hooked up with them and I made a big thing of saying goodbye to my new best friends, accepting their kind offer of a couple of free VIP tickets. The Swedes were definitely obsessed with anything VIP or "Wee-Eye-Pea" as many of them called it, charmingly.

As I left, I took Stefan to one side and began to quiz him on the extent of his bear transportation skills.

Back at the Sporthotellet, I was lying on my bed, just resting and reading a book, when I heard a very well spoken English girl's voice in the corridor. I couldn't think who it was so leapt off the bed and stuck my head out of the doorway to see Ulrika. She had made her second surprise visit to town and it was nice to see her again. She was having a quiet time in Sälen and had arranged to meet her English boyfriend, Ben, here who was due to arrive later in the day. She had been to see us earlier in the season but it was at a time when John and I had hardly seen each other all week as I was socialising with the Duved crowd.

She had been walking along the corridor with John and doing all the talking. I said that I thought it had sounded like a very prim and proper Chelsea girl's voice, it was such perfect English. She switched to Swedish, being so keen to test me on my Swedish, and was notably impressed with my progress. It never ceased to amaze me how proficiently most of them could switch from one language to another. I had been sitting in the staff dining area of the Åregården only a few days previously, talking to the *fruckost flickorna* (breakfast girls) after their shift as we were planning a morning's skiing. Two of them got up to leave and walked off still talking English to each to other and turned around to me asking: "What are we doing? We're speaking English to each other now!"

They were doing it without even thinking about it.

John, Ulrika, Ben and I met up for a few drinks that evening and Ben and I immediately got on well together, having the same sense of humour. We arranged to meet for a beer and burger the next night, as John and Ulrika were sorting something out relating to the marketing of the resort in the company brochure. We agreed to meet at Broken Dreams, the burger bar and American style diner in the town square. It was great to have a fellow Brit to converse with, and have a laugh and a few drinks with. I told him that I was having the time of my life living in the mountains, skiing almost every day, going to the bars, snowmobiling, going out on the husky dog trips and, of course, discovering the merits of the wonderfully friendly Swedish girls.

I had had a few too many beers, I think, as I hadn't let him speak much at all.

"How strange," I observed, jubilantly, "to be sitting here in a place called Broken Dreams when everything is going so well."

He went very quiet.

"I think Ulrika and I are splitting up."

"Oh."

"We've been together now for ten years and I feel we're drifting apart, her being back in Sweden and me being in London."

From then on, the conversation took on a more sombre tone and the name, Broken Dreams, became more poignant.

I had passed by the old church on the southern edge of the town so many times on the transfer but still not yet walked out to investigate it. Thinking it would make for some spectacular photographs I wanted to capture some images before the snow began to melt. I stepped out one mid-morning after being in the office and was relishing doing something normal for a change, breaking the routine that had set in. I felt like a tourist and taking a stroll through the village on my own with no ski business to do lifted my spirits more than I was anticipating. Having walked the same streets, being confined to the same part of the village for so long, it was refreshing to explore a new area.

I was ambling along the pavement by the side of the road, admiring a different view of the frozen lake and watching the tower of the church getting closer with every step, when a yellow VW Golf estate pulled up alongside and stopped just ahead of me. The tyres scrunching on the snow as the car drew to a halt. I recognised the three crowns symbol of the Swedish postal service on the doors. The window was wound down and the driver reached out an arm and pushed a bundle of letters and magazines through the opening of a mail box on a post at the road side and then drove off, the tyres spitting off tiny oblongs of snow that had got caught up in the tread. Nothing unusual in all that, but something was bugging me. Something wasn't right, or rather it was but I couldn't work out why it didn't feel right. Was I over tired? And then it dawned on me – it was a right hand drive car. How very sensible and how very typically Swedish that was.

The Romanesque church was called, imaginatively, Åre gamla kyrka (Åre old church) and was constructed in the 12th century. According to local history, once it was built the villagers had been encouraged to convert from their old beliefs of Norse gods and start believing in a bloke who died thousands of miles away in the Middle East before coming alive again a few days later. Remarkably, the church survived, probably due, in no small way, to a convincing marketing campaign on behalf of the Christians.

The church had been formed in two structures; one a rectangular stone walled building under a pitch roof. The other was a much more ornate, smaller but taller square tower structure also of light coloured stone. At first floor, there was an elegant dark timber balcony running around all four sides under a small four pitch roof. This rose up to a pointy octagonal onion-like spire sat on top of what looked like an observation floor with tiny windows looking out on all four sides. Since the ground was permanently frozen during the winter, it was impossible to bury any villager who died during the cold months. This tower was where they kept the bodies in their coffins until the ground had thawed enough for the grave diggers to start their work.

I wasn't sure whether someone was pulling my leg but, just in case, I didn't try to open the small wooden door to the tower to take a nose around. Instead, I busied myself with taking what I considered to be some very arty shots. When I had passed this church at night time the bright spotlights that were pointed at it made it look quite spectacular so I decided I should return that evening for another photo session.

The temperature gauge outside my window read minus eighteen degrees but that did not deter me from my evening stroll. I did wonder if my camera would still be functioning twenty minutes later when I would arrive at the church so I put it deep inside an internal pocket in my jacket. As I left the warmth of the Sporthotellet, I looked up to see a wonderful dark blue cloud-free sky awash with stars. It was 9pm but the sky was no longer completely dark. Encouragingly, there was a hint of lighter evenings to come as Spring approached. The snow cover on the ground was still a reminder of the winter's grip on the landscape, and the freezing temperature confirmed that.

I cut across some open space away from the main road and negotiated my way around the back of the Hotel Åregården, finding a little used pathway that led down towards the lake, across what I presumed were the gardens of people's houses. After five minutes, I had reached another smaller road and followed this towards the church, the treaded soles of my new boots making a pleasing crunch as they gripped the snow reassuringly. Elated again to be walking along a route I had not done over the last few months, it was good to strike out on my own, even doing something as simple as this night time stroll. I was keeping the cabin/resort fever in check.

The church looked even more spectacular at night time and I was in my element as I set about taking some more artistic photographs. I was so focussed on what I was doing, I almost forgot where I was and started to think about how we had been going non-stop for almost four months pretty much every day, usually burning the candle at both ends. In any normal job, I would have had the weekend off or a couple of quiet nights in. Adrenaline had sustained me for quite some time and this simple half an hour of photography, not thinking about guest lists and where I had to be next, was a welcome relief.

As I moved around the outside of the church, I suddenly felt a little dizzy. My vision of the snow seemed to go in and out of focus and a green shade of light appeared around my periphery. Was the tension and stress that had built up manifesting itself in some sort of migraine attack? As I looked at the snow, the ground started to pulse in green and now yellow waves and I felt unsteady on my feet, like the snow was moving under my boots. I straightened up and looked around for something to hold onto and, as I lifted my head, I saw the whole sky was pulsing with green and lemon waves.

It was the Northern Lights, of course; a most spectacular display of energy being released in the upper layers of the atmosphere. I stood there, wide eyed and mouth open like a small child seeing Santa Claus in his sleigh flying across the sky. All feelings of weariness and tension and stress left me and I wanted to be carried up into the sky and along on those glowing waves of light. The luminous pulsating waves then began to twitch and jump like smoke billowing up from a giant sky wizard's fire pit. I have absolutely no idea what giant sky wizards are, of course, but if they exist I'm sure the smoke from their fires would be just like this.

After a few minutes, the light waves poured down the sky like a slow motion waterfall before subsiding and retreating to the horizon. And then they were gone. And so too was my opportunity to take any photos of the light show because, through all of this, I had just held on to my camera and forgotten to actually lift it up and press the button, so in awe was I of the display. What was more, I hadn't been able to take my eyes off the sky for fear of missing one single second of it. But the images would be imprinted on my memory forever. *It was a pity no one else was there to witness it with me*, I thought, but then again it was like having a very private, VIP showing, if you like. I hung around for a while longer, hoping the lights would rekindle, but they didn't and I walked back into the village feeling like I had just experienced a close encounter of a different kind.

I began to wonder how many others had seen the show or, more worryingly, if when I returned to the village I would be the only person still alive. But that was just silly. The road back was unusually quiet though, I thought, and I couldn't see any cars moving about up ahead of me. Off to the right of me, beyond the cluster of village buildings, I spotted a very bright light heading skywards. I watched it climb steadily upwards for a bit before realising it was a piste basher. As I neared the edge of the village, a ski bus went past me and I could hear Toni Braxton singing inside. All was as it should be.

The Swedish Alpine Championships came to town for a week in mid-March with the downhill and Super G races taking place on the downhill course, the giant slalom on the Gästrappet run, and the slalom on the slalom course by the World Cup lift. The downhill practice began on a Sunday and the week's events culminated in the slalom for men and women the following Saturday. The arrival of this ski circus caused another buzz of excitement around town and, although some of the runs were naturally cut off from the general public's use, no one seemed to mind. There were a whole host of commercially sponsored Audis and BMWs parked up all over town and a fair number of TV crews and camera vans scattered about.

Colourful banners and flags promoting all manner of ski related equipment were hastily erected on almost every structure, giving the town a carnival atmosphere, and the bars were populated with even more fit, healthy looking and athletic types – mostly, I observed, sporting ridiculously large thighs.

John and I were busy as normal, but we did get to watch the slalom races standing to the side of the finish line bowl. Naively, when I was growing up watching *Ski Sunday* on the BBC and before I had even contemplated the notion of going skiing, I really believed that all the slopes would be lined with people ringing cow bells and hollering out. I was therefore very disappointed to discover on my first ski trip to Italy that there was no one standing by the trees watching and shouting out encouragement all the way down the slopes. It had been so eerily quiet at times. After that first week's let down, secretly, every time I went skiing, I had hoped my childhood vision would come true. *Maybe they just didn't do that in Italy?* I had thought to myself. Austria failed to live up to my dream in that respect, followed swiftly by France and then even Switzerland, home of the cow bell. What was wrong with these places? All the resorts had failed dismally until now.

We spent a cold evening with our colleagues from Ski Skandinavia, watching the floodlit event grateful for the protection our head gear gave us, not from the cold but the incessant and very loud commentary from the loud speakers dotted around the area. Further up the mountain, I could see people lining the sides, shouting and sounding off air horns when their favourite skiers whizzed by. At last my vision had been realised, although sadly they wouldn't be there the next day when I was out ski escorting.

I caught the freestyle mogul finals and marvelled at the punishment those skiers put their knees through. Most of them had ski pants with black square patches on the knee, which emphasised the quick up and down pummelling movement.

The aggressive music that blasted out of the loud speakers surrounding that event helped to generate a lot more excitement in the noticeably younger crowd than those who attended the race and slalom events and would certainly have pumped up the performances of the participants.

On the final day of the competition, Sweden's top skiing star of the time, Pernilla Wiberg, made an appearance, much to the appreciation of the enthusiastic crowd. She had already won gold medals at two Olympic Games; the 1992 Albertville Giant Slalom and, in 1994, across the border in Lillehammer in the Combined event. That and three World Championship gold medals had made her a legend in Sweden and worth watching her in action close up. She was also drop dead gorgeous, had a radiant smile, exuded that healthy Scandinavian glow, but also had preposterously powerful Olympian thighs.

By the end of the month, the sun was rising at about 6am and setting about 7pm. I would still often find people stood statue-still in the town square, their heads raised up towards the sun like spring flowers searching for every bit of the sun's warmth.

However, in spite of this, we had some wildly fluctuating days, temperature wise, and were not yet out of winter.

Mellissa from Ski Skandinavia had complained to her management team that, although they were living in a nice apartment, they felt a bit isolated being based out in Duved and taxis were costing them a fortune when they wanted to get back from the nightclubs and bars after the ski buses had finished. It had become critical to her deciding to stay on longer than her original end of March contract so a budget had been secured to buy a cheap car.

She had managed to get hold of a ten year old Volvo 340GL with *only* 265,000 kms on the clock and a petrol engine rather than diesel, so the fuel didn't freeze. She had invited me over to see the car after I had done a welcome talk at the Hotel Renen and we could have a drink locally then she would drive us, Katrina/Natasha and Daniel into Åre for a Thursday night out. She was happy not to drink, so pleased was she with her new found freedom.

After the welcome meeting, I walked across to street to their apartment and joined them for a box of Pringles and a beer. We had one other person join us – Marlene, the Duved 'village host' who had begun to hang out with them. As far as I could tell, Marlene's job, was to walk around the village dragging her *spark*, a flimsy frame of a structure with metal runners about two metres long and a chair mounted to it. I had seen a few people propel them by kicking the ground and running behind them along the Duved snow-covered streets, usually weighed down with shopping, beer, firewood or small children. Sometimes, all of those things. Marlene's was loaded up with large thermos flasks of strong coffee and leaflets on the local area. Her role was to hand out free cups of coffee to new arrivals at the train station, and anywhere else she found new tourists. She was an intelligent girl, studying economics and accountancy, with a wide smile and bright big eyes that lit up beneath the baseball cap that read *by värd* (village host) across the front. One wondered why she had taken this job of all jobs to while away the winter days?

After a couple of beers, Mellissa ushered us all out of the apartment, eager to show us her new toy, and we filed down into the small car park next to the apartment block to see the vehicle. It was dark but under the streetlights we could tell it was a drab grey-blue colour that probably hadn't looked any more inspiring in its earlier life than it did now, although it probably had more of its chrome trim attached to the bodywork. Sat there, nose into the corner of the car park, it looked as if it had been there a long time.

"Does it actually work?" I asked.

"Of course it does!" Mellissa replied indignantly. "I drove it here the other day."

Daniel looked at me dubiously. "It looks... very sad," was all he could say.

We surrounded it and Mellissa proudly opened the doors for us, except the rear right which had to be opened from inside. Daniel jumped into the passenger seat and I hopped into the back, sandwiched between Katrina and Marlene. For a safety-conscious brand of car in a safety-conscious country, it was alarming to see no seatbelts at the back.

"I think somebody's had them out," said Mellissa when we questioned her, "but you're all tightly packed in back there."

Amazingly, the car started first time and she reversed it back across the snow, slipping about a bit as the tyres were crossing previous tyre marks that had turned hard and crusty in the cold night air.

"You have got winter tyres on this thing, haven't you?" asked Daniel.

"Err... ooh, I don't know... I think so."

"Do they have studs?"

"No."

"Oh. Then you have summer tyres."

"Is that bad?" asked Katrina.

"Not really, but it's just about OK if we don't hit any fresh snow or any *thing*. The main road is fairly clear right now," Daniel replied, adding, "we won't be insured, though, if we have an accident because it's too early in the year not to have winter tyres."

On that less than reassuring note, we headed out onto the main street, where there were no cars, and took a right turn out towards the main E14 road and the scene of my earlier skidding to a halt in the Mean Machine *with* studded winter tyres and *with* four wheel drive.

Mellisa was doing a great job, smoothly accelerating and slowing down with only a short controlled, graceful slide to the junction and a bit of a wheel spin when she got the car going again up onto the main road. After about half a mile, there was a white splodge on the windscreen, followed by another and another and then another. The chattering in the car stopped as we all watched the windscreen fill with more and more splodges. Before too long we were driving through a full blizzard that had come out of nowhere. That was to be the tone of the weather over the next few weeks; just when we thought we were on the verge of waltzing into spring, Jack Frost dragged us back onto the dance floor of winter.

Mellissa sensibly slowed the car to a steady speed and, looking at things positively, we were on a straight main road, not the winding lake shore road. What wasn't so good was we couldn't really see a thing. The headlights on full beam simply lit up the hundreds of thousands of clumpy wet snowflakes that were coming our way so she had to drive on dipped beam, and that merely picked out the white road surface no more than ten metres ahead. Mellissa turned off the radio so she could concentrate on the road ahead and all five pairs of eyes were straining at the thick snowfall. The silence in the car added to the tension.

"Oh crap! I'm really not liking this at all," she exclaimed. No one else was either but we were all silent watching out for the first sign of traffic coming out of the dark from the other direction.

"I can't see the edge of the bloody road!" she added in what sounded like a much more northern accent than her usual one. It was the stress of the situation. It was only five miles to Åre but at no more than twenty miles an hour it was going to be a very long, tense car journey.

"We're lucky no one else is on the road," chirped Katrina, trying to buoy us all up.

"That's cos no other bugger is so stupid to be driving in a blizzard like this," snapped Mellissa.

"Your summer tyres are doing well," offered Daniel, rather dryly.

Suddenly there was a scratching on the windscreen, which made us all jump.

"What the bloody hell is that?!" exclaimed Mellissa.

"I think it's your windscreen wiper about to break off," said Daniel. "Yep, there it goes!"

It flapped about a bit and then vanished, leaving an area in front of Mellissa's head quickly filling up with snow like and egg timer filing up with sand.

"I can't see anything now!" she shrieked.

Daniel's side of the windscreen also start to fill up as his windscreen wiper, although still attached, had given up trying to shift the accumulating snow from the glass. "Neither can I now," he said. "Guess there's only one thing I can do," and he wound down the passenger side window and, freeing himself from his seatbelt, he reached out with his right arm and used his gloved hand like a windscreen wiper to clear the snow.

Mellissa had by now slowed to almost jogging pace but Daniel assured her he could see where we were going and told her to speed up as he called out steering directions to her, all the while brushing the fresh snow away from just his side of the windscreen.

And that's how we continued our journey all the way to Åre; Daniel leaning half out the window acting as wiper blade and navigator, shouting commands to Mellissa (driving literally snow blind) whilst we three sat in silence in the back in trepidation. It was dangerous, ludicrous and irresponsible but, at the same time, it was ingenious teamwork. Miraculously, we made it safely without hitting anything or going off the road, which was quite an achievement, bearing in mind the edge of the road was indistinguishable from the road itself.

After twenty long minutes or so of darkness and thick blizzard, we neared the village and the street lights began to improve visibility. It was only after we had circumnavigated a roundabout and headed down into the village that we slid a bit more than we were all comfortable with. We all held our breaths but we just rebounded off a kerb and slid merrily on our way down the sloping street until it flattened out. Mellissa started to giggle, first with relief as much as anything else, and that infectious laugh spread throughout the car as we realised we had made it. She calmly selected a gear and accelerated gently along the lower road towards the town square to find a parking space.

When the car had come to a halt and the handbrake was applied, we all congratulated Mellissa on her sublime driving skills and thanked God for delivering us safely to our destination. We headed into the Country Club nightclub in a buoyant mood and enjoyed the rest of the night. Of course, the whole point of Mellissa getting the car was so she could drive back to Duved without the need for an expensive taxi which ironically is what they all had to do at 2am in the morning when we left the club.

I very generously, albeit rather half-heartedly, offered them the floor of my room to sleep on and they could toss a coin to see who would get the sofa bed but, as I had no spare duvets or blankets, they decided to opt for a taxi back. Feeling a little uncomfortable at their misfortune, I wished them a good night and then slunk off the short distance to the warmth of my room.

In the morning, I pulled back the curtains to see we had indeed slipped back into winter mode. All the branches on the trees carried a thick line of snow that traced their wiggly growth routes back to the trunk. Snow was stacked up on car roofs and bonnets and all was very still. I dressed and headed outside to check on Mellissa's car, which showed no signs of having been driven into the village last night.

All traces of tyres tracks had been covered, as was the car itself, under a sort of jelly mould shape.

After breakfast, I popped into the small newsagents on the corner of the square to buy an English newspaper for the same price as I would pay for a magazine, some stamps and a few *Plopp* chocolate bars because they tasted good and the name still amused me. I bought extras to send home to friends but ended up eating them all over the next few days. Saga, was the name of the girl behind the counter. She had piercings all the way up the side of each ear; varying shades of purple, blue and blonde hair, cut short on one side; and a floppy fringe that hung over part of her face.

She wore bangles up one arm and was charming, but I think slightly mad. She was always very chatty and the first time I went into the shop to buy some stamps she told me she already knew my name and introduced herself as "Saga. You know what that means?" and, not waiting for a reply, "It means fairy story."

"OK."

"Do you know what your name means?"

"Err... no I don't," and added "Sorry" for some reason.

"You should always know what your name means."

"OK."

"Would you like me to find out?"

"Erm…" I was stalling for time, unaccustomed as I was to this line of questioning, when buying stamps. "Yeah… if you like…", not wishing to seem ungrateful.

I paid and turned to leave with a "Thanks, bye", trying to distance myself from her by speaking English rather than Swedish.

"Saga is also the Norse goddess of poetry," she told me.

"Oh. Is that right?… Well it's a nice name."

"Thank you," and she smiled sweetly, "Bye Andrew"

"Good bye."

When I got back to the office, I asked John about her and he confirmed my initial thought: "Ah, Saga, a lovely girl; mad as a box of frogs, though. Did she ask you about your name?"

"Yes, she did. She's going to find out what it means"

"Yes, she did that for me. And for Bob. She'll probably tell you there was a Norse god with a similar name and that hers is a name of a Norse goddess."

Considering her passion for mysticism and Norse deities, it seemed appropriate that Saga would appear at odd times around the resort. I would often meet her on a ski bus going somewhere or see her standing waiting at a bus stop in the middle of nowhere. Once, I was riding a snowmobile back across the frozen lake on the return leg of an excursion and there stood Saga, sharp metal saw in hand, looking at the circle she had just cut in the ice. Next to her was a small wooden stool, a bag, and a fishing rod. Although totally absorbed with the hole, she had just happened to look up at me as I went by. On another occasion, I found myself in the candle and craft shop and she appeared from the stock room carefully carrying a tiny orange painted wooden horse to place on a display shelf. I could have sworn that one evening I saw her from a distance, watching the frozen waterfall from the other side of the frozen river. Although it was most bizarre it wasn't freaky at all as she was so pleasant. Perhaps she really was a little Norse goddess, sent to watch over me?

The warmer weather and longer days meant that the frozen waterfall was not so frozen. Consequently, it was a much harder job for us to sell the trip to the frozen waterfall and the floodlight or moonlit walk down through the forests was less appealing without floodlights and now, more often, merely a dark grey sky.

It was not surprising, therefore, that I found Bertil late one afternoon in a bar a little bit the worse for wear. He sat with his back to the door and had clearly spent the afternoon decanting the vodka from the large Absolut bottle positioned in front of him into his body and was now comparing the level of the shot in his small glass with the level still in the bottle, wondering where it had all gone and realising he only had another few shots left.

I didn't realise it was him at first when I walked up to Erik to get some more beer vouchers for the recent influx of guests. Our vouchers "entitle the bearer to one free medium strength beer" and were a good way for the bar to attract new business among our guests. We handed them out before going on the bar tour, or if we had a surplus, then we gave them out to the nicer guests at the Welcome meetings.

I was standing next to Bertil, aware of him, but not recognising him and never expecting to see him there, whilst Erik counted out the vouchers for me.

"A good season, Andrew?" he said to me in Swedish. I turned to face him.

"Bertil ?!"

"It is I," he exclaimed in English in a vaguely theatrical way, waving one finger about unsteadily as if to confirm it was he.

"Sorry, I didn't recognise you. Are you OK?" He ignored the question.

"Not a bad one, eh?" his finger still raised and wavering about in the air between us.

"Well, it's still going strong for me."

"There's been too much wind." I wasn't sure if he was referring to himself or the weather for the hand with the pointy finger dropped onto his stomach with a smack.

"Too much wind, too much snow, and now it's melting." The alcohol had given him confidence to speak more English than the stock welcome speech at his waffle house. He still sounded just like the Swedish chef though but I resisted the urge to tell him.

He continued: "You can't see a frozen waterfall if there is no frozen waterfall…" That was very true, of course, and it dawned on me how much his livelihood relied on the freezing cold temperatures and darkness for full effect.

"Yes, that's very true," and I looked at Erik, who gave a sympathetic nod and moved away to clear some glasses.

"But you have had an OK season?"

"Arh," he squawked.

"And what will you do in the spring and summer?" I was becoming concerned.

"We open the waterfall," and he downed his shot in salute to the opening.

"Oh, I see, you open up again?"

"Yes, we open for all the tourists to see the waterfall, not the frozen waterfall," and with that he began to laugh at his own joke.

"So, you'll make some more money in the summer then?"

"But, of course we do," he replied, as if I was being stupid, which I probably was, thinking the poor chap has just lost his entire income until the next winter. When he had stopped guffawing at his humour he straightened up as if to leave and then fixed me with a stare. "Do you still want to buy that bear?"

"Err... yes... very much so," I was taken aback at his sudden seriousness.

After a little more negotiating, we finally fixed the deal at the equivalent of two thousand pounds and shook on it, celebrating with a shot of vodka each from the bottom of his bottle.

At last the deal was done and we talked some more.

"What will you do about replacing the bear?" I asked.

"Oh, I think I have another one in the barn," he answered.

And with that and me still a little stunned, thinking it was a precious family heirloom, he pushed himself up onto his feet with one hand on my shoulder for support, and headed towards the door saying, "Call me when you want to come and get it."

I left the bar and headed straight for the office to tell my Soho friends the good news. They were beyond ecstatic and then I set about trying to get hold of Stefan to see what vehicle he could offer us.

The problem we faced was that it was a very large bear. It was also fixed in its stance with its arms outstretched, so couldn't easily be bundled into the back of a taxi, even one with a large sliding door as the seats would get in the way. I wondered if we might be able to slide it into the baggage area of one of Sven's coaches but, having surreptitiously measured the door opening one day, stood by the side of a coach, I reckoned that wasn't going to work either. Stefan came to the rescue with the suggestion that a friend of his had a flat bed pick-up truck. We could load the bear onto the back, strap it down and ride with his friend, Oskar, to the airport.

John and I took a ride out with Oskar in his matt grey '79 flatbed Ford 4x4, complete with 22 inch custom wheels, to Bertil's in order to assess the logistics of move. Stefan was already there when we arrived and was talking to Bertil. It amused me to think that organising the transfer of the bear had taken priority in his daily job above any paying customers. But that was the kindness of Stefan, always willing to help out and never demanding payment from us. We were still always chasing him up to come into our office so we could run through his invoice and make a payment. We jumped out of the truck and all marched into the waffle house to admire our purchase.

Oskar reckoned the bear would require three of us to manhandle it, and one of us might have to sit on the back with the beast. John and I looked at each other and then back at the truck outside. Neither of us fancied sitting on the back for an hour and a half's journey to the airport.

"Surely, we can all sit in your cabin, can't we?" asked John.

"OK, maybe," replied Oskar, taking a step forward to make a closer inspection of the bear.

Stefan suggested, "You need to wrap it up because, if it snows or we get rain, you don't want it getting wet."

"It's a bear, Stefan – surely it's used to getting snowed on?" I said.

"Best to wrap it up as you don't want to give other drivers a scare or have the local *polis* getting interested."

"Yeah, maybe, I think it's best," concurred Oskar.

"OK, so we'll find some plastic sheeting to wrap it up," I said to John.

"Ski school might have something we can use," he suggested.

Then we all just stood in silence for a moment or two, looking at the creature while it glared back at us with glassy eyes and a fearsome open jaw. It was an uncomfortable moment and, breaking the silence, John asked, "How are we going to get it out of here?"

We looked around and he had a point. It was standing in a corner of the entrance hallway but the front doors were too small for it to fit through and, besides, we would have to negotiate our way around a tight corner.

Stefan called Bertil over, who was busying himself in the kitchen sorting out what sounded like pots and pans.

"Do you have another door at the back?" asked Stefan in Swedish.

"Yes, but only a personnel door."

"How do we get the bear out? He won't fit through here," and he gestured with his hands.

"You can pass him through the window over there," he said, pointing to a large window looking out towards the waterfall. We all looked puzzled.

"It lifts up. The whole window," he explained. "In the summer we have it fully open." I got the gist of what he was saying from his arm movements but Stefan translated. Bertil moved across the room to unlock it at the base at table height and swung it upwards and outwards towards the overhang of the roof. "You will have to pass him through on his back. That's the way he came in. It was now a four or five man job because the ground outside the window was at a lower level than the floor inside so, as well as being fed out through the open window, the bear then had to be lowered to the ground and probably stood upright before being laid flat again for the carrying around to the front of the building via the footpath to Oskar's truck. Bertil reassured us that the five of us could lift and carry the bear and we agreed to meet back here once we he had spoken to customs at the airport and fixed a date with them to receive it.

Back in the office, I phoned Jenny in the ski school to arrange *fika* with her, where I would buy her coffee and cake to discuss the loan of some plastic sheeting, slalom poles and rope. I have no idea why I asked her for slalom poles – it seemed logical at the time and was clearly something they had a plenty of. John, meanwhile, had the harder task of discussing the arrival and storage of the bear with the airport authorities. According to him, I found out later, they had been expecting his call, so the prospective owners back in London had been as good as their word in making the necessary phone calls. We could take the bear any day we wanted to – they were ready for us. It was all going far too well at this point.

Checking the forecast for the next few days, we selected a likely snow free day and one that both Stefan and Oskar could make and Stefan called Bertil. As Stefan and Oskar drove us out in convoy to Bertil's after lunch one day, with our borrowed equipment rolling about in the back of Stefan's taxi, I had trouble shaking the *A Team*'s theme tune out of my head.

Bertil had cleared away some of the tables, so we had a clear way through his restaurant from the bear's corner to the open window. Stefan and Bertil moved into position beneath the window, ready to receive our bear. John, Oskar and I got into positions around him, two of us grabbing a leg each and an arm around his back, and Oskar squeezed in between the bear and the wall to support the head and shoulders. On the count of three, we tipped him back on his feet and grabbed hold of him.

He was much heavier than we expected and I wondered what he had been stuffed with but, because his body was rigid and hairy, we couldn't get a very firm grip on him. We began to edge across the room with the bear looking straight up to the ceiling and his arms outstretched, like he was in goal waiting for the penalty kick to be taken. It must have looked such an undignified scene and not his finest moment.

We set him down just before the window, leaning him back against a pile of tables as we prepared for the great lift through the open window and the pass down to the other two. He went through feet first, lying on his back, and was carefully grabbed by Stefan and Bertil. As we eased his bulk out, one of his paws got caught on the edge of the window. His claws had wedged themselves into the groove along the outer edge of the frame, like he didn't want to leave. We struggled to lift him back up and out and didn't want to force him, for fear of breaking the claws.

Bertil and Stefan were now taking most of the weight between them and we were trying to extricate his paw by repeated short lifts. Annoyingly, he was stuck, with his legs hanging out into the cold. We couldn't lift him upwards without banging his paw against the top of the window opening. All the while, it felt as if he was getting heavier. Oskar announced he was going to let go, since the two outside confirmed they could probably take the weight if John and I were still holding on around the armpits. Oskar's plan was to clamber up onto the stacked tables to see if he could wriggle the claw free.

"OK, but do it quickly," gasped Stefan. John and I sniggered and then Bertil started to chuckle under the strain of the weight.

"Stop it!" cried Stefan. "Bertil, are you really lifting your side?" he asked irritably.

John and I snorted with laughter but held on tighter to try to regain control. The normally calm and laid back Stefan had suddenly shown an angry side and it was funny to us to see him in such a state.

"Come on Oskar, hurry up!" he cried out as he started to sink down to his knees a little, getting redder in the face. Oskar got the claws out with his fingers and then shouted down to Stefan "*Han är ledig* (he's free)! Let him down!" and, with that, John and I gradually released our grip and let the bear slide down to Stefan and Bertil and the ground. Stefan let out a cry of relief and stepped back, rubbing his hands while Bertil steadied the wavering bear, still chuckling at Stefan.

Loading him up onto the truck was a lot easier and we soon had him tied down securely and covered with sheeting. His arms were outstretched and raised up, but we figured we had done a good job with the pieces of sheeting and ropes that we had to keep him covered properly. We set off on our most unusual airport transfer in an ebullient mood.

Luckily, there were no mishaps or dramas or *polis* on the way to Östersund airport. We regularly checked through the rear window of the cab to see if the bear was still there but, with three of us jammed in to the old Ford on a bench seat, all we could do was strain our necks round, while Oskar could use his rear view mirror. It was just possible to see that the bear was still there, lying on his back, and while there was a small area of sheeting flapping about everything appeared to be securely in place. We drove through one patch of light snow, which lasted for about twenty minutes, but our bear behaved himself and kept his head down.

We pulled up into the car park at the front of the main entrance and, with our load still covered up, John went in to make contact with Lars Eriksson, the man in charge of bear transportations. After a few minutes, they both reappeared, Mr Eriksson looking very important in his blue uniform, gold pips on his jacket shoulders, and a smart police-style cap with a braid trim across the front.

After acknowledging Oskar and me, and warmly shaking Stefan's hand like the old friend he probably was, he turned his attention to our precious cargo. His gloved hand pulled back some of the sheeting rather too easily to reveal a soggy snow-soaked bear. Part of the sheeting had been tugged away in the wind to expose a bit of the bear. Quite a lot actually, as we were about to discover. At rest and out of the wind, the sheeting had flopped back down to cover the fur but, as Mr Eriksson pulled away more sheeting, we saw that the bear had got a proper soaking in that short period of snow fall. His right arm, most of his chest and belly were wet and the water had crept down his sides.

We asked him where we needed to take the bear and he replied that, ordinarily, we should drive down to the end of the buildings, through a security gate and into one of the cargo hangars, but the military had some sort of top secret operation going on so: "Are you OK to take it through here?" He pointed to the main entrance door.

Sure, I thought. *Why are you asking me? It's your airport, after all.* I think what he meant was: can you carry it through the main doors? They looked big enough so we started to unload our bear, very carefully. He had got wetter than we expected and consequently he was heavier. The four of us started to unwrap him and slide him off the back, receiving some odd looks from passengers driving through the car park.

We became more of a spectacle when we entered the arrivals / departures hall, leaving a trail of clear liquid in our wake as the water dripped off the creature. Not surprisingly, people stopped in their tracks and stared at us, mouths open. Lars led us quickly to an interrogation room to the side of the hall, where we stood him upright, water pooling around his feet (the bear that is, not Lars).

He had certainly got a good soaking out on the back of the truck and Lars said we needed to dry him off before he went into storage. We all stood there looking at each other, regarding our furry beast. It must have looked an odd sight from beyond the glass window to the hall. There was frosted privacy glass up to about chest height but clear higher up, so all people could see was the chests and heads of four men talking to one airport security official all surrounding one large brown bear who stood very still with his arms reaching out high as if he was being searched. It was about to get more comical as we needed to dry him off and we didn't think towelling him down was going to be the best way.

Lars thought he had an idea and announced, "I'll be back with some forms you will need to fill in and something that will help you."

Within five minutes, he had returned. In one hand, he held out a Cargo Registration Form, in the other, a hair dryer.

6
APRIL

S.O.S.

The heavy hand of winter seemed to release its grip a little on the very first day of April. I noticed a few more birds flitting about between the trees. The air had an ever so slightly more earthiness about it. There were more exposed branches and, in the relatively milder air we now experienced, I noticed the odd small patches of sodden grass. A few more determined strands had even begun to poke through, reaching up for air. It amazed me how any grass could survive such a suffocating winter submerged under the heavy mass of snow. Mostly, though, the sand coloured grass that was exposed still lay compressed, flat against the dark damp soil in spite of the more generous hours of daylight that were now bestowed upon us.

We had a new resident move in to a room in our corridor – Tibbe. He was a tall guy with a healthy beard and long straggly brown hair. He had a relaxed, gentle air about him and a cool dog called Victor, who was very friendly and would often wander into my room to see if I had any spare food, and usually leave with a sock or a boot that I would have to retrieve from Tibbe's room. Tibbe said Victor must like me because he and I both came from London so he sensed some commonality.

He had been working in the Alps most of the winter, running his parapenting business and had come back to Sweden now the weather was producing some thermals of a kind. His business card promoted him as "instructor, *tandempilot, världscupvinnare*" and he kept promising to take me up for a tandem flight when we got a clear day weather-wise and diary-wise. It would have been a great experience to be flown by a world cup winner but, disappointingly, our free days and good weather days never matched up and the nearest I got to one of the oversized rucksacks that sat in the corner of his room was pulling out one of my socks from a pocket that Victor had tried to hide for himself.

As the ski season drew to a close in the Alps, there were still many people wanting a week's skiing and they could guarantee good snow conditions where we were. The Arrivals Sheets were still looking healthy. On 27th March, we welcomed thirty-six arrivals, mainly due to *Påsk* (Easter) and on 30th March, twenty-eight arrivals. There was more ski escorting, more late nights, but more snowmobiling and more husky dog rides too. There was a different crowd arriving now and less had pre-booked anything, which meant more commission for us.

Easter had come and gone in a proliferation of colourful feathers fixed to birch twigs displayed in shops, hotels and restaurants, together with painted eggs and, more strangely, witches or, more specifically, models of witches; the Swedish Easter witch. As I headed off to another snow scooter safari rendez-vous on the Thursday before Easter, I noticed a large number of younger girls scurrying around town dressed in old shawls and rags with rosy red painted cheeks and freckles. They were pretending to be witches but wishing people "*Glåd Pask*" and asking for sweets and treats. The custom derives from an old superstition that witches flew off to dance with the devil on a meadow called Blåkulla but now it seemed to be just an excuse for kids to dress up and beg for free sweets. Outside our doors in the Sporthotellet all the staff and a couple of extras like us ski reps woke on Good Friday to Easter to receive an Easter sock full of chocolates and a "*Glad Pask* önskar vi varandra (Happy Easter – we wish each other)" message from Jahne, the hotel staff manager.

In the Hotel Åregården's reception area, we saw daffodils appear in vases and a particularly garish one foot high Easter chicken made of china, which got moved around the room by guests and staff only to be swiftly returned to the reception desk by Maga. It brought about a welcome splash of colour to the resort and, although no longer widely celebrated as a major religious festival in Sweden, it was none the less embraced.

In other parts of the country, where the snow had gone, people were opening windows and sweeping out the winter dust from their houses. Up here, the temperature lifted a little but every now and again the snow still fell, like winter was desperately needing to remind us it was still there, just waiting in the clouds. We weren't permitted to get on with spring until it had decided *it* was good and ready. In the warmer sun, the orange-tiled roofs cleared themselves more quickly and tree branches regained their skeletal shapes only for the snow to sprinkle itself again and again.

At the end of the first week of April, Pete, a friend from London, arrived. It was so good to see a familiar face at the airport – one I had known since student days – and I couldn't wait to catch up with him and show him the sights, both on the slopes *and* in the bars. We had had a lot of guests promising to come back but all of them would be booking up for the following year. We had one exceptional guest, Adrian from Southport, who loved the place so much he came back a couple of times. He ran his own business so could afford to take the time off and he was very generous with buying drinks and meals. He had become a friend and, as a result, we managed to get him into the nightclubs ahead of the queues and it was a pleasure to have him out to stay. He also made friends with some of the locals so, although he came out on his own, he soon felt at home.

However, having one of my best mates out for a week was something else. We had learned to ski together in Zell Am See with a group of college friends and subsequently done a week in Mayrhofen where our claim to fame was skiing with Bonnie Tyler's leopard print all-in-one ski suit. I'll clarify that; we met a couple of girls, one of whom said she was a friend of Bonnie Tyler and had borrowed her ski suit for the week.

Pete arrived on a Sunday evening transfer and we wasted no time in heading out for a few beers at the Diplomat Bar. This particular Sunday night saw the usual suspects in their usual states of merriment celebrating the guest changeover day. It was when most staff had their one night off a week and, as we generally socialised much more with the locals than the tourists, it was our big night too. Tonight, there was the added attraction of the Smirnoff vodka girls parading around in tiny white Smirnoff tee shirts with ammunition style belts of shot glasses. By the time Pete and I arrived at the party, it was in full swing and the vodka in full flow. Curtis Mayfield's *Move on Up*, appeared to have become a theme tune of the bar.

The moment we had entered the building, Pete, who had always had a soft spot for blondes, had struggled to keep his lower jaw from dropping off the bottom of his face. "Oh, my God...!" was the first thing he said once he had surveyed the room. "I see what you mean." He was like a kid in a candy shop.

"I told you" and, smiling, I moved my hand to lift his jaw back into place.

For much of the first half hour, he didn't drink a great deal of his beer, as I caught him standing all agog. He was in a state of shock.

I recognised one of the Smirnoff girls – Lena – from nearby Östersund town. She was a fairly regular visitor to our corridor in the Sporthotellet since she was employed as a promotions girl from time to time partly, I think, because of her wonderful smile and white teeth, but largely because of the size of her breasts. She was busy entertaining a couple of gangly youths when she saw me and, to their dismay, she waved and came sashaying across the room to give me a big hug and, to my surprise, a very sloppy kiss. She had clearly been participating in a few to many vodka shots herself and hung on with one hand around my neck pressing her left breast into my chest.

"Those guys were assholes," she shouted in my ear. I introduced her to Pete and she kissed him and poured him a vodka, which he accepted into his spare hand. Then, with one arm wrapped around my neck, she started to holler, "Yeah, London", "Yeah, England", "Yeah, Andrew" and "Yeah" everything, including the name of our ski company, whilst waving a vodka bottle around in the air with her other hand. It was a good first night in Åre for Pete and he was warmly welcomed by all the guys with whom we were working.

The heavenly clutches of Lena marked the start of Pete's adventurous week for he experienced all that the resort had to offer but within a few days we were both to experience the hellishness of the mountain.

The particular day had begun well in fine sunny weather. After a few hours skiing, we were sat on the terrace of Hummelstugan restaurant, sipping hot coffees and gazing down at the lake where the snow scooter safaris trailed across to the other side. Looking up, we saw the colourful swirling wings of the paragliders riding the thermals. The tiny wooden hut located near to Hummelstugan was a real winter treat. The smell of wood smoke drew skiers in as they approached it from higher up on the run above and the piping hot thick soup set them up for the black mogul field the other side of the lift station on Hummelbranten.

The whole of *Backsidan*, the backside of Åreskutan, was off-piste. You really needed a guide in that area to navigate your way around avoiding the unskiable precipices and to seek out the *ravines* as the Swedes called them. Solravine was about fifty metres from the top and then there was Hällfjallet, which I liked to think of as Hell Mountain, with its steep slopes of between thirty five and fifty five degrees. Blåsten was the 'nose' of the mountain, which protruded below a steep northern facing expanse of snow and ice. It was fifty degrees steep and sat above a cluster of rocks almost five hundred metres further down. You certainly did not want to have a 'moment' there.

The Banana ravine was the lower ravine and you would not want to find yourself on that by accident. It was a narrow, hundred and fifty metre long chute with no way out once you were in it. Below, it was a slightly wider ravine, but only slightly less steep. Eventually it fed into a river but you couldn't see that from the top. Beyond that, it was kind of bent like a banana and had been described to me as "steep as the wall of a house and slippery as a banana skin." Only fools went there. Fools, or people skiing with John, who was obviously trying to show off.

It so happened that John had come across us having our leisurely coffee and, full of boyish eagerness, had before we knew it, managed to persuade us to explore the other side of the mountain. I had been fortunate enough to have greatly improved my skiing since being out in the resort. When you can do it every day and have some free one-to-one ski lessons with the very lovely Maria – long blonde hair, blue eyes and a body honed by skiing every day of the winter – you get better very quickly.

My fitness levels had gone up several notches too. Although I'll admit I wasn't as toned as Maria – not quite – I could actually feel and see my body changing shape as the weeks progressed. Anyhow, John decided that it was time for him to take us on an exploratory ski, to show us a different part of the mountain and demonstrate what a very capable skier and guide he was. Riding up the in the cable car with him, I made sure to remind him that Pete had only done about eight weeks' skiing so implored him to take it easy. He heard me but clearly he wasn't listening. We whizzed around quite freely to start with and it was certainly nice to be guided around for a change and not have to think about how all the runs connected up and which lift would take us where. We covered a lot of ground and stopped for a chat with a couple of the guys from the ski hire shop we had met at Hummelstugan. All was good so far. Pete was keeping up remarkably well. It was then that it started to go a bit pear shaped, before it went banana shaped.

"Do you fancy going up to the top and over to Backsidan?" John asked.

Pete hadn't a clue what that entailed but I asked John if he thought it was suitable for Pete, not wishing to confess I was wondering if it was suitable for me too.

"Yes, I think he'll be fine," John assured us both.

We handed over our Kronor for the one way tow up to the very top and, a little apprehensively, skied over the edge, following John down and round to the right. It was a very different scene over there being devoid of any lifts, huts, restaurants or indeed any signs of the fun part of skiing.

It was stark, empty and unpisted, although the snow was very good.

We swooped down, zig-zagging over some rough lumpy areas of snow, all the while moving around to the right of the mountain, when eventually we came to a ridge where we stopped and looked over the edge. From here we could see the lake and the town far below, and the straight line of the road and railway cutting through the countryside heading south eastwards. Further away, on the other side of the frozen lake, the tree covered hills rose and fell as far as you could see until they became blurred in a light grey haze.

Immediately below our ski tips, the ground fell away at such a startling angle that I backed away a little, steadying myself by pushing my ski poles hard into the snow to prevent any possible forward movement.

After 'wowing' at the view, Pete and I looked up to John for directions. He looked a bit concerned and kept turning his head up towards the top of the mountain, about two to three hundred metres away. We could see a handful of skiers had stood still on the edge in a line and one-by-one were easing themselves over the edge before plunging down the slope beneath them. It looked quite steep where they were and there was some degree of hesitation before they pushed off.

"I don't think I would want to be where they are!" I commented, flippantly.

"Er, well, no. Actually, on the contrary, I think that's exactly where we ought to be," said John, rather sheepishly.

"What?!"

"Yeah, I think we've come too far down," he added.

Pete gave me a look of panic knowing that there was no way we were going to be able to climb up three hundred metres to get to where the other skiers were and his face said 'what the hell are we going to do now?'

"Yes, I think that's the ravine we should be on. This one's the steep one," said John.

"I can see it's steep! I wasn't expecting that we were going to have to ski down it. In fact, how *do* we ski down it? It's almost vertical!" A high degree of panic had come across me, which I could hear in my voice. God knows what Pete was thinking with his rusty eight weeks of skiing. He was probably hoping we were both having a joke and winding him up.

"Well, we can't get up there," John nodded towards the higher ravine.

"Jesus!" exclaimed Pete through gritted teeth as he stared down into the abyss.

The ravine seemed to grin at us, beckoning and challenging us saying, "come on, if you dare."

The snow was virtually unblemished with only three pairs of ski tracks that I could see. Some of the snow had become dislodged and formed snow balls that had run down the slope, gathering mass and momentum, leaving little wobbly trails marking their route downwards. Most of the balls were small but some had grown large and had smashed themselves to pieces on the rocks that stuck out of the snow like blisters on an otherwise smooth skin. We stood poised in our boots, supporting our weight on our poles, staring down the steep bowl of snow.

"We're going to have to go down it," John said, reluctantly.

It was so steep I couldn't see how we wouldn't all just fall to the bottom as soon as we pitched over the edge. "Best thing to do is to enter side on and traverse all the way round, losing a bit of height as you go."

"And then what?" asked Pete apprehensively.

"Then you'll have to jump turn and traverse all the way back round here again, losing as much height as you can."

Pete turned to me in horror, his lips pursed to make an "F" sound then shook his head. I felt very responsible for him and disappointed and annoyed that John had been so irresponsible.

"We'll just take it easy and take it as slow as possible."

The traversing bit would be OK. It was the jump turns that would be difficult because if you got that wrong you would certainly tumble down a long, long way, just by slightly over-balancing.

John edged himself into position, pointing his skis away from us and almost parallel with the top lip of the bowl, aiming to cross the lip at a fine angle. We braced ourselves for what he was about to do and then he shoved himself off and over the edge. He soon picked up some speed as he traversed twenty metres across and had to carefully edge his skis in order to scrub off some speed before coming to a halt at the end.

While he plucked up the courage for his jump, Pete had already gone, traversing in a tense nervous style but at a more controlled speed. His problem would be that he hadn't really lost much height and ended up about ten metres above John. I went next and concentrated hard at keeping my skis under control whilst side-slipping down a little every horizontal metre of traverse. John had already made his turn and was heading back across by the time I looked up and Pete was about to make his jump. I decided it was every man for himself and I had to concentrate on what I was doing.

Mercifully, I had become fit through all the skiing I had done. It took quite a bit of effort to bend down then jump up and spin around on my skis. Out of my peripheral vision, I was vaguely aware of the other two at stages of our descent. Once settled and steadied after each jump, we had to push off along the horizontal, dreading reaching the side of the bowl and having to perform another jump turn. There was a lot of swearing as we wavered about, teetering on the very edge of being in balance at any one time and from the increasing effort in doing yet another jump turn. I could liken it to doing your first tightrope walk except we weren't practising it a foot off the ground. My mouth went very dry and there were several moments when I thought I had overcooked the turn and was about to plummet all the way to the bottom. We carried on like this, each utterly absorbed in our own concentration, for about twenty minutes. Each time I reached the end of a traverse, I had to psyche myself up to make the jump around. It was slightly easier if you kept a bit of momentum going, as you could use the forward motion to carry you through the turn, reaching out with the downward ski pole to mark what you hoped would be the centre of your turn.

However, as I descended, each turn became more exhausting through the sheer physical and mental effort and the stress of holding it all together. This was the kind of slope I had seen on extreme skiing videos; one mistake and you fell a long way to who knew what outcome. When we finally reached the bottom, the slope began to level off. I was by now furious with John for being such a total idiot and bringing us down that way and let him know about it. To this day, I don't know how I made it down it in one piece, let alone Pete with so much less time on skis. His regular gym work probably helped him out. He remained silent when he got to them bottom. John wasn't that apologetic merely saying "Well, we all made it", but I think he had given himself a scare too and realised he had been foolish.

We followed him on down a little way and it was only then that I realised I was dripping with sweat, absolutely knackered and my body was shaking with adrenaline. John paused by a pile of boulders and a spindly tree that arched over the gulley whilst we caught up with him.

Rather sheepishly, I thought, he announced: "Err… it looks like we have to follow the course of the river. It's the only way down from here."

He was right. Ahead of us lay a narrow, frozen river bed, scattered with all sizes and shapes of boulders that we would have to ski around. We were going to have to do more quick turns if we were going anywhere. There was no other option so we pressed on in silence, pushing ourselves through the pain of exhaustion until we got to the end where we could easily ski out over a bank and re-join a piste with welcome relief.

Back in my room, Pete and I drank our beers with great enthusiasm and huge relief that we were still alive. I was now maintaining a small stock of beer cans buried in the snow on my balcony outside my window; the temperature was just right. Rummaging around for a second beer for each of us, I came across something soft and a bit squidgy. It had straight edges and was about an inch thick. I scooped some more snow away so that I could get a firmer grasp to yank it free. With a couple of wiggles, I pulled it out and to my amazement it was a half-eaten pizza from a few months ago!

Deliriously happy from still being alive and slightly drunk on two beers in the aftershock of our trauma, we decided to celebrate by taking the pizza up to the café upstairs to ask the girls if they could defrost it and heat it up in their microwave. They thought the idea was 'gross', of course, but as we all know, warmed up next day pizza tastes so good. When you have just had a near-death experience and the pizza is a couple of months old, it tastes sublime.

Something else that tastes so good is your mother's traditional Christmas cake, which I had transported all the way from Austria and had not tucked into until Christmas itself. Rationing myself to a slice every now and again I had treated a few friends to a taster. The head chef at the Åregården Hotel and creator of some fantastic dishes – which we rarely got to taste, seeing as how we ate with the regular staff most days – was a woman called Pernilla. A tall, striking looking woman with piercing blue eyes, short dark blonde curly hair she had a deep brown tan the whole season. She had a very strong, athletic figure, I presumed from healthy eating and plenty of Cross Country skiing, as she had told me.

Being head chef, her staff feared her, of course, but I always thought she was gentle and charming although I wasn't working for her in the pressurised environment of her kitchen. I got talking to her one morning as she was sat in the hotel lobby having a coffee. I had just collected a fax from the hotel office. It was one of the rare times I had seen her out of her white chef's jacket and chequered trousers and I was surprised to see here, so casually attired. She was preparing new menus for the end of season and invited me to stop for a coffee. She wanted some inspiration and to know what English people would be eating at this time of year. I'm not sure I was of much help to her but we got onto the subject of Christmas cake, which she had never tasted. I gave her a description and, knowing I had some left, I offered to share some with her. My mother would have been proud and perhaps a little embarrassed that the head chef of the best hotel in the resort was eager to try her cake.

"That would be great," she said enthusiastically. "It sounds like it's a great taste. But also, I have heard of something else you eat called *Marmot*?"

An image of a cute little furry animal sitting on a rock sprang to mind. I looked at her with a puzzled expression.

"Err… no?" I was reminded of Radar asking us about eating beetles and tried to think what she meant.

"Aah… *Marmite*, you mean!"

"Yes, that's it!"

"It's probably the opposite of Christmas cake on the taste scale, but yes I have some in my room."

She seemed delighted with the opportunity to experience some new flavours. Recalling a conversation we had had weeks ago, she asked, "Tell me, Andrew. Have you been cross country skiing yet?"

"No, I haven't."

"You must do it before the end of the season and you go home to London. How about I take you *längdåkning* (cross country skiing) with my dogs one morning in exchange for your mother's Christmas cake and a taste of some *Marmite*?"

It was an extraordinarily unusual offer, but one I had to accept.

From the head chef's desire to create ever more imaginative menus, to one menu that was standard around the world. Tuesday 15th April had become a special date in the diary amongst most of the season workers in the village, not because of any religious or traditional significance, but because McDonalds was due to open in Östersund. I have never been a huge fan of the big M but the opportunity to get out of Åre for half a day and the promise of a Big Mac and fries and a few hours of relative normality were proving to be very alluring. On reflection, it was ridiculous to want to leave a lovely ski resort to travel an hour to a normal town for a burger and chips, but it was more the desire for a change of scenery than the taste of a burger. Looking at the diary, it promised to be a quiet week with a drop in the number of guests, so I was hoping I wouldn't have to take any of them out skiing or accompany them on an excursion.

The guests were starting to get in the way of having fun nowadays as I immersed myself more and more into the ski bum community and at times it was hard to remember I was here to work seven days a week. Many of the other reps were at the end of their seasons already and had ditched their uniforms for "civvies".

Various groups had been planning car sharing or researching bus or train routes into the town. It had all become a bit desperate really, like the pre-New Year's Eve mania that develops each year. It is hard to imagine the genuine excitement that was building. It had become infectious and the closer we got to the day the more people were talking about it. I had actually got a bit annoyed that I couldn't commit to any of the kind offers of a seat in a car because I didn't know, for sure, whether I would be able to make the trip. The various journeys to the town would turn out to become more of an event than simply sitting down at the restaurant and taking the first bite but I didn't want to miss out on the day. As the day drew closer, it was becoming clearer that, on the positive side of things, I would be able to be free to go but, on the negative, since I had left it too late, all the car spaces had been filled up. I couldn't justify spending my money on the train fare and the airport transfer coaches would leave the village too early in the morning or too late in the afternoon. Like Cinderella, I was beginning to think that I would have to miss out on what was turning out to be one of the season's great social events until, quite by chance, I happened to bump into my Finnish friend, Kai. He was bounding up the stairs, following a late breakfast and on his way out for a mid-morning snowboarding session, his big eyes shining brightly from his tanned, bearded face.

"*Hej*, Andrew. I was meaning to ask you if you were wanting to go to the McDonalds opening?"

"Thanks. It seems like everyone else is going so it would be a shame to miss out on the party. I'm not that fussed about the Big Mac but it would be good to get away from here for a while."

"OK, great. You know I have my car here now and I was thinking of going late morning if you wanna lift?"

"Yeah, sure. Thanks."

"Max and Henrik are going earlier, but I'm working tonight so I will have to go later on."

"Sounds great. Where shall we meet?"

"My car's in the car park behind the hotel – I've been pretending to be a guest as I'm not supposed to park there but let's meet at eleven?"

When I met Kai in the car park, he had already cleared the previous night's snow off the windscreen and was busy wiping the rear window clear with one of his big snowboard mitten. The driver's door was open and the engine was running. It was mid April, quite late in the season, and we were still experiencing big dumps of snow overnight. *It bode well for lots of sunny Spring skiing,* I thought. I helped him kick the snow away from the rear wheels of his old Opel Manta and soon we were buckling up for the ride. When the doors shut he started rummaging around for a CD, stretching forward to reach into various storage pockets. As he was doing so, I noticed how his little extra beardy thing – a tiny twist of hair below his lower lip – appeared to twitch about of its own accord with his exertions.

"We need music, I think," he announced. "Let's have some British music for you," he said, and pulled out Jamiroquai's *Travelling Without Moving* CD and slid it into the player he had wired up to his car's system. I noticed there were wires going everywhere in this car. The opening piano chords of *Virtual Insanity* prompted him to select reverse gear with his right hand and spin the steering wheel around with his left. In an instant, we were facing out across the car park towards the frozen lake and I realised it was going to be another exciting car drive. I should have anticipated it really, seeing how he was a Finn and had learned to drive on the snow and ice.

"OK – let's go…!" and with that he floored the throttle. The car spun its studded winter tyres for a brief moment before finding grip from who knows where and we launched across the car park to the downhill slope out onto the lake road. Only the day before had John and I amused ourselves for a good half an hour in the warmth and comfort of the hotel, looking out of a window watching cars and people nervously edge their way out of this car park. Most would slide uncontrollably down into the path of the lake road and either crash softly into the snow bank on the far side or into the side of vehicles already on the road. People could hardly stand up, let alone walk down the slope – many had entertained us by falling over and sliding down on their backsides as we chortled away at their misfortune. And yet here we were already doing about 25 mph as we reached the edge of the small car park.

I felt my whole body tense up and instinctively reached for the arm rests and buried my right foot into the car's footwell on the non-existent brake pedal.

Oh My God...! I exclaimed, silently, in my head. But Kai wasn't showing off. Well, maybe just a little bit. He was utterly unfazed about the conditions and had everything under total control. I have absolutely no idea how he managed to get the car down the slope and then turn left onto the lake road without ploughing straight into the bank on the other side of the road.

There was a flash of a hand on the handbrake and a deft flick of the rear of the car. It was all a blur and so natural to him. Once on the road, he continued along at a steady pace that to start with I felt was far too quick to give him time and space to stop if he needed to. He was as calm as Helsinki cucumber. When we reached the main road, he picked up the pace and slid the car round the corners with ample doses of opposite lock, balancing the car on the throttle in the style of Ari Vatanen and Hannu Mikkola. As usual, there wasn't much traffic on the road, but he didn't slow down for corners, he just changed the car's angle, like he was turning on skis. The marker posts on the edge of the highway flashed by in a blur, as did the rows and rows of tall dark fir trees. Crossing an expansive icy patch on the road made no difference to our speed; he took it all in his stride.

"Yeah, it's fun, hey?!" and he looked across at me.

"Mmm..." I whimpered, rather unmanly-like, thankful the music was so loud he couldn't hear me, then nodded my head vigorously with approval, giving him a visible sign. "How fast are we going?" I tried to sound enthusiastic, not critical.

He looked down at the speedometer whilst reaching for his cigarettes and lighter from his door side pocket. "One twenty five," he answered nonchalantly. That was about 80 mph.

"OK" was all I could say.

After a while, since we hadn't actually hit anything or flipped the car onto its roof or crashed out over a snow bank on a corner, I began to settle down and relax into it. On a long straight, he drove for a while on the left side of the road "to make me feel at home", which was very considerate of him.

"When did Sweden stop driving on the left?" I asked.

"Sixty Seven, I think," he replied, adding, "They called it *Dagen H* (H Day), the crazy Swedes. H for *Höger* (Right)." *It must have been chaotic*, I thought. They organised it with true Swedish efficiency very early one morning. All non-essential traffic had been forbidden from using the roads from 1am to 6am on the morning of 3rd September and any vehicles that were out on the road had to stop completely at 4.50am. Then they had to drive very slowly to the right side and stop again until 5.00am before moving off again. In the larger cities, the travel ban lasted much longer, most of the weekend in fact, as workers had to alter road intersections, signage and traffic lights. The more you think about what had to be done, the more of a headache it must have been. I didn't have time to dwell on it though.

As we approached yet another bend in the road he said: "You know about the Scandinavian Flick? It's really the Finnish Flick." He demonstrated it whilst talking it through, methodically turning the wheel to the outside of the bend, then into the bend and quickly lifting off the throttle. The car slid sideways facing away from the bend. Then he turned the wheel towards the bend, released the brake pedal whilst applying the throttle and the car slingshot itself around the corner. It was a great feeling, and a league above the taxi rides to Duved, although I suspect some of those drivers could probably perform the same manoeuvre if they didn't have paying customers on board.

After all that excitement, the opening of a hamburger joint seemed, perhaps not unsurprisingly, very tame, if not a bit of a let down. We must have all been suffering from the equivalent of island fever or more appropriately, resort fever, to have been so desperate to journey to the opening by train, bus, car, snowmobile or whatever. The burgers and fries tasted just like any other McDonalds, as did the Coke. It was odd seeing so many familiar faces out of context, wearing normal clothes instead of ski clothes. The snowboard dudes still had their beanies on, of course.

Once we had feasted, no one knew quite what to do. Kai and I wandered around town for a bit and I dived into a bookshop to while away half an hour and give a bit more purpose to the day. Surprisingly, there were a large number of books in English and, oddly, I enjoyed picking out books I had already read. Over the months, I hadn't read nearly as much as I normally do and so I bought a couple of paperbacks and a high gloss photo book showing Åre in all four seasons. Kai purchased some CDs and some weird flavoured tobacco for his roll ups, so he was happy, and we headed back to the car. Although looking back now it was a bit of a mad thing to do, it was nevertheless a good morning out of the familiar surroundings of the resort and I felt better for it. The journey back was just as thrilling as the drive out, although by now I was an old hand at being the rally co-driver.

Head chef Pernilla pounced out at me in the ICA supermarket from behind the cheese counter and reminded me that we still hadn't gone cross country skiing. I unshouldered my rucksack and dug out my diary, which was now looking clearer as each week passed. All I had in it for the following week was 'Haircut five weeks', which was another £30 gone for just a regular trim, on Tuesday 22nd, and *Personalfest* (staff party) from 3.30pm in the Country Club night club. If the drinking started at that time, it would wipe me out for the following morning. Looking back to the Sunday before, then we only had five guests arriving; one staying in the 'sad single room' in the Diplomat Hotel so it wasn't looking like a big week. My employment contract officially finished on 20th April and, somewhat irritatingly, I saw we had another solitary guest arriving on Sunday 27th April. That was a whole week after my contract finished. *What on earth were they thinking?*

We fixed a date for Monday afternoon and Pernilla asked me for my shoe size then told me to be by her car, a black VW Golf, outside the Hotel Åregarden at 2pm. I headed off to buy a Coke, some crisps and a filled fresh baguette from Sandys before walking over to watch the snowboard competition. I sat in the sun, forgetting all about the demanding guests for a while. Not being a snowboarder, I had no idea who I was watching but, as I discovered later, this was a big international event; the TAB X-tra Snowboard Contest, promoted by the interestingly named *G-Spot & edge*. The guys competing were in their late teens and early twenties but were to become Olympic competitors and legends in the world of snowboarding over the next few years, the sport still being relatively young in 1997. The flyers promoting the event were advertising *50,000usd till vinnaren* (US$ 50,000 to the winner). The big names in the Halfpipe *Tävling* (competition) included: Ingemar Backman, Daniel Franck, Johan Olofsson, Terje Haakonsen, Peter Line and Jeff Brushie. Alongside these top names were a lot of locals and regional competitors, of course.

Monday 2pm soon came around and I was dutifully stood

by the black Golf when Pernilla appeared from behind the hotel being pulled on the lead enthusiastically by her two beautiful huskies. She loaded them into the back of the car and we jumped into the front before setting off at a sedate pace on the road to Duved, chatting away easily. About 15 kms after Duved, we peeled off onto a narrow track, which wound its way through a small forest for a short while before reaching the edge of yet another frozen lake. This one, however, was more remote than the others. There were no snowmobiles or, indeed, any other tracks visible in the snow.

Pernilla swiftly brought down the thin, straight cross country skis from the rack on the roof and grabbed some poles and dainty little (by comparison with downhill) ski boots for me to try on. They were a perfect fit, which was lucky because I couldn't see that she had brought any others. She helped me get settled into the boots and onto the skis, which felt very different to the normal, wider, carving skis I was used to. The toes of my boots were attached but my heels were free and it was difficult to move around. I felt like a complete novice again, which was an unsettling feeling having mastered alpine skis to the point where it was as easy as walking.

I heaved up the skis, lifting them out of the snow and placed them in the direction I needed to go, rather than sliding them around. I supported myself all the while with the ski poles and had a feeling this wasn't going to go well. Even the slightest slope down onto the lake surface did nothing to boost my confidence. I couldn't get the balance right and the skis separated, forcing me to throw myself to the floor.

"It gets easier on the flat!" shouted Pernilla, as she locked up the car and attended to the dogs. She joined me on the level and gave instructions on the correct actions my arms and legs should be taking. I needed to be looking ahead, not down at my skis, and reaching up and out with grace and poise. I looked out across the pale lemon-coloured snowfield and squinted my eyes against the brightness of the sun.

"Watch me," she said, and off she went with all the grace and poise of a gazelle, her long athletic legs propelling her forward purposefully. She stopped and looked back at me while her dogs went nuts, charging around after each other in big circles, ecstatic to be out in the fresh air and wild expanse of the frozen lake. I set off in her ski tracks, copying her actions as best I could.

"Head up!" she cried out, lifting her own head with the back of her hand. "Reach out!"

It was, surprisingly, gradually coming together already. A couple of wobbles but no falls and, after a while longer, once I had got into a rhythm, I forgot about the exaggerated movement of my limbs and concentrated on getting more power into the actions. Pernilla had set off again at some speed heading towards the middle of the lake. The dogs were running and leaping alongside her as she went. I concentrated hard and began to keep the rhythm more easily. Suddenly it felt like I had changed up a gear and I was moving a lot faster. I daren't turn but kept heading straight towards Pernilla. Disconcertingly, she had now veered off to the left a bit. The centre of the lake was further away than I had first thought and it took me quite a while to reach her. When I did finally get to her, I was huffing and puffing like a train. I thought I had become quite fit, with all the skiing I had done over the last months, but I must have been exercising a whole different muscle set. She stood there quietly with an amused look on her face as I came to a stop. My entire body heaved up and down with the exertion and I couldn't speak for about a minute.

"It's a good exercise, yes?"

I looked at her, still panting, mouth open, tongue lolling about and just nodded in agreement, leaning on my ski poles for support. Slowly, I regained my composure and my breathing started to return to normal.

"It's so quiet here," she continued, looking around us. "Listen... what can you hear?"

My laboured breathing is what I could hear but, when I got that under control, I strained my ears to hear what she was listening to. "Nothing. I can't hear anything."

"Wait. You will hear it."

We were miles from anywhere. There was no traffic anywhere near us. I listened for the shriek of a bird or the wind but still couldn't hear anything.

I looked at her and shook my head, not wanting to speak and spoil the silence. "Silence!" I whispered.

"Yes!" she congratulated me like a teacher would a pupil.

We stood there just listening to nothing. The dogs had settled down a few metres away from us. I couldn't hear anything at all, no background noise, absolutely nothing. It was an odd sensation to strain your ears so much, willing them to pick up something only to experience deafness.

"Do you hear anything yet?" she asked. I wondered what she meant and gave her a quizzical look.

"Wait some more and you will hear it." *She was beginning to get a bit weird now,* I thought. *Was I about to hear one of her chef's knives being withdrawn from its scabbard?* But then I tuned my ears to a different pitch. I could hear something after all. It was the blood being pumped around my body and what sounded like other liquids and muscles moving slowly, like a muffled sort of underwater sound. What's more, I swear I could actually hear my heart beating.

I looked at Pernilla and nodded my head in realisation. She grinned back in acknowledgement. It was the complete opposite of an outer body experience.

The Winner Takes It All

As the April days passed by, I began to notice more posters up around the resort advertising ÅRE Skutskjutet, which was a downhill ski race, a *tävling för hela familjen* (competition for the whole family). The flyer appeared pinned to notice boards, stuck to lamp posts, and inserted into the local freebie newspaper, Årefjälen Idag.

More and more people were beginning to talk about it as the day of the event drew nearer and it began to feel like entry was almost compulsory. "Why aren't you entering the race?" would be the next line of questioning. I called in at the *Turistbyrå* (tourist office) just to find out a little more from my friends there, who would surely give me an honest view of what was involved. It did sound a little daunting, being a proper downhill race with people travelling from miles around and the guys in the ski hire shop discussing which wax to use on their skis.

I left their office twenty minutes later, clutching my race entry form, having paid my 150kr entry fee and signed what I think was a waiver in the event of an accident. It was a wordy form in Swedish that Bengt in the office just waved his hand over telling me not to worry, just sign on the dotted line. I walked back across the village square deep in concentration, reading the details of the competition and begun to wonder what I was letting myself in for. Although it was promoted as being open to the whole family, it looked a little more serious than I had been led to believe. Jenny from the ski school was calling my name as I stepped up onto the pavement on the other side of the square, still fixated on the words on the piece of paper I held in front of me.

"*Hej*, Andrew! Are you entered into the competition now?"

I looked up at her.

"Don't look so worried. It will be fine. Have you time for *fika*? I can talk you through it."

She led me off to the little pizza restaurant, which was now serving coffees in the morning rather than just pizza in the evening. Still holding the competition information tightly in my hand, I sat down at a table covered with a red gingham cloth. She placed a hot coffee in front of me and told me to stop trying to translate it.

She proceeded to explain that the race day was on 30th April and there was a practice day on the 29th. The race times commenced at 9am and the course started from *Stendalsravinen slut* (the end of Stendals ravine) and finished in Ullådalen, below Ullådalenstugan, which was part way round the back of the mountain in a vast open area. There were twenty five competition classes and I was entered in *Herrar Motionsklass*, which to my relief, as Jenny explained, was not the top speed competition class. I did not need to be waxing my skis but, needing to gain any advantage, I did ask the ski shop to chuck some speed wax on. Nor did I need to squeeze myself into a figure-hugging all-in-one slippery ski suit. But lots of people would. There were Competition Classes for men, women, boys born 1982–83, girls born 1982–83, boys 84–85, girls 84–85, boys 86–87, girls 86–87, boys 88–89, girls 88–89, then followed my class (11), class 12 *Motionsklass Damer, Motionsklass* boys 82–89, and girls 82–89. There were Speedski classes for men and women, snowboard classes, Telemark, Sitski classes (for disabled skiers) for men and women, and to lessen the seriousness and new for this year a *Karnevalsklass*, which was open to everyone who wanted to dress up as a zebra or a clown. For a short while, I thought about swapping to that class as it would be forgivable to fall over, but I couldn't think where I would source the appropriate costume. Jennny told me I should be happy with my general men's class, adding that the practice day was really just for the serious competitors and I needn't bother with that. Just turn up and have fun but go as fast as you dare, she encouraged.

There would be about a thousand people competing on the day, lots more watching and, if that wasn't too off putting, the TV and radio companies would be there broadcasting all day.

She said they would have a proper start area with a timing hut and commentary all the way down as well as a big crowd at the bottom to welcome all the skiers. The event was sponsored by a host of well known companies, including SAS, Telia, ICA supermarkets, SJ (the national railway), Lapinkulta (Finnish beer), as well as local Åre companies, of course. I was excited but apprehensive. It was sounding very much like a major downhill race that *Ski Sunday* could be covering. I began to have a recurring image of me disguised as a banana, under the name Freddie Fyffes, skiing in the *Karnevalklass*. But it was perhaps going to be easier just to keep a very low profile in case I crashed out at the first turn or tumbled across the finish line. That was until I saw my name highlighted on the provisional entry list as coming from **LONDON**.

I didn't really need that extra pressure and could envisage me being announced at the start gate... "And now... all the way from LONDON... number 2356... it's..." No, something had to change. Either Freddie Fyffes had to make an appearance or I had to be listed as a local. Luckily, the latter prevailed.

I had been building the event up in my mind as a much bigger thing than it really was but, as it got nearer to race day, there was a noticeable increase in visitor numbers to the resort and a palpable frisson of excitement in the air.

Foolishly, perhaps, I heeded Jenny's advice and avoided the practice day. Looking back, I'm not sure why. Knowing the direction and flow of the downhill course would, I believe, have been a *good thing* and I should have gone. I didn't have anything else on as we only had one guest in the resort, a mysterious Mr

S from who knew where. He arrived by taxi, stayed in the 'sad single room' in the Hotel Diplomat and we never saw or heard a peep out of him. Stefan had commented that he was polite enough but not chatty and had more luggage than expected. *What he was doing all week in his room was anyone's guess – writing a book?*

Wednesday 30th April arrived with hazy sunshine. It was race day and, cunningly, I had two breakfasts, thinking that as it was a downhill race the more I weighed, the better. After a big strong coffee though, the nerves saw to it that I lost some of the extra breakfast weight in a pre-race 'download'. Oh well, I'd have to reconcile myself with being lighter and fleet of foot and ski. My start time was at 11.07 and, as I left my room, I met Mariha coming out of her room opposite so we headed out to the bus stop together. She was doing her weather girl bit for Radio Rix, reporting from the race HQ. It was good to have someone to talk to on the journey to Duved. There were a large number of serious-looking skiers on the bus, clad in skin tight gear with racy looking skis. I kept checking I had both skis with me and had done nothing stupid, like put my boots on the wrong feet or forgotten my gloves.

At Duved, we all filed off the bus and headed up towards the colourful banners at the lift station, where we were checked in and were given our numbered race bib.

They were all one size – medium. That was fine if you slipped it over your second skin slippery cat suit. Not so fine if you were wearing a regular ski jacket. It kind of sat around on my chest like an ill-designed, ill-fitting bra and I had to keep pulling it down so my number was visible.

We rode the lift up to the start area together and Mariha met up with her radio colleagues who were sorting out a tangle of some wires that had been inserted into large black boxes.

I declined their request for an interview, in spite of Mariha's attempts to charm me into doing it.

"Maybe when I reach the bottom in one piece," I suggested. They all wished me luck and Mariha said she would see me at the finish area telling me not to worry.

"It's easy," she added, taking my rucksack from me.

"Yeah? Why aren't you doing it then?"

"I have to work, of course," she replied with a big smile.

"Of course."

I turned around and trudged off through the snow with my super slippery K2 USA skis in the general direction of a gaggle of small tents I had spotted at the side of a piste lined with orange catch fencing. The advertising flags and banners fluttered sporadically in the soft breeze. Somewhat unnervingly, I noticed most of the skiers standing immediately ahead of me were wearing helmets.

"Hmmm. Didn't think of that," I said to myself. This was at a time when hardly anyone wore a helmet. As I got closer, I figured they must be in the super competition classes and there were, to my relief, a fair few other skiers like me in regular ski gear. I passed by all sizes and shapes and ages of skier huddled in groups with friends or family. It was like walking through a big airport. People were stood still, sitting down, stretching, unpacking bags, taking snacks and drinks. They hugged friends before walking determinedly off to the start hut when they could see their number was getting close to the one displayed on the illuminated sign high up on a post.

One elderly gentleman could hardly walk on the snow but was gamely carrying his thin skis and poles. He seemed to know everyone as so many people wished him luck. Jenny had told me about old Rufus. He was eighty one years old and still entered the race every year. I would be happy if I could pull on my own socks at that age.

All was calm and orderly when I reached the start hut area. People were shuffling along, waiting patiently to be called into the little wooden hut. Two snowmobiles were parked up to one side, alarmingly attached to long coffin like boxes. I'm sure they were for carrying ski poles, I reassured myself. A husky dog lay by one of the snowmobiles, tethered to a post and watched me go by.

"You should be doing it as well, rather than just lying around all morning in the hazy sun," I said to him. He looked at me and yawned.

When I got closer to the starting hut, I could see that the race numbers filing through were from 648 to 686. They were young lads, keen to impress and taking it very seriously, leaning forwards on their ski poles, stretching their calf muscles and making precise but unnecessary adjustments to their helmet straps and goggles.

There was some time to go before my turn and looking at my watch it was 10.25am. *Would they really process that number of skiers in forty minutes?* I wondered. I stood and watched for a while as the numbers steadily increased. I figured I had half an hour before I needed to return and I would only get more anxious just standing there, so I walked over to a small hill beyond the starting area where I could observe the really fast racers tackle the course.

The course boundaries were marked out on either side of the wide piste with tiny gorse bush cuttings about thirty centimetres in diameter. These were placed every ten metres or so. I watched the skiers bolt out of the hut, tuck down and cut a wide arc around to the left, close to where I was standing, before carving back to the right then down a steeper section, which banked up on the right side before sweeping to the left and disappearing from view. By this point they had gathered a lot of speed. Beyond my hill, I couldn't see much of the rest of the course because it was well below my position, but I could make out small moving blobs much further down as they glided under the finish line and came to a sweeping stop in front of the crowd. It looked like a long way down, not to mention fast. I really should have come up here the day before for practice.

I was slightly mesmerised watching skier after skier pop out of the hut and speed down in a graceful arc below me, and the half hour quickly passed. When I made it back up to the starting hut queues, I took up a position in the crowd of people and noticed three guys in front of me with the numbers 2346, 2347 and 2348 on their backs. They were edging forward with their boots already clipped firmly into their skis. I didn't see any other similar numbers to mine and many people behind me were still carrying their skis on their shoulders. Others were walking their skis along beside them, ready to throw down and step into them with that distinctive click as each boot secured itself. I quickly pulled mine apart and placed them on the snow, making sure the one with the black scuff near the top was on the left side. Superstitiously, I hadn't fallen over since I had started to do that a few weeks ago.

There was much more room to manoeuvre in this queue compared to the usual lift queue. That said, apart from one or two weeks here, there were no queues to speak of at all. That could not be said of most alpine resorts; I recall queueing in Austria for thirty minutes at one chairlift, everyone pushing and shoving and standing on your skis, just to have a ten minute ski back down. As I got closer to the hut, I could hear the race numbers being called out and in the background the *beep, beep, beep, beeeeep* of the starting timer. The organisers were churning us through fairly swiftly. My heart rate started to rise as the adrenalin kicked in. I concentrated for a moment on the white flag of Åreliftarna and the yellow flag of Åre SLK, the town's alpine ski club, which contrasted against the misty blue sky as they unfurled and rolled in the gentle wind.

And then I found myself stepping into the shadow of the

start hut, pulling down my race numbered bra so the official could see it. One of them nodded, scribbled something on his clip board and ushered me further forward.

Another man with very dark sunglasses on and a white cap motioned me into the hut as he spoke into a small microphone that was wrapped around his face. As he pushed his ear piece deeper into his ear, he nodded and then gently pulled my left arm to guide me further into the dark hut.

Competitor 2355 was crouched down, gently bobbing up and down, knees bent and arms outstretched, poised to leap out. The electronic beeps counted him down, *Beep beep beep beeeep* and then he sprang up and outward, a blur of colour against the white background. His shins pushed against the needle-like timing bar and it swung back out of the way. He was off, a little ungainly at first, as he steadied himself into the tuck position.

Next up was me and I shuffled forward on my skis across the sludgy snow inside the relative warmth of the tent towards the start line. As I got closer to the opening, my eyes adjusted to the brightness of the ski piste outside and I just caught a glimpse of 2355 as he rounded a corner and disappeared from view behind a small hill. The spectators on the hill stood up and clapped him by as he descended past their vantage point. I hoped they were going to clap for me too.

One of the starter line officials guided me into the exact start point and eased me up close to the timing needle. My skis squidged flat the imprints of 2355's skis. Breathing heavily, I could feel my heart thumping harder against my chest now and my mouth went dry. I too made unnecessary adjustments to my goggles strap whilst I looked down the piste ahead of me, trying to pick out my route.

"*Två, tre, fem, sex... redo,*" I heard someone call out, followed by the *Beep, beep, beep, beeeep.*

I heaved myself out of the hut, pulling hard on my poles and then pushing away with my legs and poles, praying I would not fall over so soon. Frantically, I grabbed more holds in the snow with the ski pole tips and pushed off with a few more ice skating strides, trying to get up to maximum speed as soon as possible. Then I settled myself into a tuck, with my arms outstretched and my poles tucked into my arm pits. Soon after the initial launch, it became a lot steeper than it had looked and my speed increased so dramatically that I wondered if I had put too much effort into my initial launch. I was certainly going to have to scrub off some speed before the second turn or I would plough straight on into a bush, up the hill I had been standing on and probably get airborne.

After the big left arc, I pressed hard down on my left ski to brake a little but, more importantly, to steer me around to the right again. I made that turn successfully and then headed down a straight section which quickly became much steeper and faster. It really didn't look this fast when standing on the hill. I rounded the next left turn, which was slightly banked up to the right and used that banking to brake and turn left. That turn had a wonderful flow to it. I was now past the hill and into territory I hadn't been able to recce from my earlier vantage point. I could see the finishing area way down the slope and, only at this point, I think I took my first breath.

Perhaps it was more of a gasp as I realised how far I had still to go. After a few more hard turns, carefully staying within the boundary markers, I could feel my thighs begin to burn. Tensed up as I was, I could feel every little bump and imperfection in the surface as my legs shook and jarred, trying to absorb bumps and compressions at such speed. I have no idea how fast I was actually going but I don't think I have ever skied as fast before or since.

"Breathe again!" I had to remind myself, as difficult as it was between gritted teeth.

The rush of air made a tremendous noise, as did the skis, scuffing and scraping their route through the snow. I cut one turn a little too tightly when I should have let the skis drift out a bit in a natural arc and got punished for it by dropping down into a compression, which forced my knees right up into my chest and almost knocked the wind out of me.

I let out a gasp of air as I hit the bottom and concentrated on recovering. My trajectory was now out of alignment for this next series of curves and, once I had recovered my stance, I found myself heading out too wide to the right. There was nothing I could do about it now, other than ride it out and at the very last moment push down on my right ski with all the force I could muster in the hope of bringing me back round to the left again.

As I got ever closer to the little green leafy markers, my right leg felt like it was about to burst open with the amount of pressure I was applying. My whole body was also canted over to the left like a true Olympic downhiller. Frustratingly, I was now heading out of the course limits for a disqualification. I looked down at the outside edge of my right boot as the marker hurtled into my field of vision, waiting for the moment. But, to my astonishment, as I watched in slow motion, the little bush flashed past in a dark green blur against the white snow *on the outside of my boot.* I had made it. I was still on the course, still in the competition. Elated, and, with renewed vigour and strength from who knows where, I pressed on, carving and turning, striving to get my lines right.

The home straight finally opened up in front of me and I dropped into the full tuck again, willing myself ever faster. I crossed the finish line under the sponsor's banner and immediately found myself having to snap out of race mode and focus on finding somewhere to stop. There really wasn't much room at all in the finish arena and my leg muscles felt completely burnt out, but one final almighty push onto the edge of my skis saw me come to a halt abruptly within a hair's whisper of the orange netting kicking up a spray of snow over some people stood nearby who were gently applauding each finisher. For a brief moment, I teetered on the brink of falling over but collected myself, lamely raised one ski stick in the air in apology and stood still, my chest heaving in and out as I caught my breath. I turned my head to look up at the digital timing clock, with a pained expression on my face. I was shattered. The timer flashed: *2:36:47*. I didn't know whether that was good, bad or average. I was just mighty relieved to have made it to the finish line and to have got down in one piece.

I shoved myself off towards a gap in the fencing thinking both my thigh muscles had actually burst through the skin of my legs.

I was expecting to see the raw sinews if I removed my ski trousers. It hurt so much I could hardly move but I had to get out of the way of the next skier. Once clear of the arena I turned around to wait for the next competitor, hunched over my ski poles as I tried to recover. My eyes flitted between the timing clock and the small black dot I could see zig-zagging across the course I had just come down. It looked like it was going to be close. Closer than I would have liked. As he crossed the line the timer flashed: *2:41:24*.

"Ha!" was all could muster. At least I wasn't going to come last and, with a sense of satisfaction, I unclipped my boots, shouldered my skis and went off in search of Mariha. I spotted her walking towards me, wearing a yellow and grey Radio Rix jacket a few sizes too big for her small frame. Her sunglasses were perched on top of her head and her big smile was stretched across her face.

"See… it was easy!" she said when she got closer, turning both palms of her hands to the sky. "Well done! You finished OK. You did good!" She planted a congratulatory kiss on my left cheek, which she probably regretted as I was sweating buckets but it didn't seem to deter her enthusiasm.

"We can go and see all the times, if you like?"

We headed over to the timing tent to see all the times registering as each skier came across the line. I could see that, in the Men's "Motion" class, I was about half way up the results table. Bearing in mind some, in fact probably most, of the skiers had been skiing since they were five years old or even younger, I was really chuffed at the result, if not a little surprised.

When the full results were posted, I congratulated myself some more. The fastest man in the out and out competition class (skin tight suits, racing helmets, race skis, aerodynamically shaped poles, future Olympian downhillers) was clocked at 1:44:28. He was a chap called Patrik Järbyn and, according to a well known information site on the web, he is now described as a "Swedish former World Cup alpine skier" with two World Championship medals. He had won the silver medal at the World Championships in Sierra Nevada only the year before and continued to compete at international level for some years to come (clearly spurred on by the threat of my time of less than sixty seconds behind his). He suffered a serious crash at the Vancouver Olympics in 2010 in the men's super-G, following which he had to be helicoptered to hospital and retired in 2012. The tenth placed man in the top section posted a time of 1:51:63. The top woman skier came in at 1:55:17, the tenth placed time was 2:03:12. However the winner of my section, the men's Motion posted a time of 1:58:25 and the last placed man, 6:38:74. Perhaps the two skiers posting times of over six minutes crashed out and bravely picked themselves up before continuing, but my time gave me a respectable 104th place out of 240 in the men's Motion class.

Floating high on my achievement, I completely missed the fact that it was Valpurgis night. I wondered why an enormous bonfire had been lit on the edge of the village. It was officially the eve of spring and a time when people come out of their houses in the early evening to feel the warmth of the fire on their faces and the cold on their backs, symbolising turning their backs on winter. Choirs sing traditional songs around the fires and the first nettle soups of the season make an appearance, being one of the first plants to emerge after the snow has melted.

Thank you for the music

Up in Åre, the snow was still present and skiers were still skiing. The lifts stayed operational until well into the second week of May but, with my contract finished and no more guests to look after, it was time to pack up and head home. Several people had already left and the place quickly began to lose some of its atmosphere. Time had suddenly rushed by and, as I began to wander around the town, I remembered evenings spent in restaurants and bars, conversations snatched on the town square. Faces popped into my mind as I recalled the process of recognising people just by the colour of their ski jacket or hat as they were wrapped up against the bitter cold. Voices and laughter echoed around my head like friendly ghosts. It was definitely time to go. John had already left to do a summer season in Austria.

Kai had said he had to go to Hell, just for the craic. It was a place in Norway he had wanted to go to all season and I received a postcard showing a fiery sky above the railway station. "*Gods från Hell*" was the phrase that amused him, which apparently was written on a sign at the station. "Goods from Hell" used to be stamped on parcels. His postcard had the Hell postmark.

There was certainly an end of term feeling to the place now and I was determined not to be the last to leave. That said, I had had such a fantastic experience, and met so many genuinely friendly people, that a large part of me didn't want to leave. After spending so many months in this winter playground, breathing in such fresh air every day, how could I go back to living in London doing normal things? As well as the tremendous variety of new experiences, it would be the people I had met that would stay in my mind. I had spent almost six months in a rarefied atmosphere. Some I would stay in touch with forever and we'd see our lives develop, some I would see for a shorter time as we tried to stay in contact but inevitably that contact would fade away and be lost. Some I would never see again, but would think about from time to time, wondering what they were doing. When I thought of them, even many years later, they would always be young-faced, wearing the same colour jacket or uniform.

On Monday 5th May at 11.30am, Stefan picked me up in his luxury VW taxi minibus. He had cleaned it especially and had even put a tie on as well as his best brown leather jacket. I was the sole passenger and, after chucking all my bags in the back, I opted to sit up front with him. He was his usual jovial self but I sensed he felt a bit sad too at the end of a winter we had all shared together. He truly enjoyed the "honour", as he put it, of taxiing the Brits around. We chatted about travel and work and London and I promised him I would send him a toy London taxi to say thanks for everything he had done. At the airport, he parked his taxi right outside the main entrance and embarrassed me by insisting on carrying my bags for me. We shook hands and then he gave me a manly hug. He said "*Hej då*" and turned to leave. He looked quite emotional.

From up high in the air in my window seat on the airplane, I took one final look down at the landscape that had been so foreign to me at the outset, but had now become so familiar. I was seeing it from a very different perspective now as we banked over to head south towards Stockholm. The dark green and grey mass of the forests was still largely surrounded by snow-covered farmland; it in turn was dissected by a handful of narrow straight roads leading off to the wilderness.

I hoped to come back one day but wondered if I ever would. All I could say to the trees was, "*Hej då!*"

SNOW BUSINESS: THE SOUNDTRACK

Throughout this book, I have referred to various songs. Music is such an emotive thing and has the ability to take you back to a certain that place and time. When I hear these songs, I am transported back to Åre. These are the tracks that formed the soundtrack to the season:

1. Money, Money, Money – ABBA
2. Unbreak my Heart – Toni Braxton
3. Sankta Lucia – various choral
4. You Oughta Know – Alanis Morissette
5. Happy New Year – ABBA
6. Jump – Van Halen
7. Just Nu – Tomas Ledin
8. Move on Up – Curtis Mayfield
9. Don't Speak – No Doubt
10. Calling Your Name – E Type
11. Vänner – E Type
12. Back in the Loop – E Type
13. I Breathe – Vacuum
14. Virtual Insanity – Jamiroquai

15. Remember Me – Blue Boy
16. Ain't Talkin' 'Bout Dub – Apollo Four Forty
17. Insomnia – Faithless
18. Cosmic Girl – Jamiroquai